# CIVILIZATION
## CALL TO POWER
## OFFICIAL STRATEGY GUIDE

by Johnny Wilson and Terry Coleman

**ACTIVISION**

**||||||BRADYGAMES**
**TAKE YOUR GAME FURTHER**

## Civilization®: Call To Power™ Official Strategy Guide

### Legal Stuff

**Brady Publishing**

An Imprint of
Macmillan Digital Publishing USA
201 West 103rd Street
Indianapolis, Indiana 46290

ISBN: 1-56686-845-9

Library of Congress Catalog No.: 98-74685

**Printing Code:** The rightmost double-digit number is the year of the book's printing; the rightmost single-digit number is the number of the book's printing. For example, 99-1 shows that the first printing of the book occurred in 1999.

01 00 99                          3 2 1

Manufactured in the United States of America.

## About the Authors

**Johnny L. Wilson** has been writing about computer games for over 17 years. In addition to serving as Editorial Director for *Computer Gaming World* and its properties, Johnny has a Ph.D. in Old Testament Studies and performs one-man shows of biblical characters in costume. Johnny has been named to Who's Who in the West and Who's Who in the World, as well as Software Reviewer of the Year by the Software Publishers Association. As an author or contributor to more than a half-dozen books, Johnny hopes his next book will be fiction.

Johnny lives with his son, Jonathan, and hopes that soon after this book sees print he will be married to Wai Lam, the love of his life.

**Terry Coleman** is the Senior Reviews Editor of *Computer Gaming World* magazine. He has been writing about computer games since 1991. Terry recently launched the premier issue of *PC Gaming Expert*, serving as its Editor. This is Terry's second book with BradyGAMES Publishing, following *Why Won't This #$@! Game Work?*, which he co-wrote with Denny Atkin. While Terry graciously concedes that Johnny has won many more journalistic awards, he enjoys reminding Johnny that Terry has won a lot more gaming tournaments.

This one is for Al, Sam, and Ziggy.

Both authors would like to thank everyone at BradyGAMES, and the folks at Activision, makers of *Civilization: Call to Power*. Everyone involved was ever pleasant, despite looming deadlines.

Finally, we'd like to thank the Civilization game series, launched in 1991. If we're lucky, maybe we'll have Civilization games well into the next millennium.

## BradyGAMES Staff

*Publisher*
**Lynn Zingraf**

*Editor-In-Chief*
**H. Leigh Davis**

*Title/Licensing Manager*
**David Waybright**

*Marketing Manager*
**Janet Eshenour**

*Acquisitions Editor*
**Debra McBride**

*Creative Director*
**Scott Watanabe**

*Marketing Assistant*
**Ken Schmidt**

## Credits

*Development Editor*
**David Cassady**

*Project Editor*
**Timothy Fitzpatrick**

*Screenshot Editor*
**Michael Owen**

*Book Designer*
**Donna Cambra**

*Production Designers*
**Dan Caparo**

**Bob Klunder**

**Jane Washburne**

*Indexer*
**Johnna VanHoose**

# Civilization®: Call To Power™ Official Strategy Guide

# Table of Contents

# Concerning the Arrogance with which Men Advise Those of Greatness

## The Purpose of This Guide
### (with apologies to Nicolo Machiavelli)

From: Johnny Wilson and Terry Coleman
To: The Magnificent Prince of Civilization: Call to Power

*Those who strive to obtain the good graces of a prince (or reader) are accustomed to come before him or her with such things as they hold most precious. Desiring to present ourselves to your Magnificence (see what respect you get for plunking down a few bucks on a book?) with some usefulness, we have not found any gaming experience which we hold more dear than the games which depict the flow of civilization. Having reflected upon the lessons to be gleaned from these gaming experiences since our initial encounter with Civilization and moving on to our recent challenges in Civilization: Call to Power, we send our lessons, digested into this volume, to your Magnificence.*

*Although, in recognizing your gaming excellence, we may consider this work unworthy of your countenance, we trust much to your benignity that it may be acceptable. Outside of this brief passage, we have tried not to embellish it with swelling or magnificent words, nor with any extrinsic allurements or adornments whatever. Rather, we have focused on enriching your already legendary prowess in* Civilization: Call to Power *with the truth behind our gaming experiences and interviews with the creators of the game.*

*Nor do I hold with those who regard it as presumption if men of low and humble conditions (you certainly didn't think editors made much money, did you?) dare to discuss and settle the concerns of princes. Rather, we have contemplated the problems of the game in order to become wise and convivial companions with enough wisdom, and hopefully wit, to help you rule your civilizations more and more wisely until you know far more about the game than do even we. This humble book is intended to help you understand the relationship between the game and history; between the individual component parts of the game and the score; and to inspire you onward to greater Magnificence.*

With this paraphrase of Machiavelli's introduction to *The Prince*, we hope to suggest the spirit of this book. Each chapter title will not only hearken back to an earlier era in civilized history, but each chapter will also contain our tested, effective solutions for winning the game. It is not a book of "cheats," though it contains some. It is not merely a rehash of the manual, though, by necessity some of the material contained therein will bear further mention in this text. In such cases, we hope to present the material in more depth and in a visual form that is easier to understand. Further, this text does not focus solely upon the game itself. It is intended to stir your thoughts and challenge you to consider the historical flow of your civilization compared with those of our history.

We know that you probably don't need the book to win, but we believe that it will help you enjoy the game more and more each time you play the game and try something new. *Civilization: Call to Power* is a chemistry laboratory that enables gamers to experiment with the elements and compounds of human existence. Though the past is separated from modern man by distance, culture, technology, language, and knowledge, this digital laboratory bench of a game allows us to right the wrongs of the past and see what might have happened; to remake the mistakes of earlier eras and determine why they occurred; and to champion some of the lesser civilizations of the past in order to change the face of the historical chronology. How entertaining it is to have the Irish enslave the

English or the Indians subjugate the Portuguese! What a challenge it is to get to the Age of Reason prior to the chronology of Western Civilization!

*Civilization: Call to Power* allows us to explore the interdependencies of nations, technology, trade, faith, and education. It enables us to explore new frontiers with little authentic risk.

It is our hope that this book will help you find the subtle nuances in *Civilization: Call to Power*. Chapter 1 will break down the buildings and goods within your civilization and offer suggestions on integrating them into your overall economic strategy. Chapter 2 will muster every combat unit together and consider ways to use them more effectively. Chapter 3 will tie together the uses of those units for tactics and overall strategy. Chapter 4 will consider the governmental types available within the game and suggest optimal times to use them or lose them in a spirit of revolutionary change. Chapter 5 will discuss the institution of slavery, including insights on using slavery to get a jumpstart on other civilizations, as well as observations on slavery as an institution. Chapter 6 is one of the largest sections of the book. It will discuss the Advances of *Call to Power* and offer political, economic, and military insights with regard to each one. Each Advance section contains some historical commentary, a quick tip or two, a technological flow chart, and an analysis of the Advance with respect to actual game strategy. Chapter 7 will detail information about the Wonders of the World, as well as teach you how to exploit them and obsolete those belonging to other civilizations. Chapter 8 will teach you how to hack the code to your advantage and cheat your friends. Finally, Chapter 9 will feature tips on multiplayer play.

We hope that this book will help you to: create your own optimal flow charts on the technology tree; stimulate further research after reading our crude historical and bibliographical notes; experiment with different systems and sub-systems within the game until you discover details that we have yet to discover; and find the greatest satisfaction you've ever had in playing a computer game. If even part of these goals is met, this little volume will have been worth the price.

We have also included an index, which we hope will be useful when you are in the heat of a game and need that quick reference check. Plus, we hope the chapter-by-chapter historical notes will be of significant use to our readers in furthering their study of world history. So, without further embellishment or adornment, O Prince, we commend these pages to your wisdom. May you always show your benevolence toward your humble servants.

Johnny L. Wilson
Terry L. Coleman
San Francisco, California
February 22, 1999

# Chapter One:

# Concerning the Building of a Civilization

## How to Get the Most Out of Your Cities and Your Economy

*"Industry is the root of all ugliness."*

—Oscar Wilde

Any first-year economics student knows that the issue is, simply put: Guns versus Butter. Assuming a full-employment economy, you will always be giving up one good to produce another. "Guns versus Butter" simply means the determination of whether to produce military or civilian goods. In *Civilization: Call to Power*, you will constantly be balancing three basic resources: Food, Production, and Gold. As you balance Production, you'll have to decide whether those Production resources need to be spent on research, military goods, civilian quality of life, or improvements to stimulate the economy through more efficient Food, Gold, or Production capacity.

Depending on your style of play, whether you are building for conquest or defense, economic growth, or merely trying to find the right balance to stay slightly ahead of your rival civilizations, you'll have to make difficult choices throughout the course of the game. There is no one straight line of development that you will be able to take. Depending on the order in which your rivals construct Wonders, the type of terrain at your disposal, and the hostility of your neighbors, you may need to choose different tactics within the context of each game.

## Location, Location, Location

Knowing what the various terrain types, constructed Improvements, and Tile Improvements can do can be extremely useful for planning your development strategy. The following is a chart that should assist you in deciding where to settle cities and the best ways to develop the terrain tiles in proximity to your cities. Defense bonuses are not listed here, since they primarily determine where you will battle, not where you will construct your cities. Although many ancient cities were formed on the basis of their inherent defensive value (on top of hills, for example), this is not a primary concern in *Call to Power*. In *Call to Power*, cities are better founded on the basis of terrain resources and, assuming you wish to build Trade Routes, exportable commodities rather than defensive value.

| Terrain | Graphic | Food | Prod'n | Gold | Movement Cost | Possible Construction |
|---|---|---|---|---|---|---|
| Beach | | 10 | 5 | 5 | 1 | Undersea Tunnels, Fishing |
| Continental Shelf | | 10 | 10 | 5 | 1 | Undersea Tunnels, Fishing |
| Dead Tile | | 0 | 0 | 0 | 1 | None |
| Deep Water | | 5 | 15 | 5 | 1 | Undersea Tunnels, Fishing, Undersea Mines |
| Desert | | 0 | 5 | 0 | 2 | Roads, Farms, Mines |
| Desert Hill | | 0 | 10 | 5 | 2 | Roads, Mines |
| Forest | | 5 | 20 | 0 | 2 | Roads |

| Terrain | Graphic | Food | Prod'n | Gold | Movement Cost | Possible Construction |
|---------|---------|------|--------|------|---------------|------------------------|
| Glacier | | 0 | 0 | 0 | 3 | None |
| Grassland | | 10 | 5 | 0 | 1 | Roads, Farms, Mines |
| Hill | | 5 | 10 | 5 | 2 | Roads, Mines |
| Jungle | | 5 | 20 | 0 | 3 | Roads |
| Mountain | | 0 | 20 | 5 | 4 | Roads, Mines |
| Plains | | 5 | 10 | 0 | 1 | Roads, Farms, Mines |
| Polar Hill | | 0 | 10 | 5 | 2 | Roads, Mines |
| Rift | | 5 | 25 | 5 | 1 | Undersea Tunnels, Fishing, Undersea Mines |
| River | | +5 | +5 | +5 | $1/2$ | As Underlying Tile |
| Shallow Water | | 10 | 10 | 5 | 1 | Undersea Tunnels, Fishing |
| Space | | 0 | 0 | 0 | $1/20$ | Food Pods, Assembly Bays |
| Swamp | | 0 | 5 | 0 | 3 | Roads |
| Trench | | 10 | 10 | 5 | 1 | Fishing |
| Tundra | | 5 | 0 | 0 | 2 | Roads |
| Volcano | | 5 | 45 | 10 | 1 | Undersea Tunnels, Fishing, Undersea Mines |

In the initial stages of the game, we think that Food production is more important because you want to get your civilization's population booming as soon as possible. So, we often go for grasslands or beach when we're getting ready to found a city. Since time is crucial when you're first founding a city, it's not a good idea to wander around looking for high production terrain or exportable goods during the initial turns. There is plenty of time to find goods and mine valuable terrain during subsequent turns, but not if you don't found a city right away. Before founding a city, it is generally best to look for a grasslands tile within the green influence grid which surrounds your Settler unit at the beginning of each turn. This guarantees the best possible food supply. Barring a grasslands tile, try a beach square, as the food production there isn't bad, and you will be able to improve the nearby tiles with nets as you accumulate enough gold in your Public Works coffers. A river tile is also a good suggestion, as it adds a nice bonus.

Should you be lucky enough to have one of the Goods markers within the green influence grid that surrounds your Settler unit, this is excellent. It means that you'll be able to develop Trade Routes at an early stage in the game (even if it's only between two of your cities). If you have to move only a couple of times before getting the Goods marker in your grid, it is probably worth the risk. If it's more than two or three turns, wait until you're ready to found your second city to take advantage of the Goods. The following chart describes the exportable commodities available in *Call to Power*. Notice that all goods begin with a value of ten gold pieces, but the market economy changes throughout the game. Remember also that you can't export them until you build a Caravan unit, and you also can't export the goods if you don't control them. So, get them when you can.

| Food | Graphic | Location | Value in Gold | Rationale |
|------|---------|----------|---------------|-----------|
| Alligator | | Swamp | 10 | Eggs, Meat, Skin |
| Beaver | | Forest | 10 | Fur |
| Caribou | | Tundra | 10 | Meat, Antlers |
| Coffee | | Hill | 10 | Beverage |
| Crab | | Shallow Water | 10 | Food, Raw Materials for Cosmetics, Drugs, Fertilizer |
| Diamond | | Mountain | 10 | Gems, Ornamental and Industrial |
| Elephant | | Plains | 10 | Ivory |
| Giant Squid | | Deep Water | 10 | Food, Raw Materials for Soap, Paint, Crysta |
| Grapes | | Hill | 10 | Wine |
| Jade | | Jungle | 10 | Jewel, Building Material |
| Oil | | Desert | 10 | Lighting, Heating, Fuel |
| Pearls | | Shallow Water | 10 | Jewelry |
| Poppies | | Grasslands | 10 | Drugs |
| Rubies | | Mountain | 10 | Gems, Ornamental and Industrial |
| Sugar | | Jungle | 10 | Food |
| Tobacco | | Grasslands | 10 | Drug |
| Whale | | Deep Water | 10 | Raw Materials for Shoe Polish, Soap, Perfume and Oil |

## Food for Thought

You obviously can't grow a city if you can't feed a city. Since it takes one Food unit to feed each citizen and one half of a Food unit to feed each slave, it makes sense that increasing Food increases population. The upward spiral, of course, is that increasing population increases productivity. So, anything you can do to boost Food production in the early days of a city is going to be optimal. The most logical way to increase Food production would seem to be by building a Farm, but Farms aren't available until you get at least 200 gold in your Public Works budget. So, at the early stages, you'll just need to improve the way your civilization stores the Food.

The Granary improvement is the best way to start building your city's population. It automatically gives a 50-percent boost in Food production due to superior storage. This helps the population grow twice as fast as it does without the Granary. We like to build Granary Improvements in each city of our civilizations as soon as we're sure we can defend those cities with garrison units.

### Granary

| | |
|---|---|
| **IMPROVEMENT:** | Granary |
| **COST:** | AGRICULTURE + 540 Production Units = GRANARY |
| **EFFECT:** | +50% Food Production due to superior storage. |

Once your city is growing to your satisfaction, it's good to start putting some of your gold into the Public Works budget. Allocating a percentage of your income to the Public Works budget does this. Next to the hammer icon, which activates the Tile Improvement menu, are two +/- spinners: *PW* and *Science*. Each represents the percentage of your income being spent on Public Works and Science, as opposed to a situation where you spend every available gold piece on constructing buildings or military units. Early in the game, it's good to put the PW percentage at only 10 to 20 percent because you don't want to divert too many resources from the basic improvements you're making. Later, you can increase this, if desired.

Once you have completed a Granary, you should try to build your Public Works budget up to 200 gold. The PW funds are reported in the box over the Total Funds box in the control panel (underneath the Population and Date boxes). When you amass 200 gold in the PW box and you're ready to improve your Food production situation, you have two options: If you are near a water source and have a square that contains Desert, Grassland, or Plains terrain, you can build a Farm. To do so, click on the hammer icon on the control panel and wait for the iconic menu for Tile Improvements to appear. All the Tile Improvements which are currently within your spending range will appear in color, and those for which you have the appropriate Science advancement but not enough funds to build will be shown in gray. The default for Tile Improvements is the menu for those that are built on Land. You can also click on the Sea button in order to get to the Tile Improvements for Sea terrain. There is another button for Terraforming. Even this early in the game, you'll be able to deforest some squares and turn them into Plains squares so that you can plant Farms. Later, you'll be able to click on the Space button to get to the Tile Improvements in Space.

*TERRAIN TOOLBOX: Once you have enough money in the Public Works budget, you'll be able to purchase Tile Improvements from this menu in order to upgrade your terrain and cities.*

When you access these menus, merely place the cursor over the desired Tile Improvement, and you'll get the name of the improvement and the minimum cost. Terrain effects can drive the price up from this base price. In order to build a Farm, simply click on the icon and then place the cursor over the desired square. If you have enough funds, and the basic prerequisites for irrigation are met (the farm is next to water or another farm), you will see a ghost image of the farm turn green. Click again and you'll see the cultivated field appear. It takes two turns for the Farm to appear and begin providing an additional five points of Food production.

*FARMER IN THE DELL: The farm icon turns green under your cursor whenever the conditions are correct for building a farm.*

Note that both the Farms and Nets Tile Improvements only garner an additional five points of Food production per turn, but as you advance along the technology tree, you'll have opportunities to build Tile Improvements which add up to 30 points of Food Production per turn. The following is a chart of Tile Improvements related to Food.

| Improvement | Graphic | Cost | Terrain | Turns to Complete | Food Production Increase |
|---|---|---|---|---|---|
| Advanced Farms | | AGRICULTURAL REVOLUTION + 500 PW | Irrigated Desert, Plain, Grassland | 2 | 15 |
| Automated Fisheries | | ROBOTICS + 1,400 to 2,000 PW | Various Sea Terrain | 2 | 25/50/60 |
| Farms | | AGRICULTURE + 200 PW | Irrigated Desert, Plain, Grassland | 2 | 5 |
| Fisheries | | OCEAN FARING + 500 to 900 | Various Sea Terrain | 2 | 15/30/40 |

| Improvement | Graphic | Cost | Terrain | Turns to Complete | Food Production Increase |
|---|---|---|---|---|---|
| ...d Modules | | ASTEROID MINING +1,400 PW | Space | 2 | 40 |
| ...d Pods | | SPACE COLONIES + 600 PW | Space | 2 | 20 |
| ...d Tanks | | GENETIC TAILORING + 2,200 PW | Space | 2 | 60 |
| ...droponic Farms | | SMART MATERIALS + 1,400 | Desert, Plain, Grassland | 2 | 25 |
| ...ts | | SHIPBUILDING + 200 to 400 | Various Sea Terrain | 2 | 5/10/20 |

...you adequately budget for Public Works projects and use your
...le Improvements correctly, you should never have to deal with
...e message that tells you that your citizens are starving and
...ing. Plus, you'll be growing your population at a steady clip
...d improving your productivity.

...hile the Public Works funds are useful for maximizing terrain
...les which aren't currently doing you much good, you'll find
...at it takes a while to build up those PW funds. We advise that
...u continue to build Improvements that assist in Food produc-
...on, and alternate them with Improvements that increase Gold
...d Production. One Food-related Improvement that becomes
...ailable fairly early in the game is the Aqueduct. Much later in
...e game, the Beef Vat becomes available and ends food
...oblems for the cities it's built in.

## ...queduct

| | |
|---|---|
| ...PROVEMENT: | Aqueduct |
| ...OST: | ENGINEERING + 405 Production Units = AQUEDUCT |
| ...FECT: | +20% Food Production |
| | -2 Overcrowding |

Aqueducts are gravity flow systems that bring fresh water from a hillside water source. When most people think of Aqueducts, they tend to think of the Roman constructions with the large arches. However, fresh water conduits called *qanat* existed in the Ancient Near East prior to the Romans. Even the Greeks had Aqueducts that preceded those of the Romans. By bringing fresh water to the masses, the Aqueducts lessened the number of harmful microbes that could live in the drinking water and, as a result, improved public health considerably. Aqueducts also ensured that there was plenty of water for the fire brigades to use. This helped reduce the chance of total destruction by fire in some of the high-density areas of the city.

In *Call to Power*, Aqueducts play the same role that they played in history, reducing the effects of overcrowding and its attendant unhappiness. Also, *Call to Power* assumes that the water from the Aqueducts will allow additional fields to be irrigated and that this will boost Food production. The best thing about Aqueducts from the player's view is that they help with two problems at once: They reduce potential unhappiness by reducing the overcrowding effects, and they give a boost in Food production.

One other Improvement that solves the Food problem should be noted. In the latter part of the game, it is possible to build the Beef Vat. In the science-fiction area of the game, you get a chance to construct this Improvement based on the idea of synthetic beef creation. Within the fiction, the geneticists of your society have placed sulfide-eating bacteria from oceanic hot springs and gene-spliced them with Hereford cattle. The inherent gain was to create enough of a food surplus to quell the fictitious Amsterdam Food Riots. In game terms, this means that the cities that build it cannot starve.

### Beef Vat

| | |
|---|---|
| IMPROVEMENT: | Beef Vat |
| COST: | GENETIC TAILORING + 3,000 Production Units = BEEF VAT |
| EFFECT: | Prevents Starvation |
| DOWNSIDE: | It is a polluter |

So, depending on your Food production needs, you can add additional Improvements as the game goes on instead of depending totally on the Tile Improvements that create Food.

## The Midas Touch (Gold Production)

Of course, the major choke point in developing your civilization is usually going to be your Gold reserves. Now that you're on your way to maximizing your population growth by providing plenty of Food, you'll have to increase the flow of Gold. The fastest way to improve the Gold flow early in the game is to build the Marketplace Improvement and follow that up with the creation of Merchants. The Marketplace Improvement instantly gives you a 50-percent boost in Gold production.

### Marketplace

| | |
|---|---|
| IMPROVEMENT: | Marketplace |
| COST: | DOMESTICATION + 675 Production Units = MARKETPLACE |
| EFFECT: | +50% Gold Production; Allows some workers to be turned into Merchants, Gold Producers |

Whether it was the Greek agora or a primitive bazaar, the purpose of a Marketplace was for Trade and communication. Initially, Marketplaces were based on a simple barter economy. Eventually, cattle became something of a standard currency (the Latin term for money, *pecunia*, reflects the root idea of cattle). Since, however, the currencies used in barter are often unwieldy, it became necessary to move toward a standardized coinage. For a time, this meant copper coins backed by private citizens, but eventually it meant precious metals backed by a powerful ruler. The Marketplace in *Call to Power* reflects this because its primary function is to generate Gold; first, in giving you a 50-percent boost in Gold production, and second, in allowing you to select Merchants from your citizens, who increase Gold production as "individuals" each turn.

At other points in the game, you'll need a Gold production boost. The following is a chart that lists the Gold producing Improvements that can follow your early construction of a Marketplace.

| Improvement | Graphic | Cost (ADVANCE + production units) | Gold Production Increase | Special Quality |
|---|---|---|---|---|
| Bank | | BANKING + 1,125 | +50% | Allows Merchants |
| City Clock | | MECHANICAL CLOCK + 1,620 | +1 G per citizen of city | N/A |
| Airport | | AERODYNAMICS + 2,500 | 50% | +100% Pollution |
| Television | | MASS MEDIA + 3,000 | +5 G per citizen | N/A |

You can never have enough gold for your civilization, and knowing these Improvements can help. In addition, several Tile Improvements provide both Gold and Production. Anytime you can get both Gold and Production out of the same effort and expenditure, you should take it. The following chart depicts these Tile Improvements. The differing amounts for Tile Improvement costs, as well as Gold and Production increases, are due to terrain variables.

| Improvement | Graphic | Cost (ADVANCE + production units) | Turns to Complete | Gold Increase | Prod'n Incr. |
|---|---|---|---|---|---|
| ...ne | | MINING + 300 to 400 | 2 | 5 | 5/10/15 |
| ...vanced Mine | | ELECTRICITY + 800 to 1,000 | 2 | 5/10 | 10/20/30 |
| ...ega Mine | | ROBOTICS + 1,600 to 2,200 | 2 | 5/15 | 15/30/45 |
| ...dersea Mine | | SEA COLONIES + 400 to 600 | 2 | 5 | 30/40/50 |
| ...vanced Undersea Mines | | ULTRA PRESSURE MACHINERY + 1,000 to 1,400 | 2 | 10 | 60/80/100 |
| ...ega Undersea Mines | | FUTURE SEA + 2,200 to 2,800 | 2 | 15 | 90/120/150 |
| ...sembly Bays | | SPACE COLONIES + 600 | 2 | 5 | 30 |
| ...vanced Assembly Bays | | ASTEROID MINING + 1,400 | 2 | 10 | 60 |
| ...ga Assembly Bays | | FUTURE FLIGHT + 2,200 | 2 | 15 | 90 |

Your empire or war machine will run on Gold. Knowing how to earn more is particularly useful. We hope that these charts will assist your decision-making as you play the game.

## Happy Together (Happiness)

If you want to keep your civilization together, you'll need to remember that morale is important. A low Happiness quotient may cause your citizens to revolt. This not only costs you Production during the turns in which the revolt is taking place, but it means that you either have to: a) run the risk of losing a city or cities to a new civilization formed by the dissidents; b) send a military garrison to calm things down; or c) spend a lot of Gold on Improvements to increase the Happiness of each city in general.

We think it is better to monitor your civilization's Happiness quotient as carefully as a cardiac patient pays attention to his blood pressure. Once that slider turns to yellow, you'll need to do something about the unhappiness within your civilization. Here are some Improvements that can directly add to the Happiness quotient or indirectly add to it by reducing the negative net effects of Crime and Overcrowding.

| Improvement | Graphic | Cost (ADVANCE + production units) | Direct Happiness Effect | Indirect Happiness Effect |
|---|---|---|---|---|
| Capitol | | STONE WORKING + 405 | Slight Increase | Lowers Crime |
| Temple | | RELIGION + 270 | +2 | N/A |
| Courthouse | | JURISPRUDENCE + 270 | N/A | -50% Crime |
| Theater | | PHILOSOPHY + 495 | +1[1] | N/A |
| Coliseum | | ENGINEERING + 1,035 | +2 | N/A |
| Hospital | | MEDICINE + 2,250 | N/A | -3 Overcrowding |
| Cathedral | | PERSPECTIVE + 2,475 | +3[2] | N/A |
| Movie Palace | | ELECTRIFICATION + 1,500 | N/A | -50% War Discontent |
| Drug Store | | PHARMACEUTICALS + 3,000 | +3[3] | N/A |
| Security Monitor | | AI SURVEILLANCE + 4,000 | N/A | -50% Crime[4] |
| Aqua-Filter | | FUEL CELLS + 8,000 | N/A | -5 Overcrowding |

| Improvement | Graphic | Cost (ADVANCE + production units) | Direct Happiness Effect | Indirect Happiness Effect |
|---|---|---|---|---|
| Arcologies | | ARCOLOGIES + 5,000 | N/A | -4 Overcrowding[1] |
| House of Freezing | | CRYONICS + 5,000 | 0[5] | N/A |
| Mind Controller | | MIND CONTROL + 10,000 | 75[6] | Special Defense[7] |
| Body Exchange | | LIFE EXTENSION + 10,000 | +3 | N/A |

NOTES

Doubles the Effectiveness of Entertainers by providing a permanent venue.
+5 in a Theocracy because of boost in faith, +1 in Communism because Religion is the opiate of the masses.
+25 Production units per turn because increased health means more reliable man-hours.
-100% Pollution and +25% Production
+5 Happiness in a Theocracy because citizens can "die" and have their taste of heaven, and then come back to life. +50% Gold.
Freezes Happiness Quotient at a very safe 75.
50% chance to prevent Convert City attack and 100% chance to prevent Capture Slaves attack.

Using these references should help you to be able to keep your citizens satisfied and your civilization out of any kind of revolutionary fervor. A combination of monitoring the Happiness quotient and occasionally building these Improvements should help you keep matters in check.

## Whip It! (Increasing Production)

Everyone knows that if an organism isn't growing, it's probably dying. That's why you will consistently wish to increase the efficiency of your civilization with regard to Production. In addition to the Tile Improvements mentioned earlier in this chapter, which boost Production (specified in the earlier chart), you will want to pay attention to the following Production-boosting Improvements.

| Improvement | Graphic | Cost (ADVANCE + production units) | Production Increase | Pollution? | Special Quality |
|---|---|---|---|---|---|
| Mill | | AGRICULTURAL REVOLUTION + 1,125 | 50% | 0 | N/A |
| Factory | | INDUSTRIAL REVOLUTION + 2,025 | 50% | 100% | Allows Laborers |
| Oil Refinery | | OIL REFINING + 3,500 | 50% | 200% | N/A |
| Nuclear Plant | | QUANTUM PHYSICS + 5,500 | 50% | -50% | N/A |
| Robotic Plant | | ROBOTICS + 4,500 | 50% | 100% | N/A |
| Security Monitor | | AI SURVEILLANCE + 4,000 | 25% | -100% | -50% Crime[4] |
| Incubation Center | | HUMAN CLONING + 2,500 | 25% | 0 | N/A |
| Fusion Plant | | FUSION + 10,000 | 50% | -100% | N/A |

Unfortunately, you will note that many of the Improvements listed here have a downside. Many of them are heavy polluters as part of the price of progress. Sooner or later, you're going to have to deal with the Pollution issues, so be sure to pay attention to the Pollution section toward the close of this chapter.

## Future Magic (Science)

No matter how you play the game, though, the key to winning is pumping up your Science points as efficiently as possible. You can do this by distributing more Scientists into your labor pool, as well as by investing in some important Improvements. The following chart delineates the Improvements that will help increase your Science knowledge base.

| Improvement | Graphic | Cost (ADVANCE + production units) | Science Increase | Special Quality |
|---|---|---|---|---|
| Publishing House | | PRINTING PRESS + 540 | +25% | $+^1/_2$ Science per Citizen |
| Academy | | PHILOSOPHY + 540 | +50% | $+^1/_2$ Science per Citizen |
| University | | CLASSICAL EDUCATION + 1,350 | +50% | N/A |
| Computer Center | | COMPUTER + 2,400 | +50% | $+^1/_2$ Science per Citizen |
| Bio-Memory Chip | | NEURAL INTERFACE + 2,800 | +50% Science | $+^1/_2$ Science per Citizen |

Don't hesitate to use these Improvements, as they significantly accelerate the Advances path and put you on the road to the Alien Synthesis Project endgame.

## Special Class (Unusual Improvements)

No matter how organized your civilization happens to be, however, you're going to eventually run up against some special needs. Here is a chart that might help you find the right Improvement for the right special need.

| Improvement | Graphic | Cost (ADVANCE + production units) | Special Effect |
|---|---|---|---|
| City Wall | | STONEWORKING + 405 | +4 Defense, Prevents Slavery, Prevents Conversions 50% of the Time |
| SDI | | SPACE FLIGHT + 5,000 | Prevents Nuke attack on a City |
| Micro Defense | | HUMAN CLONING + 3,500 | Protects against Nano Attack and Infect City |
| Rail Launcher | | SUPERCONDUCTOR + 6,000 | Launches Units into Space |
| Forcefield | | UNIFIED PHYSICS + 6,000 | +12 Defense |
| Nanite Factory | | NANO ASSEMBLY + 4,000 | Rush Buy reduced to 1 G per production unit of cost |

## Hit The Road, Jack (Movement)

In the same vein as the special class of Improvements, here is a chart of Tile Improvements to speed up your movement rates.

| Tile Improvement | Graphic | Cost (ADVANCE + production units) | Turns to Complete | New Movement Rate |
|---|---|---|---|---|
| Road | | TOOLMAKING + 60 to 400 | 2 | 1/3 |
| Railroad | | RAILROAD + 120 to 800 | 3-4 | 1/5 |
| Maglev | | SUPERCONDUCTOR + 240 to 1,600 | 4 | 1/10 |
| Undersea Tunnel | | SEA COLONIES + 1,200 to 2,400 | 2-4 | 1/10 |

## Smoke 'Em If You Got 'Em (Pollution)

Even more than in earlier versions of *Civilization*, Pollution plays a critical part in *Civilization: Call to Power*. A good rule of thumb is that the larger your city and the more you produce, the greater the Pollution will be. In general, this should not be a concern for you until you reach the Modern Era. It is then, with much larger cities and the effects of modern technology, that civilizations really start to have an impact on the environment.

Global warming has always been something to worry about in the endgame of *Civilization*, but the effects were mostly a number of polluted spaces, which basically consisted of severely cutting back the food and resources that polluted spaces produced. In *Civilization II*, polluted spaces could be cleared by Settler units (albeit at a high cost of time and resources). In drastic cases, such as a planet ravaged by decades of high-tech war, global warming could turn favorable terrain into deserts, but this was not an every-game occurrence.

In *Call to Power,* the effects of damage to the environment are both subtler and more drastic over the entire game. A lot of this is due to the fact that the end of *Call to Power* takes place at or near the year 3000 AD (depending on how quickly someone wins the game), instead of the usual *Civilization* end date of 2000 to 2100 AD. With many more years to play through in the post-modern era, it's easy to see how Pollution, if unchecked, could easily cause not just one global catastrophe, but several.

These potential catastrophes occur because of two things: 1) the incidence of global warming, and 2) new to the *Civilization* series, damage to the ozone layer. For example, a major city, even in the Renaissance Era, tends to produce about five to six points of ozone and/or global warming damage per turn. This number increases as cities get larger and technology improves. While five or even ten points of Pollution damage per turn doesn't sound like much, let's place this in its proper perspective:

Let's say that your civilization, by the middle of the Renaissance Era, has 14 cities that average a population of 12 each. That equals a total of 168 Pollution spewed into the atmosphere per turn. If we multiply that by eight civilizations, it totals 1344 pollution points generated *every* turn.

On a medium map, an environmental disaster (in this case, a flood that can affect several coastal cities) is triggered when the pollution total hits 130,000. If pollution proceeds apace at the 1344-per-turn rate shown above, it would take less than 100 turns for such an environmental disaster to occur; not a terribly long time in a standard game of *Call to Power.* This doesn't even take into account the Pollution that would have been generated for several additional turns prior to the Era given in our example, much less any other contributing factors.

As Pollution continues to increase, ozone disasters will also occur, causing "dead spaces" to occur. These dead spaces rarely, in our experience, occur in deserts; they always seem to replace what were once productive and profitable spaces near cities. Once a city goes above 100 pollution per turn, it has a chance of causing a specific ozone disaster within its own city limits, above and beyond the gloominess of the overall global Pollution picture.

How does this all work? Well, as you discover new technologies and build new structures, the base Pollution of each of your cities is multiplied by the following:

## Ecological Effects of Advances

| Advance | Environmental Effect |
| --- | --- |
| Oil Refining | Doubles pollution |
| Mass Production | +50% greater pollution |
| Conservation | Halves pollution |
| Intelligent Materials | Doubles pollution |
| Nano-Assembly | Halves pollution |
| Gaia Theory | Halves pollution |

## Ecological Effects of City Improvements

| Advance | Environmental Effect |
| --- | --- |
| Airport | +100% pollution |
| Eco-Transit | -200% pollution |
| Factory | +100% pollution |
| Fusion Plant | -100% pollution |
| Nuclear Plant | -50% pollution |
| Oil Refinery | +200% pollution |
| Recycling Plant | -200% pollution in City, Lowers Pollution Worldwide |
| Robotic Factory | +100% pollution |
| Security Monitor | -100% pollution |

## Ecological Effects of Units

| Event | Environmental Effect |
| --- | --- |
| Cargo Pod Launch | +10 ozone damage |
| Nuke Detonation | +10 global warming |
| Space-Capable Unit Launch | +5 ozone damage |
| Stealth Fighter Launch | +1 ozone damage |

So, if a city that was producing 168 basic Pollution (from our example above) also had an oil refinery and mass production, fairly typical development for the early Modern Era, it would produce 420 pollution per turn. Multiply that by every city in seven or eight civilizations, and all of a sudden, that disaster is a lot less than 100 years away.

What can you do to prevent dead spaces and floods?

* The easiest solution in a game with a small or medium map is to try to win by conquering the world before Pollution becomes a serious problem, at least in game terms. Success with this approach is difficult to achieve on higher levels of difficulty and on a large or very large map before the Genetic or Diamond Age, by which time Pollution is very much a problem.

* You can build certain Improvements, such as the Recycling Plant (see the table above). But if your neighbors refuse to take precautions against global disasters, they won't necessarily be the ones who will pay the price.

* So, you can demand through your embassy that a civilization change its polluting ways. Unless you are strong enough to conquer them militarily (in which case, why bother?), or you are a valuable trading partner for them, the civilization will likely ignore your requests, especially on higher difficulty levels. The best method seems to be to offer them research and gold in an attempt to get them to see your point of view, but we've found this to be rather expensive over the long haul.

- ❧ Build underwater cities. They tend to be rather lucrative, they don't have to worry about floods, and they receive much fewer dead spaces within their city limits than do traditional land-based burgs.

- ❧ Even if you are stronger than other nations militarily, build SDI defenses to discourage the launching of nukes.

- ❧ Especially if you are winning the "research war," consider changing your government to an Ecotopia and using Ecoterrorists against uncooperative polluters.

- ❧ Similarly, if one of your rivals has two or three of the greatest polluting cities, build the Eden Project Wonder (see Chapter 7).

- ❧ If you are close to a breakthrough with the Wormhole Detector, don't worry about Pollution anymore. Just win, baby.

## Conclusion

So, if you manage your civilization right, you should be able to build either the empire or the war machine of your dreams. Using this chapter for reference should help you to build just the right Improvement or Tile Improvement at the opportune time to blitz your way through your opponents—either economically or militarily. And so, O prince, we rest our economic case.

# Chapter Two:

# Concerning the Face of Battle

## A Breakdown of Every Unit in *Call to Power*

*"An army should be ready every day, every night, and at all times of the day and night, to oppose all the resistance of which it is capable."*

—*Napoleon Bonaparte*, Art of War

*"It is a good thing that war is so terrible, lest we become too fond of it."*

—*Robert E. Lee*

Not every leader likes going to war, but your enemies may leave you little choice. Thus, it helps to know the capabilities of each unit, so that you can make the right choices to fit with both your style of play and the specific situation in each game of *Call to Power*. For the sake of thoroughness, we have listed here not only all combat units, but also important non-combatants, such as Settlers, and Unconventional Warfare units, such as Televangelists (some of these, such as Abolitionists, are covered in our discussion of Slavery in Chapter 5). Once you've familiarized yourself with this information (please don't try to memorize everything!), you should move on to the next chapter covering tactics and strategy.

navy would rule the Pacific. But an outnumbered US fleet defeated the Japanese Navy at the Battle of Midway entirely through the use of naval air power. The age of the Aircraft Carrier had begun.

### Game Notes

Since the Fighter and the Aircraft Carrier are available at the same time, it gives you a lot more strategic options. Generally speaking, you should build four to five fighters for defense and at least one Aircraft Carrier, more if you are on the brink of war. The relatively high cost is offset by the fact that Fighter units are still effective until you reach the cusp of the Genetic Age, and Carriers are good throughout the game. Though not historically accurate, in *Call to Power* Battleships move slightly faster than Carriers.

## Aircraft Carrier

| Unit Type: | Naval (Air) |
| --- | --- |
| Cost: | 3000 |
| Attack: | 8 |
| Defense: | 8 |
| Movement: | 4 |
| Ranged Attack: | 8 |
| Era Available: | Modern |
| Made Obsolete By: | Never |

### Historical Notes

After Pearl Harbor and the sinking of several United States Battleships, the world thought the Japanese

## Archer

| Unit Type: | Land |
| --- | --- |
| Cost: | 270 |
| Attack: | 1 |
| Defense: | 1 |
| Movement: | 1 |
| Ranged Attack: | 2 |
| Era Available: | Ancient |
| Made Obsolete By: | Cannon Making |

## Historical Notes

Archers have been around since the dawn of recorded history. Archers in *Call to Power* represent all kinds of Ancient missile users, from spear-throwers to slingers, in addition to the classic bow and arrow. Though Archers are no longer part of combat units (stories persist, however, that snipers used bows in both the Korean and Vietnam Wars), the technology continues to evolve, using high-tech fibers in place of the "strong yew bows" favored by the famed English Archers at Agincourt and Crecy.

## Game Notes

It's hard to fathom why these important historical units were downgraded so much from *Civilization II*, where they sported an attack value of three, rather than the lowly one they now possess. Be that as it may, Archers are still important to the defense of your kingdom in the early part of the game because their ranged attack helps support your front-line troops. You should build Archers and place them in your capital city, plus anywhere else that borders a neighboring empire.

# Artillery

| | |
|---|---|
| Unit Type: | Land |
| Cost: | 1200 |
| Attack: | 4 |
| Defense: | 4 |
| Movement: | 1 |
| Ranged Attack: | 20 |
| Era Available: | Modern |
| Made Obsolete By: | Robotics |

## Historical Notes

Artillery came into its own when it became a truly indirect fire weapons system in WWI, and it refined this process through successive 20th century wars, the period represented by Artillery in *Call to Power*.

## Game Notes

We know that you won't enjoy the fruits of Artillery for long, but you must buy at least a few Artillery pieces to show your opponents that you mean business. Artillery is the first true "city buster" in the game: With its 20 Bombardment, Artillery can soften up a defending city or reduce an enemy force in the open into molten slag.

# Battleship

| | |
|---|---|
| Unit Type: | Naval |
| Cost: | 2000 |
| Attack: | 20 |
| Defense: | 15 |
| Movement: | 5 |
| Ranged Attack: | 20 |
| Era Available: | Modern |
| Made Obsolete By: | Ultrapressure Machinery |

## Historical Notes

The Queen of the seas for over half a century, Battleship are still relevant in the modern era, especially when fitted with the latest in electronics and cruise missile platforms (which you unfortunately can't utilize in the game). The main reason that Battleships have been mothballed isn't their rumored vulnerability (the thick armor plate of most Battleships can withstand multiple missile hits), but the fact that the huge vessels take over 3,000 sailors to staff, a fiscal impossibility in today's economy.

## Game Notes

Unlike real history, where Battleships have taken a back seat to Aircraft Carriers, Battleships are effective, with a great Ranged Attack, until almost the end of the game. As there are no middle-range ships, like Cruisers, in *Ca to Power*, you should take advantage of the Battleship's prowess, and buy at least three or four of these behemoths. When war breaks out late in the game, as it almost always does, you'll thank us (even while you're cursing the high maintenance costs in the meantime).

# Bombers

| | |
|---|---|
| Unit Type: | Air |
| Cost: | 2250 |
| Attack: | 20 |
| Defense: | 4 |
| Ranged Attack: | 10 |

| | |
|---|---|
| **Movement:** | 10, with 5 turns of fuel |
| **Era Available:** | Modern |
| **Made Obsolete By:** | Advanced Composites |

### Historical Notes

As with most air units, Bombers came into their own during WWII, as the Allies dropped millions of tons of bombs on German industry. Ironically enough, bombing as a science of warfare didn't progress significantly afterwards until the 1980s, with the introduction of smart bombs and cruise missiles.

### Game Notes

It's like flying a wing of pure gold with a knockout punch, and it's awfully tempting to buy a big Bomber fleet—especially since a Bomber can carry a single Nuke. But air power alone won't necessarily win the war for you, and you should really ask yourself, "Do I need these *right now*, or can I wait for the Stealth Bomber?"

# Cannon

| | |
|---|---|
| **Unit Type:** | Land |
| **Cost:** | 540 |
| **Attack:** | 2 |
| **Defense:** | 2 |
| **Movement:** | 1 |
| **Ranged Attack:** | 6 |
| **Era Available:** | Renaissance |
| **Made Obsolete By:** | Explosives |

### Historical Notes

The Cannon proved the end of the reign of the great walled city, once metallurgy improved to the point where shells achieved sufficient velocity to breach stone defenses. By the time of the Napoleonic Wars, the Cannon had become as important as the other arms of the battlefield. Napoleon himself once cleared the streets of Paris "with a whiff of grapeshot," scattering a group of rioters.

### Game Notes

Although it offers the first really decent chance for ground bombardment, the Cannon is merely a

short-term solution at best. Unless you are in the midst of a protracted war where you need siege equipment to break an enemy city, wait for Artillery, which is only one discovery down the Defensive War pipeline.

# Cavalry

| | |
|---|---|
| **Unit Type:** | Land |
| **Cost:** | 720 |
| **Attack:** | 5 |
| **Defense:** | 3 |
| **Movement:** | 4 |
| **Era Available:** | Renaissance |
| **Made Obsolete By:** | Tank Warfare |

### Historical Notes

While it has been around for centuries, Cavalry in *Call to Power* refers to the military arm as is existed during and after the period of the Seven Years' War. During this period, Cavalry was at its most powerful, often used to shatter a routed foe. In later years, Cavalry would be reduced to an intelligence-gathering force, and finally would disappear from the battlefield altogether after WWII.

### Game Notes

While a bit expensive, Cavalry is the modern equivalent of Knights, with a lot more punch. It's absolutely crucial that you build at least a few Cavalry units for interior mobile defense, as well as for a potent counter-punching force.

# Cleric

| | |
|---|---|
| **Unit Type:** | Unconventional Warfare |
| **Cost:** | 270 |
| **Attack:** | 0 |
| **Defense:** | 1 |
| **Movement:** | 2 |
| **Era Available:** | Ancient |
| **Made Obsolete By:** | Consumer Electronics |

## Historical Notes

Most everyone has his own idea of what a Cleric should look like, how he should conduct himself, and so on. Just keep in mind that Clerics in *Call to Power* are of all faiths and denominations, and that only the Clerics of *your* empire have the One True Faith, whatever you want that to be.

## Game Notes

The fact that Consumer Electronics makes Clerics obsolete in *Call to Power* never fails to make us chuckle, because we always remember the classic Xerox commercials with Father Dominique, but we digress… Clerics offer you some of the most effective uses of Unconventional Warfare in the game. Make a point to buy these inexpensive, very effective pests, and beset them on your enemies like a pestilence from the Bible. Remembering that the Convert City attack only has a 25-percent chance of detection should your Cleric unit fail (50-percent chance of success), you can send a wave of Cleric units into an allied civilization's territory. Unless a Spy, Diplomat, or Cleric unit spots your Cleric units, they will be able to operate in stealth mode for a while—most effective stealth unit in the days before Mass Media.

## Corporate Branch

| | |
|---|---|
| Unit Type: | Unconventional Warfare |
| Cost: | 2000 |
| Attack: | 0 |
| Defense: | 1 |
| Movement: | 5 |
| Era Available: | Modern |
| Made Obsolete By: | Sub-Neural Ads |

## Historical Notes

The Corporation is a modern phenomenon. It is unique among legal constructs, because it has legal rights beyond the lifespan of the persons who found the Corporation. It's almost as if the Corporation were itself a person.

## Game Notes

Appropriately enough, the Corporate Branch is represented on the map as if it were a person, albeit a pretty wimpy one. Even so, it's an effective unit that essentially "casts a franchise spell" on an enemy city, basically, the modern-day version of black magic, and sucks out money like a vampire going after blood. No empire should be without one or two, or even three.

## Crawler

| | |
|---|---|
| Unit Type: | Naval |
| Cost: | 5000 |
| Attack: | 0 |
| Defense: | 5 |
| Movement: | 3 |
| Era Available: | Diamond |
| Made Obsolete By: | Never |

## Historical Notes

Can't touch our old Major Matt Mason crawler.

## Game Notes

Another transport, better armored this time, with a capacity of up to five units.

## Cyber Ninja

| | |
|---|---|
| Unit Type: | Unconventional Warfare |
| Cost: | 2000 |
| Attack: | 0 |
| Defense: | 3 |
| Movement: | 4 |
| Era Available: | Genetic |
| Made Obsolete By: | Never |

## Historical Notes

The logical development of hackers, though a hacker would be just as likely to prevent this from coming into existence.

## Game Notes

The techno-Mata Hari, this female has all the attributes of a spy. Plus, she adds a 25-percent defense against enemy spies. We think this latter-day Ninja is well worth the extra few yen she costs (as opposed to a mundane Spy), if only because she's much more efficient. For more, check out Chapter 4.

# Destroyer

| | |
|---|---|
| Unit Type: | Naval |
| Cost: | 1000 |
| Attack: | 10 |
| Defense: | 10 |
| Movement: | 6 |
| Ranged Attack: | 10 |
| Era Available: | Modern |
| Made Obsolete By: | Ultrapressure Machinery |

## Historical Notes

At the pivotal battle of Jutland in WWI, German forces turned away from the British line of battle, not because they feared the Allied Dreadnoughts, but because of the vaunted British Destroyers and their accuracy with torpedoes. The Destroyers in *Call to Power* also represent other escort craft, such as PT Boats and Corvettes.

## Game Notes

They're fast, cheap, and they can even harass enemy ground forces with bombardment. Destroyers are also your best defense against Submarines (big surprise). What's not to like?

# Diplomat

| | |
|---|---|
| Unit Type: | Non-Combat |
| Cost: | 135 |
| Attack: | 0 |
| Defense: | 1 |
| Movement: | 2 |
| Era Available: | Ancient |
| Made Obsolete By: | Never |

## Historical Notes

Diplomacy, in some form or another, has been with us since the first halting cities were constructed. *Call to Power*, like other games in the *Civilization* line, allows you to send emissaries without having an embassy. But if you want to do any real political work, you'll need a few good Diplomats (whether that's a contradiction in terms we'll leave for you to decide).

## Game Notes

Unlike previous *Civilization* games, Diplomats can't pull off the bloodless coup of an enemy city simply by spending money. They can still establish embassies with foreign lands, however, which is a must if you want that "Check Information" button on your Diplomacy screen to ever do anything. Better yet, after he establishes an embassy, the Diplomat doesn't get removed from play (a welcome change from *Civilization II*). Finally, a Diplomat can spy on an enemy city, gathering specific information on production, and more importantly, the exact number and type of defensive units. So, if you suspect that a nearby nation, especially one already involved in another war, has stripped his defenses on your mutual border, you can confirm or deny that assumption with your Diplomat. This information could win you a quick victory, or save you from entering into a costly and unnecessary war. Don't overdo this type of fact-finding mission, because your Diplomat may be captured and executed, and your reputation duly sullied. As a general rule, we recommend that you keep only a couple of Diplomats in play at any one time. While they are cheap to build, the maintenance costs add up.

# Eco Ranger

| | |
|---|---|
| Unit Type: | Unconventional Warfare |
| Cost: | 3750 |
| Attack: | 0 |
| Defense: | 1 |
| Movement: | 5 |
| Era Available: | Genetic |
| Made Obsolete By: | Never |

## Historical Notes

Yogi and Boo-Boo never had to deal with this kind of authority figure.

## Game Notes

It's a one-shot deal, but once the Genesis Device goes off, it doesn't matter. There are some really wicked ways to utilize these units; make sure to check out Chapter 9.

## Ecoterrorist

| | |
|---|---|
| Unit Type: | Unconventional Warfare |
| Cost: | 5000 |
| Attack: | 5 |
| Defense: | 5 |
| Movement: | 3 |
| Era Available: | Genetic |
| Made Obsolete By: | Never |

### Historical Notes

If the Unabomber was a cult instead of an individual…

### Game Notes

One of the best buys in the game, if only for the dreaded Nano attack. Like Cyber Ninjas, Ecoterrorists give an additional 25-percent defense against enemy spies, though we suggest they are better used on offense deep in your enemy's territory.

## Fascist

| | |
|---|---|
| Unit Type: | Land |
| Cost: | 1000 |
| Attack: | 16 |
| Defense: | 8 |
| Movement: | 2 |
| Era Available: | Modern |
| Made Obsolete By: | Never |

### Historical Notes

It's somehow comforting to know that Fascists don't come into pay until the Modern Era, but very disturbing to note that they never seem to go out of style. It also seems rather eerie that these iron-booted thugs tend to enter the game at around the same time as the Televangelists (draw your own conclusions). The only reason we can figure that they have such high combat factors is that they must represent the national will of frustrated countries looking for an outlet that, in this case, turns violent.

## Game Notes

A lot of gamers will be uncomfortable using these units for obvious reasons. If you want to rationalize this, think of it as putting your country under martial law, and keep in mind that even a man as good as Franklin Roosevelt was called a fascist by those who thought the President should keep us out of WWII. If you pass on these units, you give up a lot of firepower. Of course, you have to be a Fasist government to have these units, so if you've gone that far already…

## Fighter

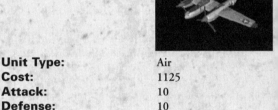

| | |
|---|---|
| Unit Type: | Air |
| Cost: | 1125 |
| Attack: | 10 |
| Defense: | 10 |
| Movement: | 10, with fuel for 3 turns |
| Ranged Attack: | 10 |
| Era Available: | Modern |
| Made Obsolete By: | Jet Propulsion |

### Historical Notes

The "Knights of the Air" in WWI notwithstanding, the fighter came into its own during the Battle of Britain in 1940, where the outnumbered Royal Air Force stopped an impending invasion of England by winning the air war against the Luftwaffe.

### Game Notes

Since the Fighter and the Aircraft Carrier are available at the same time, it gives you a lot more strategic options. Generally speaking, you should build four to five fighters for defense and at least one Aircraft Carrier, more if you are on the brink of war. The relatively high cost is offset by the fact that Fighter units are still effective until you reach the cusp of the Genetic Age, and Carriers are good throughout the game.

# Fusion Tank

| | |
|---|---|
| **Unit Type:** | Land |
| **Cost:** | 3250 |
| **Attack:** | 20 |
| **Defense:** | 15 |
| **Ranged Attack:** | 20 |
| **Movement:** | 8 |
| **Era Available:** | Diamond |
| **Made Obsolete By:** | Never |

## Historical Notes

Why buy another tank when you can buy this futuristic baby?

## Game Notes

We know it's a little expensive, but unlike a lot of the Space tech options, there is plenty of time left in the game for your enemies to seriously hurt you. Bleed a little now and buy a few of these, because you may not have enough gold to "Rush Buy" them later.

# Greek Fire Trireme

| | |
|---|---|
| **Unit Type:** | Naval |
| **Cost:** | 720 |
| **Attack:** | 2 |
| **Defense:** | 1 |
| **Movement:** | 2 |
| **Ranged Attack:** | 1 |
| **Era Available:** | Ancient |
| **Made Obsolete By:** | Machine Tools |

## Historical Notes

Archimedes, when he wasn't playing around with mathematical concepts in his bathtub (or running naked down the streets shouting "Eureka!"), was a pretty practical guy, for a scientist. He invented Greek Fire, which was an incendiary substance used by the Byzantine Greeks to flame and sink opposing ships. The most insidious thing about Greek Fire was that putting water on it didn't douse the flames. The secret of Greek Fire died with Archimedes and the Byzantines, but its spirit lives on in similarly terrible modern weapons like Napalm.

## Game Notes

For all its pyrotechnics, Greek Fire doesn't have a high combat value, and if you fall behind in the arms race, Greek Fire Triremes aren't much use against sailing vessels. They do give you the first Naval unit with bombardment capability, but that's not saying much for something that costs as much as this does. Only if you are having a lot of trouble with Pirates should you bother with this. Wait for better vessels with more firepower and seagoing capability.

# Infector

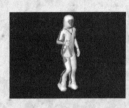

| | |
|---|---|
| **Unit Type:** | Unconventional Warfare |
| **Cost:** | 3750 |
| **Attack:** | 0 |
| **Defense:** | 1 |
| **Movement:** | 3 |
| **Era Available:** | Modern |
| **Made Obsolete By:** | Never |

## Historical Notes

Biological warfare is something we have to live with even now. The thought that special forces units will continue to develop tactics to spread deadly diseases is not at all farfetched, and that's scary as hell.

## Game Notes

The bio-attacks aren't always as effective as those of the Ecoterrorist, but you can get Infector units a lot sooner in the game. Always a good thing to have up your sleeve when threatened with war or Nukes.

# Interceptor

| | |
|---|---|
| **Unit Type:** | Air |
| **Cost:** | 1500 |

| | |
|---|---|
| **Attack:** | 15 |
| **Defense:** | 12 |
| **Movement:** | 15, with 2 turns of fuel |
| **Ranged Attack:** | 12 |
| **Era Available:** | Modern |
| **Made Obsolete By:** | Smart Materials |

## Historical Notes

The logical outcome of early experiments with jets in WWII by both sides, today's Interceptors can destroy enemies from beyond the horizon.

## Game Notes

For the slight bump you get in Attack and Defense, Interceptors are relatively expensive. Basically, players who always buy these remind us of gamers who buy every iteration of a PC processor, rather than skipping a generation. If you want to get two or three to have the longer-range capability, fine. Just don't get into an air spending war if air superiority isn't that critical to your long-range plans.

# Knight

| | |
|---|---|
| **Unit Type:** | Land |
| **Cost:** | 540 |
| **Attack:** | 3 |
| **Defense:** | 2 |
| **Movement:** | 4 |
| **Era Available:** | Ancient |
| **Made Obsolete By:** | Cavalry Tactics |

## Historical Notes

While they didn't technically appear until the Dark Ages in Europe, the Knights of *Call to Power* represent heavy cavalry, which came about due to the invention of the stirrup. Although, at first, Knights mounted on horses were only slightly more armored than the rest of the armed forces, eventually they became synonymous with heavy plate mail, to the point where once a Knight was unseated, he was so heavy that he became easy prey for lightly armed foot soldiers. Even so, the charge of a group of mounted Knights was terrible to behold, simply because of the sheer massed weight of their charge. Once high-velocity crossbows and longbows capable of piercing even the thickest armor became available, the Knight's days on the battlefield were numbered.

## Game Notes

The Knight, like so many other Ancient units, has been downgraded from *Civilization II*. Still, the Knight, with its attack of three, is the best all-around Ancient unit in *Call to Power*, and its cost is not out of line, considering its incredible mobility. Once you have the ability to build Knights, they should become the mainstay of your army, at least until you discover Gunpowder.

# Lawyer

| | |
|---|---|
| **Unit Type:** | Unconventional Warfare |
| **Cost:** | 450 |
| **Attack:** | 0 |
| **Defense:** | 1 |
| **Movement:** | 3 |
| **Era Available:** | Renaissance |
| **Made Obsolete By:** | Never |

## Historical Notes

Most of the written records we have of early civilizations concern the passage and proper enforcement of laws. However, most of the discussions concerning laws, and the development of learned professionals to carry out those discussions, came to Western culture through the Greeks, and especially the Romans, who developed a rigorous legal system. You have to wonder what the Romans would think of our present legal system, with its heavy emphasis on lawsuits, or our criminal system, with the incredible amount of time it takes for the appeals process to run its course.

## Game Notes

Lawyers are a necessary evil in *Call to Power*, just as they often are in real life. Despite the fact that Lawyers have no standard Attack value, they can really disrupt an opponent's civilization by using their special Lawsuit and Injunction attacks (probably the most underrated attacks in the game). It's the Nineties: when in doubt, slap a subpoena on your foes, and always keep a couple of well-dressed lawyers on the payroll.

# Legion

| Unit Type: | Land |
|---|---|
| Cost: | 200 |
| Attack: | 2 |
| Defense: | 2 |
| Movement: | 1 |
| Era Available: | Ancient |
| Made Obsolete By: | Gunpowder |

## Historical Notes

Weapon for weapon, the Legion, with its short swords, would seem to be disadvantaged versus the Phalanx and its incredibly long spears. Yet the Romans used the Legion to beat the Phalanx more often than not, even besting the great Carthaginian general Hannibal in the end. The Legion relied on tactical flexibility more than sheer mass or shock value, which gave it a distinct advantage over rough and uneven terrain.

## Game Notes

In all *Civilization* games, the Legion seems to have a different value. In the original *Civilization*, it was 3/1/1 (attack/defense/movement), and in *Civilization II*, it improved to 4/2/1. In *Call to Power*, the Legion is a wimpy 2/2/1. So, in a normal fight, an attacking Legion is the same as a defending Phalanx, and worth less if the Phalanx is fortified. Why? We don't really know, but we suggest that you keep your purchase of Legions to a minimum. For offense, you are better off buying Samurai, and for defense, Phalanxes are cheaper. The only exception to this rule would be if you have a chance to overwhelm an enemy early in the game, and you can't build Samurai.

## Leviathan

| Unit Type: | Land |
|---|---|
| Cost: | 9000 |
| Attack: | 40 |
| Defense: | 40 |
| Movement: | 1 tile per turn |
| Era Available: | Genetic |
| Made Obsolete By: | Never |

## Historical Notes

As far as a Panzer freak's dream, the old Ogre (from game designer Steve Jackson) moved a heckuva lot faster.

## Game Notes

If other nations are building them, you can, too. If possible, however, you should concentrate on winning the Wormhole race.

## Longship

| Unit Type: | Naval |
|---|---|
| Cost: | 720 |
| Attack: | 2 |
| Defense: | 2 |
| Movement: | 3 |
| Era Available: | Ancient |
| Made Obsolete By: | Mass Production |

## Historical Notes

The Longship is synonymous with the Vikings, brave explorers and feared raiders from the Baltic Sea to the coast of Spain. In *Call to Power*, Longships represent the early age of sailing vessels.

## Game Notes

While Longships seem fairly expensive, they are a lot better buy than Triremes, if only because they actually have a decent movement radius. Unless you have a far-flung island empire, however, you really shouldn't build more than a handful of these. Instead, wait for the much more versatile Ship of the Line to advance your power at sea.

## Machine Gunner

| Unit Type: | Land |
|---|---|
| Cost: | 800 |
| Attack: | 8 |
| Defense: | 8 |
| Movement: | 2 |
| Era Available: | Modern |
| Made Obsolete By: | Technocracy |

### Historical Notes

The Gatling Gun gets the nod as the first true Machine Gun, but it wasn't produced in sufficient numbers to have an impact on the American Civil War. By the First World War, however, the Machine Gun had developed such a killing efficiency that thousands of men could be killed in a scant few minutes while fighting over mere yards of terrain. *Call to Power* reflects the short dominance of the more bulky and relatively fixed Machine Gun at the turn of the 20th century, rather than the portable Machine Guns of today, such as the AK-47 and related models.

### Game Notes

The Machine Gunner is one of our favorite units for a non-Fascist government. It's fairly inexpensive, durable, and more mobile than earlier types of infantry units. You'll definitely want to build several of these to use as your base units in city defense. Offensive players will find that they need them for a balanced attack, as well—Machine Gunners certainly make for excellent occupation troops.

## Marine

| Unit Type: | Elite Land |
|---|---|
| Cost: | 1000 |
| Attack: | 12 |
| Defense: | 8 |
| Movement: | 3 |
| Era Available: | Modern |
| Made Obsolete By: | Fusion |

### Historical Notes

Marines have been around since the days of the Greeks and Romans, but in *Call to Power*, they represent the classic WWII soldier with amphibious assault training.

### Game Notes

A little improved from *Civilization II*, Marines are often mainstays of a well-rounded army in *Call to Power*. Don't forget that, like Samurai, Marines cost you the full "At War" maintenance cost, regardless of whether the rest of your units are on standby or standing down. Still, it's hard to resist infantry that move at a speed of 3 and have the ability to amphibiously assault, as well.

## Mobile SAM

| Unit Type: | Anti-Air |
|---|---|
| Cost: | 2000 |
| Attack: | 4 |
| Defense: | 4 |
| Movement: | 6 |
| Ranged Attack: | 12 |
| Era Available: | Modern |
| Made Obsolete By: | Robotics |

### Historical Notes

Originally begun as an attempt to counteract nuclear missiles, surface-to-air missiles eventually moved to the more practical and achievable use of anti-aircraft defense, where they have been a fixture on the electronic battlefield since the 1970s. So sophisticated are these weapons today that even hand-held launchers have claimed several aircraft kills.

### Game Notes

It never hurts to have a few of these to stave off enemy Bomber attacks. But if you are going to spend a lot of money on these, you might as well be building Interceptors.

## Mounted Archer

| Unit Type: | Land |
|---|---|
| Cost: | 270 |
| Attack: | 1 |
| Defense: | 1 |
| Movement: | 3 |
| Ranged Attack: | 1 |
| Era Available: | Ancient |
| Made Obsolete By: | Gunpowder |

### Historical Notes

In most areas of the world, Mounted Archers weren't found as early in history as you are able to build them in *Call to Power*. The Egyptians did employ Chariots, which featured a limited missile capability. But while Chariots were found in *Civilization II*, they are conspicuously missing here, and the Mounted Archers are nowhere near the same things. These seem to be modeled more along the lines of scouts, and as such, there is a general historical context for them, but that's it.

## Game Notes

We recommend that you build one and only one Mounted Archer. Use it to explore the countryside at the beginning of the game, where its relatively high movement rate is helpful. Once you get a reasonable road network set up, you no longer need these weak, expensive units, especially since you can build two Phalanxes for the same price. The ranged attack of 1 doesn't make up for the high cost, since Mounted Archers lack punch.

# Musketeers

| | |
|---|---|
| Unit Type: | Land |
| Cost: | 560 |
| Attack: | 4 |
| Defense: | 4 |
| Movement: | 1 |
| Ranged Attack: | 4 |
| Era Available: | Renaissance |
| Made Obsolete By: | Mass Production |

## Historical Notes

The life of a Musketeer probably wasn't as romantic as Dumas portrayed it, but D'artagnan and his less fictional mates certainly lived in interesting times. Musketeers fought in every corner of Europe for both religious and secular causes, where they were renowned for their courage under fire, their talent with the newfangled weaponry, and their sense of flair.

## Game Notes

This is one unit in *Call to Power* that is actually improved from *Civilization II*. In particular, Musketeers are some of the most versatile units in the game due to their ability to fight equally well from the front or back ranks. This is due to their good (for the time period, anyway) Ranged Attack. If you are fighting an offensive war, you'll need at least half of your army to be Musketeers. Those more concerned with defense will want to mix in a few Musketeers with the much cheaper Pikemen.

# Nuke

| | |
|---|---|
| Unit Type: | Air |
| Cost: | 4000 |
| Attack: | 100 |
| Defense: | 1 |
| Movement: | 20 |
| Era Available: | Modern |
| Made Obsolete By: | Never |

## Historical Notes

One of the great "what-ifs" of history is what would have happened had Truman not given the order to drop Atomic Bombs on Japan. Given that he did, and it's been over a half century since another nuclear weapon was used in war…

## Game Notes

The Nuke's special ability is to destroy both 75-percent of City Population and all units and Tile Improvements within a one-tile radius of ground zero (aside from any Pollution aspects). Any game where you blithely toss Nukes around tends to bother us, so fortunately, there are defenses against Nukes in *Call to Power*, and consequences for using them. Sad to say, but the old Mutual Destruction Madness, where everybody has The Bomb, is a lot safer than only one side having it. If any of the computer players think you won't retaliate, none of them show much reluctance to use Nukes. Keep in mind that the Nuke only has fuel for one turn; regardless of whether it moves one space, or the full twenty, the Nuke will blow up. So, make sure that you can reach your target *before* you launch—Nukes are too expensive to waste.

# Paratrooper

| | |
|---|---|
| Unit Type: | Land/Air |
| Cost: | 2500 |
| Attack: | 10 |
| Defense: | 10 |
| Movement: | 3, with the Paradrop ability |
| Era Available: | Modern |
| Made Obsolete By: | Never |

## Historical Notes

Paratroops were used throughout WWII, notably at Crete and Operation Market Garden. Though lightly armed, paratroops were often used during invasions to secure bridges and perform other behind-the-lines duties.

## Game Notes

There are many nasty but effective ways to use Paratroopers. You should always have at least two or three in your force mix, even if you don't plan on going to war (see Chapter 3 for more details). Best of all, these units never go obsolete.

# Phalanx

| | |
|---|---|
| Unit Type: | Land |
| Cost: | 135 |
| Attack: | 1 |
| Defense: | 2 |
| Movement: | 1 |
| Era Available: | Ancient |
| Made Obsolete By: | Agricultural Revolution |

## Historical Notes

The Companion Cavalry grabbed all the headlines, but the backbone of Alexander the Great's steamroller Macedonian army was the Phalanx. In combat, each man in the tight formation would thrust forward with his more-than-20-foot spear, while simultaneously guarding the man to his left with a large shield. Phalanxes weren't particularly flexible, and they were vulnerable to attacks from the flank and rear. But used properly, they were tough do beat, as 600 Spartans proved against several thousand Persian troops at Thermopylae.

## Game Notes

Phalanxes aren't very mobile in *Call to Power*, either. But they are cheap, and quite effective against Barbarian incursions, provided you fortify them in your cities; build a City Wall around them for additional city defense as soon as you can afford it. Never make the mistake of using a Phalanx in open combat; they almost always get slaughtered.

# Phantom

| | |
|---|---|
| Unit Type: | Space |
| Cost: | 6750 |
| Attack: | 40 |
| Defense: | 10 |
| Movement: | 3 |
| Era Available: | Diamond |
| Made Obsolete By: | Never |

## Historical Notes

Not related to the old *Phantom* comic (no indigenous peoples were harmed in the making of this quip).

## Game Notes

While they are a bit on the pricey side, these slick "Space Stealth Interceptors" are a great late-game gambit to try and slip through your enemy's defenses, due to their cloaking ability (especially if he is trying to "wormhole" his way to victory). Unless you have a lot of gold, though, you'll probably want to mix these in with a few Swarm for balance.

# Pikemen

| | |
|---|---|
| Unit Type: | Land |
| Cost: | 270 |
| Attack: | 3 |
| Defense: | 3 |
| Movement: | 1 |
| Era Available: | Renaissance |
| Made Obsolete By: | Explosives |

## Historical Notes

Pikemen were traditionally effective against mounted units such as Knights. The Swiss Pikemen went undefeated in battle for hundreds of years, and their battlefield dominance only began to slip as gunpowder rose into ascendancy.

## Game Notes

Not only is the Pikeman an effective and balanced unit, the cost is a bargain. Pikemen have three times the Attack and 1.5 times the defense of a Phalanx, but cost only twice as much. And by this point in the game, you should easily be able to afford a lot more Pikeman than you could afford Phalanxes at the beginning of the game.

# Plasma Destroyer

| | |
|---|---|
| Unit Type: | Naval |
| Cost: | 4500 |
| Attack: | 30 |
| Defense: | 15 |
| Ranged Attack: | 15 |
| Movement: | 8 |
| Era Available: | Diamond |
| Made Obsolete By: | Never |

## Historical Notes

This is the quintessential futuristic naval unit.

## Game Notes

You might think that by this time in the game, the only reason you'd need another naval unit is if you are close to conquering the world. Actually, Plasma Destroyers offer a reasonably priced combination of anti-air and anti-sub defense with enough mobility to defend the area around your wormhole if needed.

# Plasmatica

| | |
|---|---|
| Unit Type: | land |
| Cost: | 4500 |
| Attack: | 15 |
| Defense: | 15 |
| Movement: | 6 |
| Era Available: | Genetic |
| Made Obsolete By: | Never |

## Historical Notes

Sounds like a band that once opened for the Sex Pistols.

## Game Notes

All things considered, this is a pretty cheap and solid unit on both attack and defense for the remainder of the game, very mobile.

# Samurai

| | |
|---|---|
| Unit Type: | Elite Land |
| Cost: | 335 |
| Attack: | 3 |
| Defense: | 1 |
| Movement: | 2 |
| Era Available: | Ancient |
| Made Obsolete By: | Explosives |

## Historical Notes

The term covers a lot of ground, but Samurai usually refers to professional soldiers of feudal Japan. These warriors adhered to a strict moral code, Bushido, where how you fought and the manner in which you maintained your honor was as important as the actual combat result. So, even when early gunpowder weapons, such as the arquebus, became available, the Samurai refused to use them, feeling that they were a dishonorable weapon, fit to be used only by the untrained peasants, or ashigaru.

## Game Notes

While it's laudable that Samurai are included in *Call to Power* (they weren't in previous versions of *Civilization*, save in add-on scenarios), they have caused our favorite ancient unit, the Legion, to be downgraded. Basically, you pay a lot more for a Samurai to get essentially the firepower that a Legion gave you in the original *Civilization*. Then again, if you want to have some offensive punch, you are better off purchasing three Samurai than four or five Legions, simply because the Samurai have the punch to take out a fortified Phalanx, and the Legions don't. Keep in mind that Samurai, due to their status as Elite troops, always cost you the full "At War" maintenance. Therefore, don't buy a lot of them unless you plan on going to full wartime status.

# Sea Engineer

| | |
|---|---|
| Unit Type: | Non-Combat |
| Cost: | 4500 |
| Attack: | 0 |

| Defense: | 1 |
| Movement: | 5 |
| Era Available: | Genetic |
| Made Obsolete By: | Never |

## Historical Notes

For fans of *Voyage to the Bottom of the Sea* and a few Roger Zelazny stories (like us).

## Game Notes

The futuristic equivalent of Settlers, these are a must if you need underwater cities to escape the effects of worldwide pollution.

## Settler

| Unit Type: | Non-combat |
| Cost: | 540 |
| Attack: | 0 |
| Defense: | 1 |
| Movement: | 1 |
| Era Available: | Ancient |
| Made Obsolete By: | Never |

## Historical Notes

Whether it's the early nomadic tribes, or the Pilgrims, who left for the New World to escape religious oppression, there are examples throughout history of population movements and shifts. In *Call to Power*, these shifts are represented as Settler units, with the added benefit that you control where they go to found new cities, a luxury not available to historical leaders.

## Game Notes

In earlier versions of *Civilization*, Settlers performed all sorts of functions, from mining and irrigation to road building and terraforming. In *Call to Power*, all of these functions are performed through Public Works (see Chapter 1), leaving Settlers with but one reason to be in the game: building cities. As such, one of the most common *Civilization* tactics, that of building settlers to control runaway population (each time you build a Settler, the population of that city is reduced by one), is less effective. Because new Settlers you build can't be used to improve your empire, they must either build new cities (which can cause unhappiness in your empire) or you must disband them, a terrible waste of resources. This situation is exacerbated since Settlers are now more expensive to

build than ever. For example, in *Civilization II*, Settlers cost the same as two Phalanx units. Now, they cost the equivalent of *four* Phalanxes. What can you do? Keep tabs on your city growth so that the population of your largest cities doesn't get out of control; use your Max Gold or Max Science buttons to keep your workers off the farms. And don't build a Settler unless you need to start a new city.

## Ship of the Line

| Unit Type: | Naval |
| Cost: | 855 |
| Attack: | 4 |
| Defense: | 4 |
| Movement: | 4, can transport 3 units |
| Ranged Attack: | 4 |
| Era Available: | Renaissance |
| Made Obsolete By: | Mass Production |

## Historical Notes

While Frigates like "Old Ironsides" might capture our fancy, it was the Ship of the Line that ruled the seas. In fact, England's empire was largely based on its capability to project naval power throughout the world. In *Call to Power*, the Ship of the Line represents the apogee of sailing ships, armed with lots and lots of cannon.

## Game Notes

One of the best combat unit buys in the game, period. Not only can the Ship of the Line easily take out any ship from an earlier era, it's also the first really effective ship used in a bombardment role. Amazingly, this versatile vessel doesn't become obsolete until the dawn of the Genetic Era! If you want to keep your strategic options at sea open, build at least six to eight of these, and use them to keep your shores free from worry. If you have a largely island empire, build a dozen.

## Space Bomber

| Unit Type: | Space |
| Cost: | 7500 |

| | |
|---|---|
| Attack: | 6 |
| Defense: | 6 |
| Ranged Attack: | 50 |
| Movement: | 2 |
| Era Available: | Diamond |
| Made Obsolete By: | Never |

## Historical Notes

Bomb the earth from Space—cool!

## Game Notes

Don't let the low movement number fool you; two movement points in Space lets a unit move 40 tiles in a turn. And their ranged attack packs a heck of a punch. If things are to the point where you're desperately fighting over the Wormhole, money has less meaning—go for it!

# Space Engineer

| | |
|---|---|
| Unit Type: | Non-Combat |
| Cost: | 7500 |
| Attack: | 0 |
| Defense: | 3 |
| Movement: | 5 |
| Era Available: | Genetic |
| Made Obsolete By: | Never |

## Historical Notes

A little different from the way Robert Heinlein saw the future, but what the hay?

## Game Notes

It's highway robbery, but you are going to need this to win via the "alien" method.

# Space Fighter

| | |
|---|---|
| Unit Type: | Air/Space |
| Cost: | 2250 |
| Attack: | 16 |
| Defense: | 16 |
| Movement: | 15 |
| Ranged Attack: | 16 |
| Era Available: | Genetic |
| Made Obsolete By: | Never |

## Historical Notes

They may look like a geometry experiment gone haywire, but Stealth Fighters are very effective.

## Game Notes

This is a reasonably priced and good all-around attack and defense plane, with the added enticement of space-capable combat and movement. It's a good choice for a peaceful player determined to defend his wormhole.

# Space Plane

| | |
|---|---|
| Unit Type: | Air/Space |
| Cost: | 2250 |
| Attack: | 0 |
| Defense: | 3 |
| Movement: | 15, can transport 5 units, 2 turns of fuel |
| Era Available: | Genetic |
| Made Obsolete By: | Never |

## Historical Notes

Seems to be the next step beyond the real-life space shuttle.

## Game Notes

It can carry a few units, but it also trashes the ozone layer, which is usually already in pretty bad shape by this stage of the game. You'll need these for your Space Colonies, but use them with discretion.

# Spy

| | |
|---|---|
| Unit Type: | Unconventional Warfare |
| Cost: | 1500 |
| Attack: | 0 |
| Defense: | 1 |
| Movement: | 4 |
| Era Available: | Renaissance |
| Made Obsolete By: | Neural Silicon Interface |

## Historical Notes

It seems appropriate that just as Printing Presses are getting up and rolling, the Spy should put in an appearance. Information, especially written records, is the magnet for espionage.

## Game Notes

Spies aren't really changed all that much from *Civilization II*, except that they cost more. On the other hand, they are available a lot earlier in the game, and they stick around for a long time. Spies can do everything a Diplomat can do, but better. The Spy's most terrible attack is to plant a nuclear device in the city of an enemy. So, if you're going into Tom Clancy novel withdrawal, by all means, keep a couple of Spies around—you can always deny everything later to the Congressional Committee.

## Spy Plane

| | |
|---|---|
| Unit Type: | Unconventional Warfare |
| Cost: | 2815 |
| Attack: | 0 |
| Defense: | 2 |
| Movement: | 10, with 10 turns of fuel |
| Era Available: | Modern |
| Made Obsolete By: | Never |

## Historical Notes

The U2 spy plane being shot down over the Soviet Union was one of the defining moments of the Cold War.

## Game Notes

Not really worth the cost, unless you're desperately trying to find your opponent's wormhole. If it's info you are looking for, consider the GlobeSat Wonder (see Chapter 8).

## Star Cruiser

| | |
|---|---|
| Unit Type: | Space |
| Cost: | 7500 |
| Attack: | 30 |

| | |
|---|---|
| Defense: | 20 |
| Movement: | 5 |
| Ranged Attack: | 30 |
| Era Available: | Diamond |
| Made Obsolete By: | Never |

## Historical Notes

This is the stuff of which space operas are made.

## Game Notes

Once you find the Wormhole, you'll need at least one of these, expenses be damned.

## Stealth Sub

| | |
|---|---|
| Unit Type: | Naval |
| Cost: | 6000 |
| Attack: | 30 |
| Defense: | 10 |
| Movement: | 3, can carry 4 Nukes |
| Ranged Attack: | 30 |
| Era Available: | Genetic |
| Made Obsolete By: | Never |

## Historical Notes

The logical extension of modern super-quiet nuclear Subs, but why is it so slow?

## Game Notes

Even the peaceful-minded will want to build a few of these to either take out a potential invasion fleet, or to have a hidden nuclear deterrent at sea.

## Stealth Bomber

| | |
|---|---|
| Unit Type: | Air |
| Cost: | 3375 |
| Attack: | 16 |
| Defense: | 8 |
| Movement: | 10, carry 2 Nukes, 5 turns of fuel |
| Ranged Attack: | 22 |

| | |
|---|---|
| **Era Available:** | Genetic |
| **Made Obsolete By:** | Never |

## Historical Notes

Once considered the brainchild of science fiction, the Stealth Bomber acquitted itself well in Desert Storm.

## Game Notes

This is the Bomber we recommend, no strings attached.

## Storm Marine

| | |
|---|---|
| **Unit Type:** | Space |
| **Cost:** | 4500 |
| **Attack:** | 24 |
| **Defense:** | 20 |
| **Movement:** | 3 |
| **Era Available:** | Genetic |
| **Made Obsolete By:** | Never |

## Historical Notes

Where did I put my lightsab… Oops! Wrong game.

## Game Notes

A reasonably priced space unit for once, with amphibious assault capability to boot.

## Submarine

| | |
|---|---|
| **Unit Type:** | Naval |
| **Cost:** | 1500 |
| **Attack:** | 20 |
| **Defense:** | 8 |
| **Movement:** | 5 |
| **Ranged Attack:** | 20 |
| **Era Available:** | Modern |
| **Made Obsolete By:** | Sea Colonies |

## Historical Notes

Once Jules Verne introduced us to Captain Nemo and the Nautilus in *20,000 Leagues Under the Sea*, the waves have never seemed the same. Submarines in more primitive

forms have actually been used in combat as far back as the American Revolutionary War, but the *Call to Power* subs represent the sleek underwater killers of WWII and beyond, particularly the famous (or infamous) U-Boats.

## Game Notes

With their special Underwater Attack ability, Submarines are well worth the money. Make sure to keep them away from Destroyers, however, as Subs have a mediocre defense. If you have the opportunity, it's well worth sacrificing a Sub for an enemy Carrier.

## Sub-Neural Ads

| | |
|---|---|
| **Unit Type:** | Unconventional Warfare |
| **Cost:** | 2250 |
| **Attack:** | 0 |
| **Defense:** | 1 |
| **Movement:** | 5 |
| **Era Available:** | Diamond |
| **Made Obsolete By:** | Never |

## Historical Notes

Having run movie theatres in an earlier life, Terry can vouch that the old subliminal trick of splicing a single frame of a well-known beverage product into the movie *does* actually increase concession sales (just kidding). All we know is that this unit seems worlds beyond our parlor tricks.

## Game Notes

A really good way of disrupting your enemies in the endgame. They work better when you sic them on several enemy cities at the same time. Keep in mind, however, that moving to these units makes your Corporate Branch units obsolete, and you should only do this if you feel the additional harassment is warranted.

## Swarm

| | |
|---|---|
| **Unit Type:** | Space |
| **Cost:** | 5250 |
| **Attack:** | 20 |
| **Defense:** | 20 |

| | |
|---|---|
| Movement: | 3 |
| Era Available: | Diamond |
| Made Obsolete By: | Never |

## Historical Notes

Starfighters, basically.

## Game Notes

Worth the price to protect your Wormhole rights.

## Tank

| | |
|---|---|
| Unit Type: | Land |
| Cost: | 2000 |
| Attack: | 16 |
| Defense: | 10 |
| Movement: | 6 |
| Ranged Attack: | 16 |
| Era Available: | |
| Made Obsolete By: | Fusion |

## Historical Notes

At the Battle of Cambrai, tracked, armored vehicles armed with Machine Guns blew through German lines, winning more ground in a day than either side typically did in a period of months. The name "Tank" was originally a code name to confuse the Germans (as in "fuel tank"), but as with most good monosyllabic nicknames, it stuck.

## Game Notes

"The Battleship of land," as the Tank was once called, is a tough call. It's fairly expensive, even given where you are in the game (just compare it to the costs of Fascists), but it packs a wallop, and it's so mobile. If you have any intention to fight an aggressive campaign, you really need to have a core of Tanks, if only to take advantage of their superb Ranged Attack ability. On the plus side, Tanks do stay effective until most of the way through the Genetic Era.

## The Televangelist

| | |
|---|---|
| Unit Type: | Unconventional Warfare |
| Cost: | 1000 |
| Attack: | 0 |
| Defense: | 1 |
| Movement: | 3 |
| Era Available: | Modern |
| Made Obsolete By: | Never |

## Historical Notes

The Televangelist unit in *Call to Power* is the epitome of the stylish television preacher who inspired Ray Stevens' musical question, "Would Jesus wear a Rolex if he had a TV show today?" These slick provocateurs have no inherent offensive capacity, but they can be most effective at aiding one's allies or disrupting one's enemies, all for a price. Also, in keeping with the real-life fund-raising capacity of these priests of the broadcast cathedral, they are extremely valuable economic units.

## Game Notes

While they cost a lot to spread the Word, these folks sure know their medium inside out. Televangelists are much more effective than Clerics at Converting Cities, Selling Indulgences, and Soothsaying, and they are less likely to be caught. If you find these units too distasteful to use, you're missing out on a lot of the game's satire, and you really reduce your options of messing with your opponents without having to go to war.

# Trireme

| | |
|---|---|
| Unit Type: | Naval |
| Cost: | 540 |
| Attack: | 1 |
| Defense: | 1 |
| Movement: | 2 |
| Era Available: | Ancient |
| Made Obsolete By: | Machine Tools |

## Historical Notes

Triremes in *Call to Power* represent all kinds of early oared sailing vessels, from canoes and Biremes to Catamarans, Quinquiremes, and larger. While recent research by Thor Heyerdahl and others suggest that these types of ships were capable, in some rare cases, of oceanic travel, the game chooses to limit Triremes to local sea travel.

## Game Notes

In earlier versions of *Civilization*, you were allowed to try to sail your Trireme away from shore, but there was a 50 percent chance it would sink if it ended a turn not adjacent to land. *Civilization II* added the Lighthouse Wonder, which allowed free movement by Triremes in seas and oceans, but that's not an option here. So, the compromise the designers made in *Call to Power* is that you only have to be within two spaces of the shore, instead of directly adjacent, but that's the limit, always enforced. So, keep moving around your local sea-lanes, and use narrow straits to bridge the water gap between continents. If you're persistent (and a little lucky), you may find an untouched continent ripe for the plucking.

# Troop Ship

| | |
|---|---|
| Unit Type: | Naval |
| Cost: | 1200 |
| Attack: | 0 |
| Defense: | 2 |
| Movement: | 5, transports 1 to 5 units |
| Era Available: | Modern |
| Made Obsolete By: | Never |

## Historical Notes

The unsung workhorses of D-Day, they were also traps for the men inside once they hit the beach and opened the "front door." If you wonder what being in one of these was like, check out some of the recent movies dealing with WWII.

## Game Notes

The Troop Ship can carry five units and move five spaces, so it's a must if you plan an amphibious assault. But it's as fragile as an eggshell, and expensive to replace (not counting any transported troops that sink with it). So, make sure you send it out with an escort. If you don't have any enemies overseas, you can pass on this one: In *Call to Power*, unlike *Civilization II*, you don't need Troop Ships to transport Caravans.

# Warrior

| | |
|---|---|
| Unit Type: | Land |
| Cost: | 135 |
| Attack: | 1 |
| Defense: | 1 |
| Movement: | 1 |
| Era Available: | Ancient |
| Made Obsolete By: | Bureaucracy |

## Historical Notes

These represent the first halting beginnings of an organized fighting force in history.

## Game Notes

The sooner you can replace Warriors with Phalanxes, the better.

# War Walker

| | |
|---|---|
| **Unit Type:** | Land |
| **Cost:** | 3000 |
| **Attack:** | 12 |
| **Defense:** | 12 |
| **Movement:** | 5 |
| **Ranged Attack:** | 24 |
| **Era Available:** | Modern |
| **Made Obsolete By:** | Never |

## Historical Notes

This is the logical unit for fans of Giant Robots.

## Game Notes

This is a fairly versatile unit, with a great Ranged Attack. It also moves through mountains much faster than the usual rate. If you can afford a few War Walkers to go with your Space Marines, the combo makes for a good endgame defense.

# Wormhole Probe

| | |
|---|---|
| **Unit Type:** | Space |
| **Cost:** | 9375 |
| **Attack:** | 0 |
| **Defense:** | 3 |
| **Movement:** | 5 |
| **Era Available:** | Diamond |
| **Made Obsolete By:** | Never |

## Historical Notes

It's been speculated that stable Wormholes exist, but we're a long way from proving it.

## Game Notes

The key to winning the game peacefully.

# Chapter Three:

# Concerning the Use of Force

## How to Move, How Combat Really Works, and How to Get the Most Out of Your Forces

*"War is the continuation of national policy goals no longer attainable by other means."*
—Carl von Clausewitz

Combat in *Call to Power* is not always desirable, not always decisive, and not even always necessary. But it is inevitable in a game of *Call to Power* that you will have to fight sometime, and often not at a time or place of your own choosing. If you prefer building to fighting in *Call to Power*, you have several options:

1. Play at a lower level of difficulty, where rival civilizations are less likely to attack you.
2. Play on a large map, where you will have less direct contact with other civilizations until later in the game.
3. Similarly, play with fewer opponents.
4. Finally, build certain Wonders of the World that help prevent wars, such as the ESP Center (see Chapter 7).

## Concerning Costs vs. Goals

Many of us, however, find combat to be simply part of the game, and an often-fascinating part, at that. It's a challenge to be in a situation where, for example, your Legions are outnumbered by the enemy on the Roman border, and you think to yourself, "What would Julius Caesar have done here?" *Call to Power* has no pretense of being tactically realistic. And it's a good thing, too, because the game would be

terribly complex, and likely would never end. However, it does give you the broad picture of how and why wars are fought.

First, wars cost money, a lot of money. You have to spend production units and/or gold toward the purchase and support of military units that could potentially be used to build theaters, hospitals, Wonders, and the like. You have to spend for City Walls and other defensive structures. And when you lose units in battle, or they become obsolete with the passage of time, you have to spend all over again: Muskets cost more than swords, and space-faring units cost more than prop-driven planes.

If *Call to Power* always fell into the same predictable pattern every time you played, it wouldn't be much of a game. Because the designers introduce enough randomness to keep things hopping, you don't know whether your neighbor is going to attack your peaceful cities because he lusts after your oyster trade, or whether you should forego your usually peaceful nature to free your neighbor from the "burden" of growing all that tobacco.

Therefore, the first question inevitably is, "What is my strategic goal in this particular game?" The second question that follows from this is, "Can I afford to undertake my chosen goal?" What newcomers to *Call to Power* often fail to ask is, "Can I afford *not* to undertake my chosen goal?" Or worse, they have no goal at all.

One thing we can assure you, however, is that if you simply go along, letting the game play *you,* instead of you playing the game, your civilization will be left in the dustbin of history. Therefore, whenever you are faced with the possibility of military conflict, ask yourself:

1. *Does the potential enemy pose an immediate threat to the well being of my empire?*

    In the early part of the game, for example, tough-looking Barbarians may be unable to plunder much of your well-defended empire. Therefore, it might be better to wait and let them attack at favorable odds for you, at least until you build units with higher attack strengths to drive the Barbarians off.

2. *Will this fight start a long, protracted war?*

    We've found in testing that most computer-controlled empires, especially early on in the game, are amenable to peaceful resolutions to problems, provided that you honor your agreements. But eventually another nation will continually encroach on your territory, and you will have to decide when to boot them out. Generally, the AI will move units into your territory only if it considers you to be weak. So, don't play into the computer's hands. Often, you'll just have to suffer the indignity of having foreign troops on your soil for a few turns until you are better prepared to go to war.

3. *Why am I going to war?*

    If you are fighting to protect your own borders, fine. But many wars in *Call to Power* aren't that clear cut. You have to sometimes go to war to either help out an ally, or to prevent another empire from becoming so powerful that it threatens to run away with the game. If you are ill prepared to do these things, it's often better to try to resolve the situation through Trade or Tech concessions than to end up on the losing side in a protracted war.

4. *How much can I afford to lose?*

    When you go to war, you risk losing not only units, but also cities, trade, and gold. If you are a primarily peaceful nation, you will likely have to put much of your research on hold, or switch it toward more military-oriented Advances. You may even have to forego building Wonders that would benefit your civilization. Especially with more advanced forms of government, such as Democracy, it helps to set reasonable limits on how long you will fight and how much you can afford to spend, as your citizens will get increasingly unhappy the longer you are involved in the conflict. The big exception to this is if you have a major rival determined on taking you out (or that you are determined to remove from the game). If that's the case, consider switching your government to something more efficient for a wartime economy (see Chapter 4 for more details on various types of Governments).

5. *Will this war help me win the game?*

    At the risk of sounding cynical, we tend to go to war when it is most practical to do so. For the Alexander-style player, this might be 90-percent of the time (yet you still don't want a war forced on you before you're ready). Even if you're a player whose style is better suited to economics and production, you're going to eventually reach a point where you are entangled in a "World War" that will continue over a long number of turns. In either case, you are going to have to decide whether: a) crippling your opponents is enough; b) you should take an opponent entirely out of the game; or c) you can derive a lasting advantage without expending as much effort.

TIP: With Friends Like You: It's advantageous to work on alliances early in the game. Often you can help an ally by going to war (at the ally's request) with a distant enemy who really can't do much damage to you. You can even fight a couple of meaningless battles at sea and sign a cease-fire with your "enemy," and you've still gained whatever Tech or gold concessions were used by your ally to entice you into the conflict.

*I'D LOVE TO HELP YOU, BUT... Don't be shy in forming alliances early in the game. Not only can they help against over-aggressive enemies; alliances can also gain you Trade and Tech concessions when you help out your friends later in the game.*

Now that we've given you some food for thought on how to formulate goals, we're going to spend the rest of the chapter on helping you reach those goals. We're going to discuss in detail how movement and combat work, with concrete examples. This way, you'll have a better idea of when to rush that enemy Phalanx or when to intercept an enemy Bomber. We'll show you what terrain to defend tenaciously, and what terrain you wouldn't want your units to be caught dead in—literally (just keep in mind that it's only a game).

Throughout this chapter, we also get down and dirty with specific tactical tips. We'll unlock the keys to Submarine attacks, show you how to keep those pesky Barbarians off

your back, and much more. Well, what are you waiting for? There's a newly generated world out there, ripe for the plucking!

## Concerning Land Movement

Before you can fight an enemy, you have to move to meet it on the field of battle, or else it has to meet you. In fact, combat itself can even be partially considered a function of movement in *Call to Power*, because you must, in most cases, attempt to move into an opponent's space to initiate a battle.

As with most strategy games, the map of *Call to Power* is divided by a grid used to regulate movement. Just so you know, this phenomenon is not restricted to turn-based games like *Call to Power*. Popular real-time strategy games also divide the map into a grid; they just don't show the grid to you. While you can turn on the grid in *Call to Power* (the default is off), we don't recommend doing so, because it tends to make the map look too busy.

If you've ever played a classic board game like Monopoly or Parcheesi, the movement of each piece in those games is determined by what you roll on a pair of dice; toss a seven, and your piece moves seven spaces. While this method might offer a simple way to determine movement, it's very luck-dependent, and hardly what Julius Caesar had in mind when he uttered his famous line, "The die is cast." So, most sophisticated strategy games regulate movement by assigning each piece (or unit) a set movement capability, which is expressed as "movement points." Movement points vary per unit type. Cavalry, for instance, has more movement points than infantry, like Marines or Legions, because generally speaking, you can go a lot farther on horseback than you can on foot in the same amount of time.

How movement points work in *Call to Power* is pretty straightforward once you get used to it. If you are in "open terrain," such as grassland, your movement points tell you how many spaces you can move. In difficult terrain, like mountains, it will take longer (more movement points) to move through.

Every unit can always move at least one space every turn, no matter its movement points or the type of terrain its moving through.

## Example 1

Let's say a Mounted Archer, which has three movement points, is moving this turn through a combination of two grassland and one plains space. Since both of these types of terrain cost one movement point apiece, our Mounted Archer could move all three spaces.

If our Mounted Archer were moving through a desert, on the other hand, it would be able to move only one space. Our Mounted Archer would use up two of its three movement points for this turn moving into the first desert space, and would have only one movement point left, not enough to enter the next desert space, which costs two movement points to enter.

## Land Movement Costs

| Land Terrain | Movement Point Cost | Build Roads/ Railroads/Maglevs? |
|---|---|---|
| Dead Tiles | 1 | No |
| Deserts | 2 | Yes |
| Desert Hill | 2 | Yes |
| Forest | 2 | Yes |
| Glaciers | 3 | No |
| Grasslands | 1 | Yes |
| Hills | 2 | Yes |
| Jungles | 3 | 50% Yes |
| Mountains | 4 | 100% Yes |
| Plains | 1 | Yes |
| Polar Hill | 2 | Yes |
| Swamps | 3 | 50% Yes |
| Tundra | 2 | Yes |

Roads are different in *Call to Power* than in earlier versions of *Civilization*. Roads now offer no trade benefits, but they are still critical because they let units move over them at one-third of one movement point per space. This means that if you built a connected road over two hills and a mountain, instead of the movement point cost being eight total for the three spaces, it would only be a cost of one. Thus, a Legion could move over all three spaces in a single turn, instead of it taking him three turns per usual.

Similarly, Railroads allow you to move at one-fifth movement point per space. Maglevs (which you can build once you gain the Superconductor Advance in the Genetic era) are even faster, costing only one-tenth movement point per space.

> **TIP:** No Free Ride—In *Civilization II*, your units had an unlimited movement allowance along Railroads. In *Call to Power*, that benefit is reduced considerably. This difference is only a problem later in the game, but it's something to keep in mind. You can't, for instance, automatically send a ground unit from one end of your far-flung empire to the other over a Railroad in a single turn.

## Concerning Sea Movement

Naval units, which spend one movement point per space, undertake movement over the seas. Water in *Call to Power* is pretty much the same all over the world. Certain units, such as Triremes and Troop Ships, can carry ground troops, and Aircraft Carriers (true to their name) can carry combat aircraft, such as fighters.

> **TIP:** Escort Those Transports! When you transport troops on naval vessels, the defensive values of the ground troops are irrelevant; only the naval vessels count toward defense in sea combat. So, make sure to escort your valuable troop transports by keeping other naval vessels, such as Battleships, in the same space with them.

## Naval Movement Costs

| Naval Terrain | Movement Point Cost | Undersea Tunnels? |
|---|---|---|
| Beach | 1 | Yes |
| Continental Shelf | 1 | Yes |
| Deep Water | 1 | Yes |
| Rifts | 1 | Yes |
| Shallow Water | 1 | Yes |
| Trenches | 1 | No |
| Undersea Volcano | 1 | Yes |

Like Sea movement, all Air movement costs are one movement point expended per space entered. In Space, movement cost is 1/20.

## What's a ZOC, Dad?

Well, kiddo, back in the prehistoric days before computer games, things were different. Our strategy games were turn-based, a lot like *Call to Power*, but we played 'em on paper maps with cardboard counters and plastic pieces. Anyway, one of the things that game designers figured out was that nobody in a battle (nobody in his right mind, anyway) would let some enemy walk right up to him and kill him, you know, like you can do pretty easily in some computer games today.

Once you saw an enemy and they saw you, it makes sense that you'd both get into fighting position. So, game designers tried using concepts like "reaction rates" and "field of fire" to simulate this, which worked okay until you got to troops that fought hand-to-hand with swords and spears and whatnot. What designers eventually came up with was the idea of a Zone of Control, or ZOC for short, which made a moving unit stop when it got next to an enemy unit. The use of ZOCs assumes that the defending unit would react to the moving unit in a manner that stopped or impeded its continued advance. For strategic games like *Call to Power*, this concept, some four decades old, still works quite well, especially in a turn-based environment.

Those veteran gamers among you should keep in mind that the ZOCs in *Call to Power* are "rigid," in that they prohibit movement from one enemy ZOC to another. You can't slip and slide through enemy units. However, the ZOCs are also "inactive," meaning that you can be in an enemy ZOC without being forced to enter into combat.

## Exceptions to Zone of Control Rules

1. All stealth units (Clerics, Spies, Ecoterrorists, and so forth) may freely ignore ZOCs.
2. All aircraft ignore ZOCs.
3. Aircraft lack a ZOC of their own.
4. If you are adjacent to one of your own units or cities, you may move into the space with it, regardless of the presence of enemy ZOCs.
5. If you are adjacent to an unoccupied city, you may move into it, regardless of the presence of enemy ZOCs.

TIP: Lack of Control—Because of the ZOC exception rules, any time you have an empty city it's in grave danger. You might think that moving a unit next to the city would protect it. You would be wrong. If an enemy moves next to your wide-open city, it will be able to move in there and capture the city, and your forces next door will be on the outside, looking in. Luckily, the opposite is also true. If an enemy moves next to your city, it doesn't automatically prevent you from moving into that city and reinforcing it.

## Concerning the Art of Combat

When you attempt to enter the space of an enemy piece, combat occurs. Remember how movement through open terrain was fairly simple to figure out? Combat in open terrain is fairly simple as well. This is because you can make a rough estimate of your chances in a given combat by comparing the attack value (of the unit moving into the space) versus the defense value (of the unit already in the space).

Combat percentages are always figured from the attacker's point of view, as follows:

> **Attacker value is divided by (Attacker value + Defender value) = Chance of a Hit**

If the Attacker makes his Chance to Hit, he scores a single hit on the Defender, who loses one hit point. If the Attacker misses his Chance to Hit, he loses a hit point himself. This continues until one of the units has lost ten hit points and is eliminated.

## Example 2

A Phalanx, with a defense strength value of 2, defends in Plains (whether or not the Plains space has a road, it's still considered open terrain). Assume that a Legion, with an assault strength value of 2, attacks the Phalanx. The odds are even, which you'd expect from two units with the same value. But let's go through the process anyway:

> **Legion Attack is 2, Phalanx Defense is 2**
>
> **2 (Legion attack value) divided by (2 [Legion attack value] + 2 [Phalanx defense value]) = Chance for the Attacking Legion to Hit the Defending Phalanx**
>
> **2 divided by 4 = 1/2, or a 50% Chance to Hit for the Legion against the Phalanx**

At this point, the computer program would generate a random number from 1 to 100, much like rolling a pair of ten-sided percentile dice. If the number in this case came up as, say, 43, then the Legion would have made its Hit Chance, and would inflict a Hit on the Phalanx. If the random number were a 51, or a 99, for example, then the Legion would have failed its Hit Chance and would take a hit itself. The process repeats until one of the units loses ten Hit Points and is eliminated.

Keep in mind that all units on At War status have a full allotment of ten Hit Points. Units that are Standing Down, however, can have no more than 75-percent of their normal Hit Points, making them brittle in combat.

> **TIP:** Unless you are so removed from other civilizations as to have no danger of conflict, you should keep your forces on At War status early in the game, when your cities are at their most vulnerable. One way to keep Military Readiness costs down is to build the Sphinx Wonder, a move we heartily recommend (see Chapter 7).

## Example 3

Now, let's see what would happen if the battle were fought the other way around.

The Phalanx is less effective on Attack, with an assault strength value of only 1. The Legion, a better-rounded unit in *Call to Power*, is a defense strength of 2. Let's assume that the combat takes place again in the open (say, in a Grassland or Desert space), which, again, has no terrain effect on combat.

> **(Phalanx Attack of 1) divided by (Phalanx Attack of 1 + Legion Defense of 2)**
>
> **1 divided by 3 = 1/3, or 33%**

Obviously, the Phalanx is not very useful to wage an offensive war, since it is twice as likely to take a Hit in this example than it is to give one.

## Example 4

Now, let's return to our earlier example, with the Legion as attacker. But this time, let's place the Phalanx in some decent defensive terrain: a forest, which gives an additional 50-percent to the basic defense value.

Legion Attack is still 2.

Phalanx Defense is 2 + 1, with the addition of one reflecting the 50-percent boost provided by the forest terrain, for a total Defense of 3.

Using the regular process:

(Legion's Attack of 2) divided by (Legion's Attack of 2 ÷ Phalanx's Defense of 3)

2 divided by 5 = 2/5, or 40% Hit Chance for the Legion

So, merely stationing the Phalanx on a hill effectively improved its final defense by ten-percent, not the straight 50-percent that the basic defensive modifier for forest would lead you to believe. Still, a ten-percent improvement is nothing to gripe about, especially since these Hits add up. If the Phalanx were to Fortify on the hill, it would be even more difficult to defeat.

## Unit Combat Modifiers

| Unit Condition | Combat Effect |
|---|---|
| At War status | Normal |
| On Alert | -12% |
| Standing Down | -25% |
| Fortified | +50% |
| Unit has 2/3 of a movement point left | -33% |
| Unit has 1/3 of a movement point left | -67% |
| Veteran unit | +50% |

TIP: The Temptation Defense—Normally, units controlled by a computer player are less likely to attack when they have less than a movement point remaining (if they have been moving down a road, for example). If you move your unit to where it is at the far end of the computer unit's movement range (such as just alongside, but not on, a road) the computer's unit is likely to move next to you, but not attack you at unfavorable odds. This allows you to attack the defending computer unit on your next turn, or to reinforce with other units if the odds are unfavorable for you.

## Example 5

We already know how just putting a unit in a forest can add to its defense. Let's take a different unit, the Machine Gunner (which has a

good basic defense of 8), and see how tough it can be when defending in the right terrain.

If our Machine Gunner is defending, and it's attacked by a Tank unit, the combat would go as follows:

16 (Tank Attack) divided by (16 [Tank Attack] + 8 [MG Defense])

16 divided by 24 = 66.7% Chance to Hit for the Tank

Not very good odds for our defending Machine Gunner, are they? What we should do here is to build a Fortification, which would improve our defense strength by 150-percent. Let's see how the combat would go now:

16 (Tank Attack) divided by (16 [Tank Attack] + 20 [MG Defense of 8 + 12 for the Fortification bonus])

16 divided by 36 = 44.4% Chance to Hit for the Tank

Such an improvement, and all because we built a Fortification.

## Terrain Effects on Combat

| Terrain/Improvement | Combat Effect |
|---|---|
| City Walls | +4 defense |
| Forcefield | +12 defense |
| Forests | +50% defense |
| Fortification* | +150% defense |
| Hills | +50% defense |
| Jungles | +50% defense |
| Mountains | +100% defense |
| Swamps | +50% defense |
| Unit Fortified | +50% defense |
| All Other | Normal |

* Fortification is a structure you build, different from the Fortify command you give a unit.

## Example 6

Now that you've had a chance to look over the tables and see all the various defensive modifiers, let's go back to our defending Machine Gunner unit. Since all combat modifiers in a space add up, just how tough a defender can we make it?

Let's assume our unit is a Veteran (because it's won a few battles), and that it's Fortified within a Fortification:

> 8 (Basic Defense Value) + 50% (for Veteran status) + 50% (for Fortified status) + 150% (for Fortification)
>
> 8 + 4 + 4 + 12 = 28 Total Defense Value

That's not bad for a single Machine Gunner unit! The process works the same, regardless of whether you are in the Ancient, Modern, or even the Diamond era. So, don't consider City Walls a luxury, consider them a necessity.

## Concerning Combat with Multiple Units

### With a Single Defender

If there are multiple attacking units, and only one defender, the process is similar to that of *Civilization II*. Each of the attacking units, starting with the best unit, attacks the defender. If the initial unit is defeated, the process repeats until either the defender dies or all of the attacking units are defeated. The process is much the same with a single attacker, but it's even less likely that the attacker will win.

### With Multiple Units on Both Sides, but No Ranged Units

When multiple units are involved in a battle, they are matched up, one Attacker to each Defender, highest value to highest value, and so on down the line. Units fight in the usual manner through a series of combat rounds.

If, after each round, there are still survivors on both sides, units are matched up again, highest

to lowest, and combat continues until one side is totally eliminated, with no unit on a side fighting twice until everyone on that side has fought. Thus, the side with numerical superiority benefits by having its freshest units rotated to the front with each new round of combat.

## Example 7

There are six units attacking five defenders. The attackers have two Samurai, two Legions, and two Phalanx units. The Defenders have three Phalanxes and two Warriors.

**Round One.** The units are matched up as follows in the first round of combat:

> The best two attackers, the Samurai, versus two of the three Phalanxes;
>
> The two Legions versus the other Phalanx and one of the two Warriors;
>
> Finally, one of the two Phalanx units versus the final Warrior unit.
>
> One attacking Phalanx is held in reserve.

Round one ends with both Samurai winning, but one of them takes 8 Hits in the process.

Meanwhile, one Legion wins (while taking 7 hits), and the other loses to the defending Phalanx.

The Phalanx loses a close battle to its Warrior foe (which takes 9 Hits).

**Round Two.**

> The less-damaged of the two Samurai (the highest-ranking attacker) *versus* the last remaining defending Phalanx;
>
> The "fresh" Phalanx (which didn't fight last turn) *versus* the final Warrior.

If, after round two, there are any more defenders left (doubtful in this example), other combat rounds would follow, with the best of the remaining attackers matched up against any remaining defenders.

TIP: Elite (and Expensive)—Elite troops, such as Samurai, were historically expected to carry the fight to the enemy and to be an example for the rest of the army. In keeping with this tradition in *Call to Power*, the best attacking units are the first to fight in situations featuring multiple units. Therefore, when you are attacking units in good defensive terrain or behind City Walls, your elite troop casualties will often be disproportionately high.

Don't risk your best units to win a narrow victory. Maneuver to attack another city of your enemy that you can beat more easily. Whether your enemy counterattacks (as he almost certainly will), or stays within the defenses of his cities, you will have more of your elite troops remaining to continue the campaign.

## Concerning Ranged Attacks

Ranged combat is new to the *Civilization* series, but it's not terribly complicated when compared to other strategy games; just different.

1. Basically, all units with a Ranged Attack (Archers, Musketeers, and so forth) are placed in the "back row" of each side, as long as they have normal land combat units (Marines, Phalanxes, and the like) in front of them in the "front row."

2. When combat begins, the Attacker's Ranged Units fire on defending enemy units in the front row, and the defenders do likewise at the attackers in the front row. The combat is resolved similarly to the usual fashion, except that:

   a) Each back row unit attacks with its Ranged Attack value.

   b) Each Ranged Unit attacks, or "fires" 10 times (with arrows, musket balls, or whatever).

   c) Anything that would normally count as a Hit to the Ranged Attacker has no effect (since they are firing from a distance too far for units with non-ranged weapons to really hit them).

3. Next, the front row troops conduct combat as normal.

4. This continues until all front row troops of one side are eliminated. Then, the Ranged Units of that side must move up to the front row and use their normal (non-Ranged Attack) values. Now that they are in the front row, enemy units in the second row (using their Ranged Attack) may fire upon them.

5. Combat continues until all units of one side are eliminated.

### Example 8

Two Roman Knights and one Legion attack a group of three Greek Phalanxes and one Archer on a hill.

1. Even though the Greeks are the defenders overall, the Archer still gets to "Attack" the Romans by using its Ranged Attack value.

2. The Archer opens fire on one of the two Knight units, firing 10 times:

   (Archer Ranged Attack of 3) divided by (Archer Ranged Attack of 3 + Knight Defense of 3)

   3 divided by (3+3)

   3 divided by 6 = 1/2, or 50%

Let's say that in this example, the Archer does slightly less than the average damage, scoring 4 Hits on the Knight.

3. The fresh Knight (the one that took no Hits) defeats the opposing Phalanx, but loses 8 Hit Points in the process.

4. The other Knight, damaged by the Archer, loses to its opposing Phalanx.

5. The Legion loses a close battle to its opposing Phalanx.

6. Outnumbered, the Knight takes 5 Hits from the Archer's Ranged Combat and is easily dispatched by the Phalanx.

It should be noted that without the Archer unit, the Knights would have probably had enough firepower to take out the Phalanxes.

> TIP: Most units with Ranged Attacks are much more effective in the second row than in the first. So, make sure that you have a balanced force, with plenty of front line troops to protect your Ranged Attack units. A good example of this would be to have only half as many Archers, for example, as you have Legions, Samurai, and/or Phalanxes combined in a particular force.

## Concerning the Bombardment of the Enemy

Bombardment is also new to the *Civilization* series. In *Call to Power*, units with Bombardment capabilities act like "Super Ranged Attack" units. Basically, you fire at units, using your Ranged Attack values, *before* entering into standard combat. This allows you to damage the defensive troops and "soften up" tough defensive positions, like hills and City Walls, increasing your chances of success.

> TIP: *Call to Power* rewards the use of "combined arms." Therefore, you should note that Bombardment alone will not win most battles for you. Unless you follow up immediately with ground troops to take the position, most enemy units, particularly those fortified behind City Walls, will "heal" just as fast as you can Bombard them.

While we offer breakdowns of each of these units in Chapter 2, here's an at-a-glance view of all units in *Call to Power* with Bombardment capability:

## Bombardment Values

| Unit | Bombardment Value |
| --- | --- |
| Artillery | 20 |
| Battleship | 20 |
| Cannon | 6 |
| Destroyer | 10 |
| Leviathan | 40 |
| Plasma Destroyer | 15 |
| Ship of the Line | 4 |
| Space Bomber | 50 |
| Star Cruiser | 30 |
| Stealth Bomber | 22 |
| Stealth Sub | 30 |
| Submarine | 20 |
| War Walker | 24 |

## Concerning the Incursions of Barbarians

As a rule, Barbarians are in the game as a sort of practical application of chaos theory. They vary from troublesome nuisance to sheer waves of terror for your civilization, especially early in the game, before you've had time to erect proper defenses.

In fact, we've found in our testing that Barbarians gravitate to lightly defended cities. Barbarians will always attack if they feel they have anywhere near a 50-percent chance of success. Moreover, they always seem to magically find any empty cities, regardless of how far off the beaten path you might have them located. Unwary or reckless players will find themselves losing a city to the Barbarians if they leave that city open for more than a handful of turns after building it. It's hard to recover from such a loss—it might even knock you totally out of the game!

> TIP: Build for Quality Defense—Early on in a game, replace your Warriors with Phalanxes and immediately Fortify them in your cities. Then, build City Walls as you can afford them. As soon as your Phalanx becomes a Veteran (usually after two or three successful battles, on average), the adjusted Phalanx

Defense of 2+1+1+4 = 8 makes it almost impossible for a single Barbarian unit to capture one of your cities. You can then focus on building your empire.

Should the Barbarians actually capture a city, they won't go around founding a bunch of other cities and building an empire. They will, however, build military units and attempt to conquer other cities. As you show the ability to adequately defend your cities, Barbarians will then plunder your resources, especially mines, so consider garrisoning them, as well.

TIP: Counterattack Barbarian Hordes—Once you start to build units with some offensive punch, you no longer have to react passively to annoying Barbarian incursions. Station a Samurai unit in your most critical city (generally, that's your capitol), and others around the perimeter of your empire as you can afford them. If you think this is expensive, keep in mind the amount of gold and production you lose every time a Barbarian plunders your territory.

When a Barbarian moves adjacent to one of your cities, attack and destroy it. You should have a 60- to 70-percent chance of winning the battle. Just make sure that you have the city garrisoned with a Phalanx unit as well, in case your karma is low that turn, and your Samurai loses!

BARBARIAN STANDOFF: *It's not worth risking our Phalanx unit in a low-odds attack against this Fortified Barbarian defender. We should build a Samurai as soon as possible.*

The frequency of Barbarian incursions varies according to a number of factors that change from game to game. Nevertheless, here's a good rule of thumb: The more technologically sophisticated you are, *and* the more sophisticated *all* nations are as a whole, the more Barbarians you will see, and the better armed they will be.

Veteran players will want to include Barbarians in every game, if only because they tend to keep things from being predictable. We suggest that those of you not terribly familiar with games of this kind should place the Barbarians on the lowest occurrence setting while you learn the game. But do this only for the very first time you play. Once you have the mechanics of the game down, you should at least bump the Barbarian occurrence level up a notch. Why? Because they affect your opponents, whether computer-controlled or fellow human, just as much and sometimes *more* than they mess with you.

TIP: Cover Your Assets—Once you begin to discover units such as Samurai, and especially Knights, you will see an immediate upswing in the danger presented to you by Barbarians. At this time, you should make a point of adding ranged units, such as Archers, to each of your cities for defense. In critical cities, such as those where you are building most of your Wonders, you should have two front-line troops (Phalanx and either Samurai or Knight) and a ranged unit.

## Mobile Defense

*UPWARDLY MOBILE: Here, our Cities are garrisoned well enough that we should start building a Mobile Defense group. Placing three or four Knights in Sparta means that we can rush them, en masse, to any of our endangered Cities in only one turn.*

Whether you're an Alexander-style leader concerned with bringing an enemy to his knees, or a basically peaceful soul who just doesn't want to be pushed around, you share the same problem: how to build a solid defense without ruining your economy or sacrificing your overall goals. There's no pat answer because every game is different. Nonetheless, we recommend one simple method that we guarantee will help save you from a lot of headaches: the Mobile Defense.

After garrisoning each of your cities as we've described earlier in this chapter, you need to build a centrally located force that can reach all areas of your empire, even remote ones, quickly (preferably within a single turn). This isn't so hard once Maglevs are available (see *Movement* at the beginning of this chapter), but we'd like you to be free of worry during the Ancient, Renaissance, and Modern eras, too.

The solution is to build a group of tough, fast units that can both defend and counterattack against an invading enemy force. The first unit that meets our criteria is the Knight. With its movement of 4, the Knight can potentially reach an enemy 12 spaces away, but only over Roads.

Which brings us to the second important point: You must connect *all* your cities on the same continent with a Road network for the Mobile Defense to work. Whether you upgrade those Roads to Railroads eventually is less important than keeping your units updated, first to Tanks, then to War Walkers for the endgame.

In general, once your empire grows larger than seven or eight cities, you'll need two groups for Mobile Defense. Each of these groups should have at least three, and preferably four, Knights/Tanks/War Walkers. This approach allows you to deal with a Barbarian incursion on one front, and an enemy "probe" on the other.

> TIP: Don't "Mount" This Defense—While it might be tempting, don't try the Mobile Defense with Mounted Archers. They're far too expensive for the minimal punch they give you. Wait for Knights instead.

## Naval Warfare

The most common assumption in Naval Warfare is that you don't really have to worry about terrain. Nothing could be further from the truth.

1. You must be able to repair your ships, so Cities that serve as Ports are critical and must be defended.

2. Similarly, you must be able to defend your Trade Routes from Piracy during war and peace.

3. Placing ships in narrow straits prevents the movement of other nations' navies from one sea to another.

4. Having ships patrolling off an enemy's home coastline may make him think twice before starting a war.

5. Control of the sea means that you can launch amphibious invasions of an opponent's land territories with impunity.

As you can see, therefore, there are a lot of reasons to have naval superiority, if only for the strategic reach such power gives you. Without overtly starting a war, you can keep the pressure on your opponents.

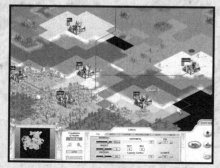

*THE THIN BLUE LINE: These long overseas Trade Routes are an invitation to Pirates. We need a protective fleet, and soon.*

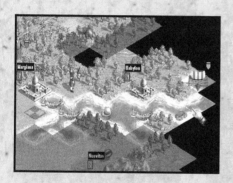

*CONTROLLING THE SHALLOWS: By placing a Trireme at the mouth of this estuary, we would avoid Barbarian seaborne incursions, and also protect our valuable oyster and crab trade. Later on, we'd want to upgrade to a Ship of the Line.*

TIP: Fast Attack Boats—Unlike previous versions of *Civilization*, Battleships in *Call to Power* aren't lumbering behemoths. Not only are they actually faster than Aircraft Carriers, Battleships don't go obsolete until the Diamond era. Build them early and as often as you can, because these big gun platforms are versatile, with great Attack, Bombardment, and Defense ratings. Watch out for Subs, though!

*QUEEN OF THE GREY SEAS: Battleships in Call to Power are a better buy than in other versions of Civilization, and they don't go obsolete for a long time.*

## Don't Overlook the Power of the Blitz Attack

Why would a single attacker be foolish enough to attack multiple defenders, you ask? Normally, this *is* a pretty lopsided situation because the multiple defenders would be able to wear down the attacker, or defeat him outright. However, if you break through the outer defenses to the innermost cities of an empire, these tend to be more lightly defended than cities along a rival border.

Therefore, it's not only possible, but also likely, that you'll be able to do some serious damage in the rear areas. We've found that breaking through and then exploiting with Tank units tends to cause some grief to the AI, and even to human opponents who have too much confidence in their outer defensive perimeter. The Tank, with its attack of 16, can generally overpower anything less than a Machine Gunner, even if the defenders are in pairs.

Better yet, you have a good chance of catching Air and Naval units unprotected in the city. These are easy for a Tank to kill, and very expensive for your opponent to replace. A good rule of thumb is to break through with four tanks, and send one or two Tanks to each inner city you intend to attack. The next turn, have Infantry units with decent defensive values ready to move into the cities you've just captured. This allows your Tanks that are beaten up to catch some R&R, and your still-fresh Tanks to move on to the next minimally defended cities.

## See Me, Feel Me, Touch Me...

If you can't find the enemy, it's hard to kill him. All units in *Call to Power* have a range limiting what they can effectively "see," the area that becomes visible to you as you move units around the map. Most units, especially ground troops, are limited to seeing only one space in all directions. The following should give you an idea of the "vision" of your units:

### Vision Ratings

| Unit/City | Vision (in spaces) |
|---|---|
| Aircraft Carrier | 2 |
| All Cities | 2 |
| All Subs | 2 |
| Battleship | 2 |
| Cargo Pod | 2 |
| Corporate Branch | 2 |
| Cyber Ninja | 3 |
| Destroyer | 3 |
| Diplomat | 2 |
| Ecoterrorist | 2 |
| Fascist | 2 |
| Fighter | 2 |
| Fusion Tank | 2 |
| Interceptors | 3 |
| Leviathan | 3 |
| Marine | 2 |
| Mobile SAM | 3 |
| Paratrooper | 2 |
| Plasma Destroyer | 2 |
| Plasmatica | 2 |
| Space Bomber | 2 |
| Space Fighter | 3 |
| Spy | 3 |
| Spy Plane | 5 |
| Star Cruiser | 2 |

| Unit/City | Vision (in spaces) |
|---|---|
| Stealth Bomber | 2 |
| Storm Marines | 2 |
| Subneural Ads | 2 |
| Tank | 2 |
| Televangelist | 2 |
| Troop Ship | 2 |
| War Walker | 3 |
| Warrior | 2 |
| Everything else | 1 |

Don't forget that:

1. Submarines can be seen only by Destroyers, Sonar Buoys, other Subs, Spy Planes, and the Crawler.

2. Most non-conventional warfare units, such as Clerics, Ecoterrorists, and Televangelists, are only visible to units of their own type. A Televangelist, for example, can see a Corporate Branch, but not an Ecoterrorist. Diplomats can see stealth units, such as Clerics, and Spies in Cities seem to see everything except Subs, Trade Units, and Phantoms.

TIP: "To defeat the enemy, you must first know him."—Sun Tzu, *The Art of War*

Military intelligence is the key to success on the battlefield. As a result, we recommend that you strongly consider building The Agency Wonder for peace of mind against domestic terrorism. If you are on the strategic offense, it's also hard to resist the GlobeSat Wonder, as it gives you radar coverage over the entire world. For more on these Wonders, see Chapter 7.

## The Wolfpack Attack

Given that Subs can only be seen by a handful of units (and Cities with Sonar Buoys), they can wreak havoc with your Aircraft Carriers and even your Battleships if left unchecked. The classic method is to seek them out with Destroyers and sink them with a combination of Destroyers and Aircraft.

So, what do you do when you want your Subs to send your opponent's tonnage to the bottom of the ocean? In WWII, the Germans developed the tactic of sending large groups of Subs, called Wolfpacks, to overwhelm unsuspecting prey. It's a little more difficult to manage this in *Call to Power*, but the idea is still valid.

The best method we've found is to form a Wolfpack of four or more Subs and hold them off a couple of spaces. Then, send out one or two other solo Subs to try to break through the "picket line" of Destroyers that's spread out, trying to protect the valuable Carriers and Battleships. If the solo Subs get through, fine, but at least one of them will likely be detected. The computer is not terribly disciplined, and it will often break up its Destroyer picket line to converge on your Sub and kill it. This generally opens up a hole for you to plunge through with your Wolfpack and head straight for the juicier enemy targets.

> TIP: Self-Sub Defense—One way to keep the Wolfpack Attack from happening to you is to station a Sub as a last line of defense near your valuable Carriers. From what we've found, the AI doesn't do this, so take advantage on your end.

## Air War—Make it Expensive

The only major campaign decided by air was not the Gulf War, but the Battle of Britain in WWII. While German bombers managed to drop their payloads on many occasions, the British always made them pay. You should set up your Air Defenses in a similar fashion:

1. In *Call to Power*, Mobile SAMs (surface-to-air-missiles) are available before Radar and before Bombers. So, if you are in or about to enter a war, start building SAM defenses.

2. Since you probably won't have all your Radar installations built before enemy

Bombers start Bombarding your Cities and units, have Fighters ready to take the Bombers out, even if it's after they attack. Keep in mind that your enemy is likely to escort his Bombers with Fighters of his own, so make sure that you send at least two Fighters after every Bomber you sight.

3. When you are getting close to discovering Jet Propulsion, start building Fighters. Then switch over to Interceptors as soon as you discover the Jet Advance, which will give you a lot of Interceptors in a hurry.

4. Don't overlook the value of having Aircraft Carriers based off the coast of your enemy. Fighters based on Carriers can often catch the Bombers in route, and can also help destroy them on their way home.

*SEEK AND DESTROY: Once they are found, Stealth Aircraft blow up as nicely as any other target, as our Interceptor shows here.*

## The MAD Defense

For a little while in the Modern and Genetic eras, until the advent of the Nanite Defuser Wonder in the Diamond era (see Chapter 7), the specter of nuclear weapons hangs over the world. Like other versions of *Civilization*, the delivery platforms of nuclear weapons in *Call to Power* consist entirely of ballistic missiles. Interestingly enough, the range of these missiles (20 spaces) is always fixed, regardless of the map size on which you play. Therefore,

Nukes can only be considered "long-range" on a small or medium map, and medium-range on larger maps. This distinction is not merely one of semantics: Missiles that fail to reach a target by the end of their 20th (and final) space are removed from play without detonation. It would therefore be reasonable to assume that if you were far removed from a potential enemy armed with Nukes, you would be relatively safe.

But the reality in *Call to Power* is that there are ways to effectively increase the range of Nukes, such as placing them on naval vessels. Submarines are really useful for this, due to their ability to hide in the open seas. While you can attempt to destroy submarines and other potential launch platforms through the use of Destroyers and aircraft, you aren't going to be successful in such a defense if your opponent starts the war and launches the Nukes before you can take them out.

In fact, until the Nanite Defuser is available, the best method of defense against Nukes is the one that has worked historically. The MAD defense relies on the principle of Mutually Assured Destruction. In other words, if you launch Nukes against me, I'll retaliate. And with the world plunged into a nuclear holocaust, we'll both lose. This method can backfire, plunging both you and your enemy into a costly spiral of Nuke-building. Therefore, the MAD Defense works best if you:

1. Have a better economic base than your enemy, allowing you to spend missile for missile with him. Eventually, he will have to concede nuclear parity to you, or risk an economic collapse—exactly what happened to the former Soviet Union in the real-world Cold War.

2. Supplement your missiles with a missile defense. SDI is available just as you are getting ready to enter the Genetic Age. But depending on SDI to give you blanket protection is iffy, especially against Nuke-happy computer players.

3. Make sure to spread out your Nukes. We are particularly fond of placing them in small cities and on Naval vessels. Subs are best for this, because of their ability to evade detection.

# Nuke N' Go

If your intelligence reports suggest nuclear war is imminent despite your best efforts, don't waste time:

1. Launch a pre-emptive strike from as many different spots as possible. This tends to confuse your enemy as to where and how to respond.

2. Have Paratroops ready to drop into the Nuked enemy cities and capture them.

3. Have transports (probably Troop Ships at this point in the game) loaded with ground troops (Marines, Tanks, and Machine Gunners) ready to hit the opponent's beaches.

4. Always keep at least two, and preferably four, Nukes for a follow-up strike.

5. If, after signing a peace treaty, the enemy nation shows any signs of building more nuclear weapons, it will almost certainly attack you again. Show no mercy: Nuke them back to the Stone Age, or at least capture all of their cities.

# Chapter Four:

# Concerning the Body Politic

## How to Use Every Government Properly

*"It is to be regretted that the rich and powerful too often bend the acts of government to their selfish purposes."*

—Andrew Jackson, upon vetoing the Bank Renewal Bill in 1832.

Why do governments exist? Plato, in The Republic, theorized that governments exist because individuals are not capable of producing everything that everyone desires. As a result, there is a necessity for a division of labor in order to assure a wide variety of products. If there is a wide variety of products, then there must be a marketplace in order for trade to be conducted. Once the marketplace becomes known for having a wide variety of goods, he hypothesized that nearby communities without as much as the original community would try to take what they wanted by force. As a result, the original community is forced to create a standing army in order to protect their superior standard of living.

Once you have a standing army, you have to have commanders. These commanders are essentially the warrior caste or nobility that we know from both the Ancient Near East and the Classical World. Unfortunately, in order for this standing army to remain prepared at all times, this means that the warrior caste created to protect this community no longer contributes labor to the production of goods. Now, there will be a necessity of creating a trading class to supplement the

original community's production by obtaining goods from other communities. With the proliferation of trade, there are bound to be discrepancies and complaints of injustice. Suddenly, there has to be a ruler or council to provide judgment on these complaints and ensure equitable economic and social transactions.

Hence, the origin of government is to be found in both humankind's greed and in the inherent untrustworthiness of the individual. As Cambridge historian Ernest Gellner observed, "Property and power are correlative notions." He went on to say that the agricultural revolution led to the storage of possessions (both necessities and wealth) which, in turn, had to be protected. Hence, the protectors became an unavoidable aspect of social life.

In *Civilization: Call to Power*, you deal with 12 different forms of government. Each has different effects on the following: Growth, Production, Science, Gold and Military Support. In addition, each governmental form has a maximum percentage limit of Gold that can be spent on Science per turn. As a result, each governmental form has an appropriate point within your strategy in which it is to be used most efficiently. In this chapter, we will consider each type of government in alphabetical order. Then, we'll touch on traditional Diplomacy as handled in *Call to Power* and offer a few types of "Dirty Tricks" as a special treat.

## Anarchy

| Government: | ANARCHY |
|---|---|
| Requires: | Nothing |
| Size of Government Penalty: | N/A |
| Science Bonus: | .1 |
| Gold Bonus: | .75 |
| Pollution: | Medium (1) |
| Production Bonus: | 1 |
| Maximum Gold for Science: | N/A |
| Growth: | Awful |
| Military: | Awful |

Anarchy is the point at which everyone does their own thing and the law of the biggest or most ruthless applies. Anarchy is a chaotic time of lawlessness that reflects the anomie between governments. Imagine all the looting and rioting which has accompanied most revolutions in our world. That is what the period of Anarchy represents in *Civilization: Call to Power*. If you're lucky, the cities will continue to function without rioting. The decline in productivity is reflected in the table above.

The most serious problem with the period of Anarchy between governments is that you have only 1/10 the amount usually provided for Science and 3/4 the amount usually garnered

in Gold. This means that the period of Anarchy is most inefficient; yet, it is a necessary period. You cannot reach a higher or more efficient form of government until you go through the lawlessness and productivity penalties associated with this governmental shift.

## Communism

| Government: | COMMUNISM |
|---|---|
| Requires: | Communism Advance |
| Size of Government Penalty: | 70 |
| Science Bonus: | 2 |
| Gold Bonus: | .75 |
| Pollution: | High (3) |
| Production Bonus: | 1.75 |
| Maximum Gold for Science: | 60% |
| Growth: | Average |
| Military: | Good |

In theory, the governmental form of Communism is merely a provisional state designed to facilitate the transition from a downtrodden mass of exploited workers to a classless utopia where all material possessions would be held in common. Since humanity is inherently selfish, a totalitarian regime was necessary in order to re-educate the minds, redistribute the wealth, and reorganize the structure of society. After Marx and Engels had presented the arguments for this classless utopia, their followers suggested different ways in which the utopia could be instituted.

In the most famous implementation of Communism, the Union of Soviet Socialist Republics, three theories were advanced. G.V. Plekhanov advocated a revolution followed by a provisional democratic government to aid the transition from decadence to utopia. V. I. Ulyanov (Lenin) taught that after the working classes threw off the yoke of oppression, there would need to be a provisional capitalist era prior to reaching the utopian ideal. Joseph Stalin recognized the dangers inherent in lapsing back into democracy or capitalism, so he instituted the totalitarian regime which we associate with the U.S.S.R.

In *Call to Power*, Communism is represented as a form of government that exchanges individual freedom for efficiency. It assumes that the central planning mechanism of a totalitarian regime can be very efficient in the short run, but forces you to pay the price in Pollution. By using the 1.75x multiplier for Production and 2x multiplier for Science, you can develop your industrial base rather quickly. Of course, your citizens will be choking on their own soot.

In short, Communism is ideal for a quick industrial boost. It severely damages the quality of life in the long term since it destroys the environment and reduces individual initiative and the creation of individual wealth by exchanging freedom for efficiency. The 3/4x modifier for Gold reflects the disincentive with regard to personal and corporate wealth building.

# Corporate Republic

| Government: | CORPORATE REPUBLIC |
|---|---|
| Requires: | Corporate Republic Advance |
| Size of Government Penalty: | 100 |
| Science Bonus: | 2 |
| Gold Bonus: | 2 |
| Pollution: | Medium (2) |
| Production Bonus: | 1.5 |
| Maximum Gold for Science: | 60% |
| Growth: | Average |
| Military: | Average |

The Corporate Republic is a fictional form of government designed for *Call to Power*. However, it could happen. As electronic banking and instant currency conversion intersects with such phenomena as the unification of the European economy and currency, there is bound to be a tremendous revolution in the way business is conducted. As traditional tariffs and protectionism become extinct, this paves the way for mega-corporations to move beyond the boundaries of traditional multinational corporations.

In the *Call to Power* fiction, the Corporate Republics began by offering social services and ended up becoming their own virtual countries, run by data transmission from an orbital network. The Corporate Republic is a libertarian dream and a marvelous piece of science fiction, but it seems highly unlikely from today's perspective.

Note that with its 1.5x Production modifier and 2x Science modifier, the Corporate Republic is nearly as effective in providing an industrial burst of energy as Communism. The advantage of the Corporate Republic is that it isn't quite as bad in terms of Pollution and is far superior in terms of wealth formation (a 2x modifier for Gold). Since the 1.25x increase in Gold is more important than the .25x you gain in Production with Communism. The Corporate Republic is superior to Democracy, Monarchy, Republic, Theocracy, and Tyranny in terms of its impact on your fiscal (Gold) and industrial (Production) status.

## Democracy

| Government: | DEMOCRACY |
|---|---|
| Requires: | Democracy Advance |
| Size of Government Penalty: | 80 |
| Science Bonus: | 2 |
| Gold Bonus: | 1.25 |
| Pollution: | Medium (1) |
| Production Bonus: | 1.25 |
| Maximum Gold for Science: | 70% |
| Growth: | Average |
| Military: | Bad |

Coming from the Greek words for demos ("people") and kratos ("rule"), Democracy is based on the ideal of ancient Athens where leaders ruled by the consent of the people. When we speak of Democracy, however, we usually do not mean the "pure democracy" of Athens. Rather, we speak of the western system of representative Democracy. This system is built upon a "give and take" principle whereby the general population allows the leadership to make certain policies related to the public good in exchange for certain recognition of individual and/or local rights which are, in turn, protected by the national entity.

In *Call to Power*, Democracy is synonymous with the ideals of the American Revolution. Freedom begets an inherent curiosity that is good for Science. Although the 2x modifier for Science seems at first glance to be equivalent to that of Communism and the Corporate Republic, note that the leader of a *Call to Power* Democracy can assign 10% more of the Democracy's Gold to the advancement of Science (70% as opposed to 60%). This represents a significant net gain as you move through the technology tree.

The downside of Democracy is related to its strength, the freedom of its people. The natives of a Democracy get restless whenever the nation engages in war. So be prepared to boost your Happiness quotient in other ways or to switch to another governmental form if you decide to declare war from a state of Democracy.

In short, Democracy is tremendously efficient in terms of Science. Only Ecotopia, Technocracy, and Virtual Democracy are better at stimulating scientific research. Further, Democracy is moderately efficient in wealth formation (Gold) and industrial efficiency (Production). Hence, it is a solid government to use when you're building up your peacetime government. The possibilities of unrest during wartime make Democracy a poor proposition for gamers who prefer to conquer above all else.

# Ecotopia

| | |
|---|---|
| **Government:** | ECOTOPIA |
| **Requires:** | Ecotopia Advance |
| **Size of Government Penalty:** | 100 |
| **Science Bonus:** | 2.5 |
| **Gold Bonus:** | 1.25 |
| **Pollution:** | Low (0.25) |
| **Production Bonus:** | 1 |
| **Maximum Gold for Science:** | 80% |
| **Growth:** | Good |
| **Military:** | Good |

Ecotopia is another fictitious governmental form in the science fiction section of *Call to Power*. As a backlash against corporate abuses of the environment in the late 21st century, environmentally conscious peoples formed the Ecotopia. The Ecotopian form of government is extremely friendly to scientific research with a 2.5x modifier. Also, since the Ecotopian form of government arose out of a violent reaction to the corporate rape of the environment, Ecotopia is an ideal government for those who wish to prosecute an efficient war. It is particularly effective when you wish to attack heavy polluters.

In short, Ecotopia has the advantage of allowing you to increase your Science pace and to still be able to prosecute warfare. It is an excellent governmental form for both gamers who prefer to conquer and gamers who prefer to build.

# Fascism

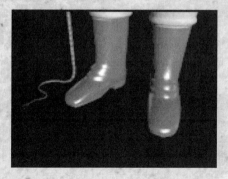

| | |
|---|---|
| **Government:** | FASCISM |
| **Requires:** | Fascism Advance |
| **Size of Government Penalty:** | 70 |
| **Science Bonus:** | 2 |
| **Gold Bonus:** | 1 |
| **Pollution:** | Medium (1) |
| **Production Bonus:** | 1.5 |
| **Maximum Gold for Science:** | 70% |
| **Growth:** | Average |
| **Military:** | Excellent |

Like the Communism of the 20th century, Fascism is a totalitarian regime that asserts the right of the state over the individual for the greater good of the nation. Like Communism, Fascism nationalized industries and eliminated certain personal freedoms. Neither freedom of the press nor freedom to assemble were available to citizens in countries like Mussolini's Italy and Hitler's Germany. Instead of perceiving this totalitarian regime as a provisional government in the Communist sense, however, the Fascist dictators expected the totalitarian regime to continue in perpetuity.

Nationalism was a major factor in incubating Fascism in our world. The countries to which Fascism appealed were countries that had experienced stinging defeats prior to rise of Fascism. Further, the countries where Fascism was birthed were countries with weak central governments as a result of those military defeats. Fascism promised a return to a national glory as of old (even if that glory never really existed) and a plan for achieving this. Fascism used propaganda to indoctrinate entire communities in the ideology (and often the racism) inherent to its domination.

In *Call to Power*, Fascism is an extremely efficient form of government. It doesn't accrue Gold as quickly as Democracy, but the Science modifier is equivalent to Democracy's and, reflective of national planning, Production is slightly superior. The best news for the conqueror-style gamer is that you get this efficiency without having to worry about unrest in your cities due to discontent over warfare. The Fascist population knew that the return to glory was predicated upon warfare.

If you happen to be a conqueror-style player, you'll be very interested in the special unit available to the heads of Fascist governments. Equivalent to Nazi Germany's SS unit and as mean as any Fascist brown shirt of any era, *Call to Power* allows gamers to build the Fascist unit. The Fascist unit has an assault value of 16 and a defensive value of 8. The downside to this unit is that, should you decide to change governments, you won't be able to keep such a fanatic around. Only Fascism allows Fascists.

Fascism is the ideal governmental form for prosecuting a war prior to the advent of Ecotopia. There are no major disadvantages for the conqueror unless you happen to build so many Fascist units that you take a significant force reduction when you change to Ecotopia or a more advanced government later in the game.

# Monarchy

| Government: | MONARCHY |
|---|---|
| Requires: | Monarchy Advance |
| Size of Government Penalty: | 20 |
| Science Bonus: | 1.25 |
| Gold Bonus: | 1 |
| Pollution: | Medium (1) |
| Production Bonus: | 1.25 |
| Maximum Gold for Science: | 50% |
| Growth: | Bad |
| Military: | Good |

Monarchy dates back to the civilizations of the Tigris-Euphrates River Valley. It is very likely that Monarchy originally combined religious and civil authority in order to encourage submission to the monarch by the people. This combination of religious and civil authority often convinced the individuals within a Monarchy that their king or leader was either a god, demi-god, or representative of a god who ruled by divine right. This is logical, of course. The successful conqueror proves himself the chosen of the gods. As a result, the loyalty of the populace was not usually questioned. The fact that this loyalty did not have to be cajoled, but was granted with a certain amount of willingness by the common people, is a major distinction between the Tyrant and the Monarch.

*Call to Power* recognizes that a Monarchy functions best when it is a tightly-knit group of people who see the monarch as somewhat superhuman or semi-divine. Therefore, the larger the empire, the less effective the Monarchy is. Early in the game, however, the Monarchy is the most efficient way to prosecute a war. Naturally, it is soon superceded by other forms of government.

Obviously, the slight bonuses for Science and Production during the early portion of the game are far outweighed by those of other forms of government as the mid-game approaches. Note also that the larger the empire, the less efficient the Monarchy government becomes. As your empire grows, don't hesitate to change to a new form of government.

## The Republic

| Government: | REPUBLIC |
|---|---|
| Requires: | Republic Advance |
| Size of Government Penalty: | 30 |
| Science Bonus: | 1.5 |
| Gold Bonus: | 1.25 |
| Pollution: | Medium (1) |
| Production Bonus: | 1.25 |
| Maximum Gold for Science: | 60% |
| Growth: | Bad |
| Military: | Bad |

The roots of The Republic form of government are to be found in the amphictyonic or cult-centered alliance known as the Delphic League. As with the ideal civilization described in Plato's *The Republic*, there may occasionally be a central leader authorized by an assembly of free citizens, but the authority for the government rests in said assembly. In Plato, this assembly was formed of philosopher kings. Surprisingly enough, however, the Republic of Plato was not "free" in the modern sense. Censorship by the government, indoctrination of youth, and disinformation from the authorities were considered to be acceptable.

In *Call to Power*, the Republic is the most efficient form of government for a medium civilization. It offers across the board bonuses to the Science, Gold, and Production modifiers. It also has the least downside of any form of government until you are able to form a Democracy.

## Technocracy

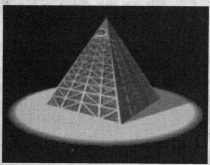

| Government: | TECHNOCRACY |
|---|---|
| Requires: | Technocracy Advance |
| Size of Government Penalty: | 110 |
| Science Bonus: | 2 |
| Gold Bonus: | 1.5 |
| Pollution: | Medium (1) |
| Production Bonus: | 2 |
| Maximum Gold for Science: | 80% |
| Growth: | Good |
| Military: | Average |

A nightmare government from the 22nd century, the technologically elite have banded together to form an efficient and enriching government on the backs of the poor and middle classes. In order to stifle dissent, the techno-elite disseminate drugs. Through a combination of coercion, robotics, and pharmaceuticals, the elite have managed to create an efficient form of government that enriches themselves while only further impoverishing those to whom they are giving drugs as a literal "opiate of the masses." This is a useful but inhumane form of government, since it has the highest Production modifier in *Call to Power*.

Technocracy is definitely the form of government to use when you're falling behind and you need to pump up Production in a hurry with no definite downside.

## Theocracy

| Government: | THEOCRACY |
|---|---|
| Requires: | Theocracy Advance |
| Size of Government Penalty: | 40 |
| Science Bonus: | 1.25 |
| Gold Bonus: | 1.25 |
| Pollution: | Medium (1) |
| Production Bonus: | 1.25 |
| Maximum Gold for Science: | 60% |
| Growth: | Bad |
| Military: | Average |

Recognizing that the Roman Catholic Church functioned in many ways like a separate country during much of world history, *Call to Power* decided to include Theocracy as a form of government. The historical background in *Call to Power* suggests an almost symbiotic relationship between the Church and the kings of Europe. With the Church's hold on education

and powerful potential for intervention on matters of diplomacy (particularly in terms of who could marry whom), education (with many of the foremost educators being priests), and warfare (the Pope could interdict any king who went to war without his blessing), it was in many ways like a powerful state itself. Wherever there was dissension, the Pope could always excommunicate a monarch, leaving said ruler to suffer the disapproval and discontent of his people, as well as to fear for his soul.

Today, the Roman Catholic Church doesn't really act much like a Theocracy, but many Islamic countries respond to their holy man leaders as though Allah were truly speaking through them. These relatively small countries are not only willing to wage a holy war or jihad, but they wish to convert their enemies, too. In *Call to Power*, this desire to "convert" one's enemies to the "right" way is reflected in the ability of a Theocracy to create Cleric units. These valuable units can provide significant income for gamers by allowing them to use the Convert City special attack. If successful, this attack lets you collect Gold from the target city as a tithe. Plus, if you have the Hagia Sophia Wonder early in the game, you can collect double the tithe from the affected city.

In summary, the Theocracy is a relatively efficient form of government. It doesn't pay dividends as big as some of the later governments with regard to the modifiers, but the Cleric attack could become a big income producer for your government. This is a very nice government in the early portion of the game for someone who prefers to build rather than conquer.

# Tyranny

| Government: | TYRANNY |
|---|---|
| Requires: | None |
| Size of Government Penalty: | N/A |
| Science Bonus: | 1 |
| Gold Bonus: | 1 |
| Pollution: | Medium (1) |
| Production Bonus: | 1 |
| Maximum Gold for Science: | 50% |
| Growth: | Awful |
| Military: | Average |

In Tyranny, a ruler controls his domain by absolute power. Often, this power is maintained by physical threat. In primitive tribes, this would have been seen in the chief who could physically defeat all contenders. As Tyranny progresses in primitive societies, this power evolves into rules with implied threats as their enforcement.

In *Call to Power*, Tyranny is the beginning government for your civilization. You are the leader and you rule by absolute power. As the game begins, you are just starting your social structure through the division of labor between the Settler unit, the Workers in your cities who must produce, the elite warrior classes represented by the military units, and Entertainers in your cities.

However, since Tyranny represents the baseline functionality for *Call to Power* and there are no advantageous modifiers in remaining under Tyranny when it is possible to move on, we advise that you change governments out of Tyranny as quickly as possible.

# Virtual Democracy

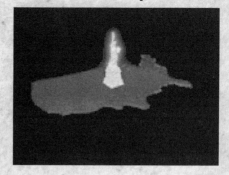

| Government: | VIRTUAL DEMOCRACY |
|---|---|
| Requires: | Virtual Democracy Advance |
| Size of Government Penalty: | 120 |
| Science Bonus: | 3.5 |
| Gold Bonus: | 1.75 |
| Pollution: | Medium (1) |
| Production Bonus: | 1 |
| Maximum Gold for Science: | 100% |
| Growth: | Excellent |
| Military: | Bad |

A highly idealized futuristic version of pure democracy, Virtual Democracy posits a true "one person-one vote" ethos in an environment where discrimination and poverty have been eliminated. *Call to Power* also says some nice words about ending human depravity. One wonders, of course, just how that happened—considering some of the corporate nightmares unleashed within the game's fiction. Nonetheless, Virtual Democracy is the best government for making progress in Science. If you're headed for the Wormhole Sensor and Alien Synthesis Project ending, this is the government you'll need to succeed.

## No Man Is An Ireland (Diplomacy)

Now that you know the basics about each governmental style, you'll need to know a little bit about how governments interrelate. The late cartoonist, Al Capp (famous for *Li'l*

*Abner*) used to misquote the classic "No man is an island" observation of John Donne by substituting "Ireland" for "island." Ironically, this malapropism turns out to be quite appropriate since the original phrase meant that humans are interdependent on each other and Capp's phrase underscored the "Troubles" which have plagued Ireland for years. In *Call to Power*, trouble is all around you and your civilization won't be able to avoid contact with potentially hostile civilizations. Being either an island or an Ireland is not going to help you win in *Call to Power*, so we offer these tips on Diplomacy as a conclusion to this chapter on the governments of *Civilization: Call to Power*.

The famous military theorist Carl von Clausewitz (see quote, Chapter 4) would have been proud of the way that *Call to Power* allows you to deal diplomatically with your rivals. In general, you'll be able to freeze the opposition with the occasional diplomatic head feint, and this will often give you time to build up your forces to either conquer them or defend against them. To open diplomatic relations with a rival civilization, you must build a Diplomat unit and move it into proximity of a target city. Then, you can use the Establish Embassy command. Once this is complete, you can use the Diplomacy screen to select the kind of action you wish to take with your rival.

*DIPLOMATIC AMENITY: This handy menu allows you to perform any one of these actions with a rival civilization with whom you've established an embassy.*

The diplomatic portion of the program in *Call to Power* uses "fuzzy logic." Each action that you take and some game states affect the artificial opponent as a positive or negative modifier. These are not hard-coded, however, but take effect to a random degree based on your actions. Think of these reactions as taking place along a continuum from Warlike to Peaceful, with Warlike meaning the negative side of the continuum and Peaceful being the positive side. Each leader profile starts at a different point on the continuum.

Here are some of the variables that affect the artificial opponents in general. First of all, the artificial opponents don't like to keep the status quo for very long. They like a dynamic world situation.

* They don't like to stay at war for extended periods.
* They don't like to be at peace for too long.
* They are less likely to go to war after a short peace.

Therefore, it is unwise to think that you are going to be able to keep them at bay with one long-lasting treaty. You need to approach them every so often with a demand, offer, or tribute in order to keep their algorithms churning. You might accidentally set them off, but we haven't found that to be likely. In fact, if the rival is Peaceful, we have found that you can even attack the rival on one occasion without retaliation. After that, of course, you're fair game.

Since it is advantageous to keep the lines of communication open with your rivals, you should keep in mind the following two variable lists—one for positive variables and the other for negative variables.

Things That Make Rivals Like You More:

* If the rival is in first place and you are in last. (Exception: When you are the rival's worst enemy.)
* If you are in first place and your rival is in last. (Exception: When you are his worst enemy.)
* If you are close to your rival and he is in a Peaceful state.
* If you accept the rival's requests.
* If you attack the rival's enemies.
* If you keep your word with regard to meeting demands and honoring agreements.

Things That Make Rivals Like You Less:

* If the rival is not in last place, but you're in first place.
* If you are close to your rival and he is in a Warlike state.
* If you use unconventional attacks on your rival.
* If you trespass.
* If you Pirate his Trade Routes.
* If you attack your rival's friends.
* If you violate a Stop Trade Agreement.

In general, it is a good idea to occasionally disturb the Diplomatic waters. This way, you'll always have some idea of what your opponents are up to by regularly opening the Diplomacy screen and checking their temperature with regard to your civilization and others. If you don't succeed in your demand or Diplomatic suggestion, usually the worst response you'll get is something like the screenshot pictured here.

*KINGSTON QUEEN: In this sequence, Elizabeth II of Jamaica expresses her frustration at dealing with you. She does nothing about it, though, and you buy time.*

## Spy versus Spy (Dirty Tricks)

Of course, dealing with your rival civilizations isn't always clean and neat. Sometimes, you just can't trust what they tell you and need to gather some intelligence for yourself. Spies, Diplomats, and Cyber Ninjas are your tools for intelligence gathering. At other times, you need to destabilize a country with a covert action. Spies and Cyber Ninjas can plant Nukes or incite revolutions. At other times, Espionage is demanded. So, Spies and Cyber Ninjas can steal Advances from rival civilization.

The procedure is fairly easy. Move the Cyber Ninja, Diplomat, or Spy into the immediate proximity of the enemy city, then choose the appropriate command and place the targeting reticule over the city. The cost of the action will immediately be assessed against your Gold reserves and the program will determine your success or failure. In the event of success, you get what you want. In the event of failure, there is a chance that the undercover unit will be killed.

[ 77 ]

The following chart shows the costs and odds for each "dirty trick."

| Unit | Dirty Trick | Effect | Cost | % for Success | % for Apprehension/ Death of Agent |
|---|---|---|---|---|---|
| **Diplomat** | Establish Embassy | See part of a city's secrets | 0 | 100% | 0% |
| **Cyber Ninja** | Spying | Reveals all of a city's vital statistics | 0 | 75% | 5% |
| **Diplomat** | Spying | Reveals all of a city's vital statistics | 0 | 50% | 10% |
| **Spy** | Spying | Reveals all of a city's vital statistics | 0 | 75% | 10% |
| **Cyber Ninja** | Steal Advance | Steals 1 of city's Advances | 4,000 | 50% | 25% |
| **Spy** | Steal Advance | Steals 1 of city's Advances | 4,000 | 50% | 50% |
| **Cyber Ninja** | Plant Nuke | Spy dies with large population | 0 | 25% | 10% |
| **Spy** | Plant Nuke | Spy dies with large population | 0 | 10% | 50% |
| **Cyber Ninja** | Incite Revolution | Causing city to overthrow government | 4,000 | 50% | 25% |
| **Spy** | Incite Revolution | Causing city to overthrow government | 4,000 | 50% | 50% |

As you can tell, the risk-to-reward ratio is high in relation to these Diplomatic "Dirty Tricks," but desperate times call for desperate measures. The time may come within some of your games that you need some of these high-risk tactics to level the playing field once again. Some gamers like to play "Gunboat Diplomacy" by rattling their swords very visibly. Others would rather flatten their opponents with the equivalent of the horse's head in *The Godfather*.

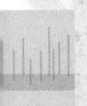

# Chapter Five:

# Concerning the Institution of Slavery

## The Economics and Consequences of Slavery and Abolitionism

The most controversial addition to *Civilization: Call to Power* is likely to be the addition of slavery. There will be those who will insist that empire building games like *Call to Power* do not need the less savory aspects of the human condition, as well as those who insist that allowing such a reprehensible institution in the game is equivalent to legitimizing it. We would suggest that placing such a mechanism within the game is not legitimization, but rather an opportunity for learning. Gamers will discover within *Call to Power*'s slavery model that while there may be economic advantages, the socio-political disadvantages are very much in attendance, as well.

Slavery, in one form or another, has existed since the first communities moved from the hunter/gatherer model to that of an agrarian/pastoral model. In a hunter/gatherer society, one wasn't likely to use many slaves because they would be likely to run away. It would have been an inefficient use of manpower to watch over large bands of slaves who would be spread out by the nature of the hunt. Indeed, it was more efficient to kill one's enemies than to put them to work, since live prisoners were additional mouths to feed and didn't significantly increase the efficiency of the hunt. Once agrarian and pastoral models came into play, however, taskmasters and slavers could watch over workers, harvesters, and to some degree, herdsmen. Production improved enough that the philosophy changed for the victors in war. Instead of the only "good" enemy being a dead one, the only good "prisoner" was a live one. I am reminded of amateur historian Will Durant's observation that, "Slavery became part of the discipline by which man was prepared for industry."

Many texts from early civilizations reflect the institution of slavery. Circa 2000 BC, texts from the Sumerian kingdom of Eshnunna listed the worth of a slave at 15 shekels of silver. Prior to the 17th century BC, the Code of Hammurabi also mentions stealing a slave (either male or female) as a capital crime. Depending on how literally one accepts the unusually round numbers in the biblical chronology, the nation of Israel threw off its enslavement in Egypt somewhere between the 15th and 12th centuries BC. By the eighth century BC, the Israelite prophet Amos castigated the Philistines for engaging in the slave trade with Edom. Herodotus, the Greek historian, mentioned the Scythian practice of blinding their slaves during the fifth century BC. Strangely enough, the purpose of the blind slaves was to stir the milk in wooden casks until the cream rose to the top—making them the first human churns.

Slaves were a vital part of the Greek and Roman economies. Plato accepts them as a matter of course. His dialogues on law insist that free citizens treat slaves properly as part of basic justice endemic to any human society. A few decades later, Aristotle likened slaves to mere tools in his *Nicomachean Ethics*. By the time of the Roman Republic (third century BC), Cato's *De Agricultura* described the exact amount of wine, clothing, wheat, and relishes necessary to keep slaves for a 150-acre estate.

Since slavery appeared in such early stages of civilization, it is no wonder that *Call to Power* allows gamers to build Slaver units from nearly the start of the game onward. With an initial city of 10,000 population and the Toolmaking Advance, it will take 12 turns and 270 gold to create a Slaver—twice the amount of time and gold necessary to build a Warrior. The Slaver has no attack value, but because of the defense value, he can garrison the city until you build a Warrior. As long as you have a Slaver in the city, no other civilization will be able to sneak a Slaver into the city's proximity.

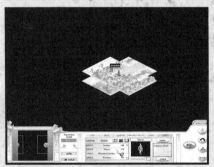

*TASKMASTER, TASKMASTER! The Slaver in* Civilization: Call to Power *has an unsavory appearance and attitude that is far from pro-slavery.*

Of course, the big advantage of building the Slaver early on is that the Slaver has twice as many movement points as the Warrior. So, you can explore the vicinity of your capitol city twice as fast as you could with a Warrior unit. Unlike the Mounted Archer, which has the same initial cost as the Slaver and can be built as soon as a civilization has the Domestication Advance, only another Slaver, a Diplomat, an Abolitionist, or a Cleric can see the Slaver unit. This makes your Slaver a valuable unit for providing intelligence about rival civilizations without them knowing that you're spying. Another valuable reason for building a Slaver early on is because the AI civilizations have a tendency to use Slavers as spies, as well. Of course, there is a slight trade-off because the Mounted Archer has a one-third higher movement rate than the Slaver.

*TAKES ONE TO KNOW ONE. Only Diplomats, Clerics, Abolitionists, and other Slavers can spot a Slaver on a mission. As a result, Slavers make excellent de facto spies—use them to get close to your enemies long before you get the Nationalism Advance and get to build an actual Spy unit.*

Unfortunately, the Slaver's ten points for defense disappears pretty fast when he faces a real Warrior, so it's a good idea for the Slaver to use his superior movement to get away from any military threat as fast as possible. To avoid hanging your Slaver out to dry (or to die!), we recommend placing him with some military units. Should you be fortunate enough to defeat some enemy units while the Slaver is stacked with friendly units, the Slaver can enslave the defeated units. Remember, though, you'll need 250 gold in order to accomplish this. If you believe that your goal in warfare is to ensure that the enemy is unable to prosecute war against you (von Clauswitz's axiom of war), this is an ideal trade-off because it converts the enslaved units into your worker units at a very advantageous wage and food consumption ratio compared to your free citizens.

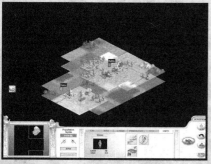

*NET PLAY. To attempt a slave raid, you need to be adjacent to the target, have 250 in gold, and have a garrisoned city. Then, click on the net icon and place the targeting reticule over the victims.*

Should you be fortunate enough to encounter a Settler unit from another civilization or get adjacent to another civilization's city when you have 250 gold in your treasury, you'll have an excellent chance to pump up your population in the best possible way—at a rival civilization's expense. You have a 75 percent chance of having the rival population drop by 10,000 and having your nearest city gain 10,000 in population. Naturally, to reflect the coercion effect endemic to slavery, you'll have to have some military units garrisoned in the city to keep

the new slaves from revolting. If you do have such a garrison in a nearby city, there is nothing more satisfying than weakening your opponent while at the same time strengthening your own position. Of course, there is a downside. A Slaver who is actively making a raid has a 50-percent chance of getting caught. As noted earlier, Slavers don't stand up long when facing Warriors and more powerful military units. So, you could lose a Slaver pretty fast by trying too many slave raids in a short period.

*NET GAIN. If the raid is successful, your nearest garrisoned city will gain one population point (10,000 in population), while your enemy's city loses one point. If you have plenty of gold, using a Slaver to reduce the population is a good way to soften up a city prior to besieging it.*

Beyond weakening your opponent, you also build up your labor pool and increase production at a very efficient cost/effectiveness ratio. The best news about this is that the one point of population you steal from your rival will cost you only half as much in food and gold as workers who are free. Those who follow the historical theory that slavery as an institution actually inhibited innovation will be disappointed with how efficient slavery is within the context of *Call to Power*. The old theory was that slavery provided such inexpensive labor that slave owners were not motivated to improve efficiency. Yet, any slave owner who is responsible for buying slaves and keeping them alive is definitely going to want to see his investment go further. Slaves are simple labor power with unrestrained sales and transfers, much like any other capital goods. As such, the owner will want maximum value.

*Call to Power* reflects the reality that on any advancing frontier, there is always a labor shortage. During the middle part of the second millenium AD, many colonial powers attempted to coerce the indigenous populations of the New World into a labor force, but soon found that transporting slaves from the Slave Coast of Africa was economically more desirable. In the 15th century AD, the Portuguese were prodigious slavers. Later in the millenium, the Dutch become prolific slavers.

> TIP: Walled cities make it tougher for Slavers to capture new slaves. Should you discover that your population has suddenly dropped by one point for no apparent reason, either build a City Wall to foil the slave raid, or produce your own Slaver to spot the enemy Slaver before your opponent has another 250 gold to try again.

Fortunately for the human spirit, the 18th century AD brought about a backlash against slavery. Voltaire praised Baron Montesquieu for recovering the title deeds to human freedom. In the United States, abolitionist fervor inspired the prohibition of slavery in Delaware, Maryland, Massachusetts, North Carolina, and South Carolina from their inception as states (and commonwealths) forward. The Constitutional Convention was rife with debate from the likes of Massachusetts lawyer Rufus King on the abolitionist side and Charles Pinckney of South Carolina on the pro-slavery side. Pinckney appealed to the classic examples of Greece and Rome while contending, "In all ages, one half of all mankind have been slaves." Naturally, seeds of the American Civil War were sown in this debate, but the ideal of abolitionism had been planted and was taking root long before the Emancipation Proclamation.

After the French Revolution, the new Convention passed the Laws of Ventose in 1794. These laws abolished slavery in both the French colonies and on domestic lands. Robespierre is said to have described slavery as a decadent reminder of the "nonsense of monarchy."

In *Call to Power*, you will also need to reach the Classical Education Advance before you can build an Abolitionist or the Age of Reason Advance before you can complete the Emancipation Proclamation Wonder. The Abolitionist is the strongest anti-slavery unit and has two extremely important uses prior to the implementation of the Emancipation Proclamation Wonder. First, the Abolitionist can attempt to free slaves in any target city. The cost for this effort, reminiscent of the 19th century's legendary John Brown, is only 50 gold and has the same odds of succeeding (75-percent in favor of success) as the slave raid, but at one fifth the price. Further, the Abolitionist's action only has a 10-percent chance of being detected, as opposed to the 50-percent chance in a slave raid.

The result of a successful attempt to free slaves is, of course, the direct antithesis of the slave raid. Instead of adding one population point of slave labor to the nearest garrisoned city while reducing the population of the enemy city (as in the slave raid), freeing slaves adds one population point of free citizens to the Abolitionist's closest city. The reduced cost in this attempt reflects the high cost of maintaining an institution that runs counter to the human spirit. It is easier to spur an individual to freedom than to keep that individual in forced slavery. Such is the ideal since the Age of Reason, and it is implemented extremely well in *Call to Power*.

*JOHN BROWN'S POSSE. Suggesting that the human spirit is innately free and that the ideal of slavery is counter to that of the human spirit,* Civilization: Call to Power *only charges one fifth of the cost to free a slave as to enslave one.*

The second important tool in the hands of the Abolitionist is the ability to incite riots in the cities of slave owners. Although this form of benevolent sedition is expensive (1,000 gold), it is effective. The Abolitionist merely moves adjacent to the city of his choice, pays the 1,000 gold, and always causes a slave revolt. This feature obviously reflects the reality that anyone who depends upon slave labor continually has his production at risk. The beauty is that such a revolt immediately impacts your enemy's production capability, giving you a chance to build faster and over-run that civilization militarily.

Of course, the Emancipation Proclamation is the best way to undo a slave-holding enemy. Proclaiming this Wonder of the world immediately converts slaves into citizens on a global basis. This causes -1 happiness for every new citizen in the city, as well as increases the city's food consumption. The Wonder also causes an additional -3 happiness in every slave-holding city for five turns. Naturally, all of this causes riots in foreign, slave-holding cities and the snowball effect could lead to revolution. Think of the effect of this Wonder on the slave-holding nations as being similar to the riots in "The Terror" following the French Revolution.

> TIP: Inciting riots may not seem like a savory activity, but it serves the purpose of immediately reducing your enemy's food and production capacity and getting his attention. Fortunately, the 1,000 gold it costs to incite a riot always succeeds.

In summary, the following chart shows the advantages and disadvantages of Slavers and Abolitionists in *Civilization: Call to Power*.

| Unit/Wonder | Action | Cost | Result |
|---|---|---|---|
| Slaver | Slave Raid | 250 | 75% Success/50% Detection |
| | | | Success creates 1 Production, costing .50 Food |
| Abolitionist | Free Slaves | 50 | 75% Success/10% Detection |
| | | | Success creates 1 Production, costing 1 Food |
| Abolitionist | Incite Riots | 1,000 | 100% Success |
| | | | Immediately causes riot in slave-holding cities |
| Emancipation Proclamation | Frees Slaves Globally, causes -3 happiness in every slave-holding city for five turns | | 100% Success |
| | | | Success creates 1 Production, costing 1 Food for each Slave |
| | Incites Riots | | 100% Success |
| | | | Success creates riots in slave-holding cities on global basis |

## Conclusion

Slavers and slavery as a system have their uses during the early exploratory periods of a game's history. Slavery is relatively cost-efficient in the early stages of *Civilization*, but becomes exceedingly more risky as humankind discovers the freedom within and is less willing to submit to outside arbiters of morality. Gamers will quickly discover that the institution of slavery is not desirable once they reach the mid-game of *Call to Power*, but the advantage is definitely there in the early stages of the game. The designers are to be commended for creating a system that reflects the appropriate flow of history.

## Chapter Six:

# Concerning the Advances of Civilization: Call to Power

## How Each Civilization Advance Can Help You

*"Ancient Astronauts didn't build the Pyramids! Human beings built the Pyramids, and they are now journeying to the stars—it all taps into the same spirit of celebrating human achievement."*

—*Gene Roddenberry, on the enduring popularity of* Star Trek

Machiavelli was correct when he said that it is difficult to be the innovator. "There is nothing more difficult to take in hand, more perilous to conduct, or more uncertain in its success than to take the lead in the introduction of a new order of things." By introducing new ideas, techniques and processes, the innovator inevitably creates enemies of those who have done well under the old order and, at best, gains lukewarm allies among those who think that the new order will work. A major part of the play balance in *Civilization: Call to Power* is the way you, as the player, choose to allocate resources for research and innovation. Each game of *Call to Power* is different, as you weave between the branches of the technology tree.

*Call to Power* contains 103 different "Advances." These are the landmark technological, sociological, or ideological shifts which form the building blocks of human civilization. Each Advance, like a Lego building block or Tinkertoy piece, allows additional Advances or Improvements to be built upon it. Within this chapter, we will attempt to give some historical background for each Advance. We'll provide a snapshot of where the Advance fits on the technology tree, as well as a table of units and/or Improvements available upon completion of the Advance. Finally, we'll give you some hints on how to use the Advance to foil your enemies or secure your civilization.

In *Call to Power*, there are ten branches on the technology tree:

1. Cultural Advances
2. Sea Advances
3. Construction Advances
4. Aggressive War Advances
5. Defensive War Advances
6. Physical Science Advances
7. Economic Advances
8. Medical Advances
9. Mechanical Advances
10. Flight Advances

Some of the Advances that bud and bloom upon these branches of the technology tree serve as forks in the road to other branches of the tree. These are called crossover technologies, because the discovery in one area opens up the way to new innovation and discovery in another area. The flow charts in this chapter should assist you in determining when to shift your research funds from one branch of the tree to another when you reach these forks. Although the technology tree provided with *Call to Power* is very useful, it is sometimes easy to get lost with regard to the crossover technologies and lose track of how they fit together. We hope that the smaller flow charts in this chapter will help you keep track of what you want to accomplish.

In order to provide two ways to cross-reference these Advances, we have presented all of the Advances in alphabetical order. In addition, we have labeled each Advance according to its position on each of the given branches. For example, Agriculture is the prerequisite to the first Advance on the Cultural Advances branch. Therefore, it will be listed as *Pre-Cultural 1*. However, Agriculture is also the first step in the Defensive War branch and hence, is also listed as *Defensive War 1*, since it is required prior to the Domestication Advance. Here's hoping that between the two approaches, you can find the information you'll need to progress more quickly in achieving the Advances that you really want.

In addition, we have listed the units or buildings that are contingent on each Advance below the appropriate Advance on the flow chart. The Improvements in *italics* are Tile Improvements, which must be built out of the Public Works budget (see Chapter 1).

# Aerodynamics

## Flight 1

Now the game gets really interesting with the introduction of Flight. Both peaceful and military strategists should attempt to gain this Advance as soon as possible after the discovery of Mass Production for the increasingly high-tech toys that are readily available, if expensive (see Chapter 2).

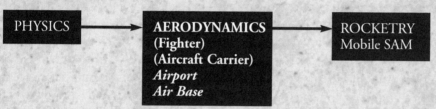

PHYSICS → **AERODYNAMICS** **(Fighter)** **(Aircraft Carrier)** *Airport* *Air Base* → ROCKETRY Mobile SAM

HINT: Regardless of your playing style, move as quickly as possible now toward the development of Nukes. At least one of your neighbors is certainly doing so, especially if you're in a multiplayer game.

# Age of Reason

## Cultural Advancement 6

The 18th and early 19th centuries are often called either the Enlightenment or the Age of Reason. In its simplest form, that rationalism of the 18th century caused the intellectuals of that century, or *philosophes*, to believe that individuals within humankind would see "reason" whenever it was exposed to them and, as a result, change their behavior based upon natural law. Such *philosophes* would look to nature for analogies and expect all of the complications of human nature to be subsumed by these analogies.

Though David Hume's criticism of the dominant philosophy eventually won out, the spirit of the Enlightenment is visible in the works of Immanuel Kant (1724-1804), who believed in a "categorical imperative" beyond the natural order. This spirit is also apparent in the works of Jean Jacques Rousseau (1712-1778), who used Nature as a pedagogical tool for espousing a democratizing sentiment. Indeed, the Age of Reason was the philosophical underpinning of both the American and French Revolutions.

Ironically, Rousseau's ideal was a patriarchal period prior to the establishment of private property. He molded his thought and observations on social theory off the idea of this primitive family. He blamed private property for the economic, political, and social inequality that he saw within the French regime of his day. His work spawned revolution, but the only lasting revolution (the American Revolution) was actually built on a capitalistic underpinning that accentuated private property rather than moderating it.

In *Civilization: Call to Power*, the Age of Reason Advance accentuates the positive by allowing you to construct the Emancipation Act Wonder, which is a useful tool when you are facing rival slave-holding civilizations. As discussed in their respective chapters, this is a powerful item to use against slave owners.

| PRINTING PRESS (Publishing House) Gutenberg's Bible | → | **AGE OF REASON (Abolitionist) Emancipation Act** | → | CONSERVATION (Recycling Plant) | → | GAIA THEORY Gaia Controller |

HINT: If you are not facing a slave-holding civilization, the Age of Reason Advance is not a high priority. The major exception would be whenever you realize that a rival civilization has become a major polluter. Then, you may want to build toward the Gaia Controller Wonder in order to exploit your advantage against your environmentally challenged opponent.

# Agriculture

## Aggressive War 1, Pre-Cultural 1

It shouldn't be surprising that Agriculture is the initial building block in both the Cultural and the Aggressive War branches of the technology tree. Agriculture is important because it allowed for the significant growth of civilizations beyond the hunter/gatherer type of society. Hunter/gatherer societies are dependent upon what they can hunt and kill. This forces migration to follow the migration paths of their prey and limits the size of the society proportional to the fecundity of their hunting grounds. Agrarian society, on the other hand, makes allowance for food storage, which can safeguard against disappointing harvests and reduce the seasonal migration patterns of the society. Further, agrarian societies tend to have more stable diets, reducing the infant mortality rate considerably.

Historians and archaeologists usually pinpoint the development of Agriculture and the attendant domestication of animals to the Neolithic Period (usually between 9000 BC and 5500 BC). In what is now the border area between Iran and Iraq, a Neolithic settlement called Jarmo proved to have had domesticated grains and evidence of domesticated goats, sheep, and pigs as early as 6750 BC (as organic remains were Carbon-14 dated). However, it appears that Agriculture was invented more than once in the history of humankind. The crops of pre-Columbian America were significantly different from those of the Middle East, Europe, and Asia. Agriculture in the Orient, where crops were largely disseminated by transplanting shoots from a parent plant, was significantly different from Agriculture in Europe and the Middle East, where crops were largely planted by sowing seed. In general, however, it was the process of adjusting to the seasons and utilizing the land to fullest capacity that enabled societies to sustain themselves continuously at given locations, whether that meant taking advantage of annual floods or developing systems of irrigation.

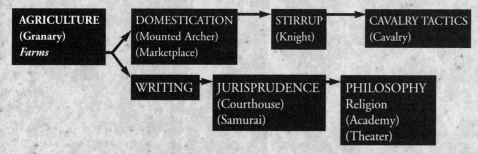

HINT: Within the context of Call to Power, everybody gets Agriculture at the start of the standard game.

However, if you choose to select different Advances when handicapping a multiplayer game (see Chapter 9), then it is absolutely vital that you get the Agriculture Advance as soon as possible. Your population is not likely to be able to grow without the Granary Improvement to enable food storage, or to maximize its potential without the capacity to build Farms. In addition, you'll need the cultural Advances available after the Writing Advance in order to progress to the Renaissance epoch. Without Agriculture, you wouldn't have the Writing Advance, which was largely based on being able to inventory the crops in order to keep track of tribute and taxation.

# Agricultural Revolution

## Mechanical Discoveries 1

During the early portions of the 11th century AD, some agricultural advances began to show up in Western Europe. Some were already known in the eastern world, but only began to be formalized in the western world at this time. In general, the agricultural lands of each manor were divided into thirds. One-third of the property was planted to wheat or rye. Another third was planted to barley or oats. The third portion was left fallow.

As time progressed, market forces began to take a role. Crop rotation became based more on price than tradition and even the balance between animal husbandry and cultivation began to be jockeyed between the prices at various town and church market faires.

This is the period in which harness makers in the west developed the stiff collar for plow animals. Since the animals no longer choked when hitting hard ground, they became more efficient and could now plow three to four times as much acreage in a day as they could prior to its invention.

More importantly, and reflected in the Agricultural Revolution Advance in *Civilization: Call to Power* was the adoption of the water mill. The mill appeared in western civilization around the end of the 12th century, though it had been known outside of Europe prior to this period. The mill provided an extremely efficient means of grinding grain, a central unifying point in many communities, and enabled oxen to be used elsewhere.

The overall effect of new efficiencies provided during this early period of the Agricultural Revolution was that individuals were not shackled to the land as much as they had been in centuries past. In *Call to Power*, the advantages of the Agricultural Revolution are presented in the availability of the Pikeman unit (essentially a medieval national guardsman) to reflect the need for less labor in the fields; the Mill Improvement, which increases Production by 50-percent to reflect the improved efficiency of the water mill; and the Advanced Farms Tile Improvement, which adds 15 Food to represent better agricultural methods, like crop rotation and fertilization, as well as more efficient tools.

CLASSICAL EDUCATION [w/GEOMETRY] (University) → **AGRICULTURAL REVOLUTION** **(Pikeman)** **(Mill)** **(Advanced Farms)** → MECHANICAL CLOCK [w/ OCEAN FARING] (City Clock) → MACHINE TOOLS (Ship of the Line)

HINT: The Advanced Farms Tile Improvement becomes available with the Agricultural Revolution Advance. This makes the Advance extremely valuable for all types of players. With one quick Advance, you can improve your military posture with the addition of the Pikeman unit, your Production capacity with the construction of a Mill Improvement, and your Food production with expenditure of Public Works funds on the Advanced Farms Tile Improvement. This is a high priority Advance for all players.

# AI Surveillance

## Mechanical 9

As we've said at length throughout this book, a persistent theme of *Call to Power* is that we are being watched. The AI Surveillance Advance, with its Security Monitor, is just more honest about it.

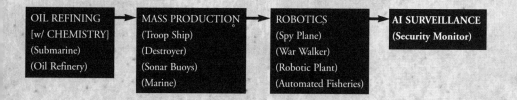

OIL REFINING [w/ CHEMISTRY] (Submarine) (Oil Refinery) → MASS PRODUCTION (Troop Ship) (Destroyer) (Sonar Buoys) (Marine) → ROBOTICS (Spy Plane) (War Walker) (Robotic Plant) (Automated Fisheries) → **AI SURVEILLANCE** **(Security Monitor)**

HINT: Security Monitors are okay, but you're better off building The Agency. The best thing about this Advance is that it puts you very near to the Wonder trio of Nanite Defuser, Primer, and Eden Project.

# Alchemy

## Defensive War 3

Alchemy, of course, is the proto-science that precedes the more disciplined science of Chemistry. It is founded upon some simple principles derived from the observations of ancient man. For example, wise men steeped in Alchemy believed that every animal is the product of sexual union, every plant of its seed, and every mineral of a mixture of earth and water. In Alchemy, there was a belief in a common and universal matter called Chaos. Within Chaos, there were the four basic elements: air, earth, fire, and water. These elements, in turn, had four basic qualities: cold, heat, dryness and humidity. By observing the interactions of these elements upon themselves and their different behaviors under the different basic qualities, an early Chemistry evolved.

In general, Alchemy taught that there were both pure and impure elements. Impure elements were those which could be dominated (that is, changed) by interaction with water (lead, tin, copper, iron, and silver). Pure elements were those such as gold, which could only be refined by interaction with fire. As observed in the section discussing the Philosopher's Stone Wonder, the most famous aspect of Alchemy was the incessant desire in both the ancient world and during the Middle Ages for alchemists to seek the reagent, which would transform common materials, most usually lead, into this perfect element called gold. Rulers had more mercenary hopes for this process, believing that these investigations and experiments would finance the expansion of their kingdoms and enhance their wealth. Alchemists hoped that by finding gold, the "perfect male body" in their cosmology, they would find some of the secrets to life.

In *Civilization: Call to Power*, the Alchemy Advance represents that which is positive in terms of the ancient discipline. As a result of ordered observation, the Alchemy Advance allows your civilization to build Archer units, construct the destructive Fire Triremes, and of course, construct the Philosopher's Stone

Wonder. Naturally, gaining the Alchemy Advance enables you to move toward the ever-important Gunpowder Advance and toward the powerful defensive capability of casting cannon.

| IRON-WORKING (Legion) | → | ALCHEMY (Archer) (Fire Trireme) Philosopher's Stone | → | GUNPOWDER (Musketeer) (Advanced Mines) | → | CANNON-MAKING (Cannon) |

> HINT: Alchemy is a significant Advance for both empire-building and conquering players. It is not only useful for the strong defensive capabilities of the longer ranged Archer units and the Fire Triremes, but it is also a vital prerequisite for the paradigm-shifting Gunpowder Advance. To win the game, you'll need to put Alchemy high on your priority list. If you're an empire-builder as opposed to conqueror, you'll want to put the Philosopher's Stone high on your list, too. The capacity for making diplomatic moves with every civilization on the map is most important for your defensive capacity.

# Alien Archaeology

## Physical Science 7

As important as the monolith was to *2001: A Space Odyssey*, so is the Alien Archaeology Advance in *Civilization: Call to Power*. You cannot win the game by using the Alien Synthesis Project objective if you don't discover the secrets of psychic communication contained with the Martian ruins associated with this Advance. The Alien Synthesis Project is actually quite intricate, but well worth the effort. Once you start the project, you'll build a Xenoform Laboratory and follow that up with an Embryo Tank, Containment Field, Gene Splicers, and Extra-Terrestrial Communication Device. And, you still aren't guaranteed success. There is a 20-percent chance of cataclysmic failure unless you build two Gene Splicers. Then, you reduce the chance of disaster to 10-percent, and you're ready for the optimal endgame.

For more information on this mode of victory, please see the discussion of the Wormhole Sensor Wonder. You should also be aware that gaining this science-fiction Advance in *Civilization: Call to Power* automatically renders the following obsolete: Edison's Lab, Hollywood, The Agency, Internet, Contraception, and the Genome Project. Assuming that your rivals have more of these Wonders than you have, grabbing the Alien Archaeology Advance can be extremely satisfying.

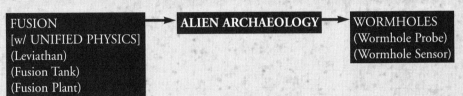

| FUSION [w/ UNIFIED PHYSICS] (Leviathan) (Fusion Tank) (Fusion Plant) | → | **ALIEN ARCHAEOLOGY** | → | WORMHOLES (Wormhole Probe) (Wormhole Sensor) |

**HINT:** If you plan to win with the Alien Synthesis Option, be sure to monitor the effects on your own civilization when you obtain the Alien Archaeology Advance. Losing the effects of several Wonders at once can become a real hardship if you are not prepared. Naturally, Alexander-style gamers may want to pay attention to which opponents have some of the Wonders on the bubble, so that the rival civilization can be exploited during the early transition from existing benefits to zero benefits from newly-obsolete Wonders.

# Arcologies

## Construction 8

For readers of science-fiction, the idea of the Arcologies Advance isn't really new. We know it from Robert Silverberg's classic *The World Inside* and dozens more. Arcologies reflect the convergence of several different trends. On the one hand, they reflect the idea that for humankind to find "Lebensraum," room to live, civilization may have to continue to expand upward. With the Arcologies Advance, there is seemingly no vertical limit to expanding upward in order to create ample living space. On the other hand, Arcologies represent the ideal of the self-supporting community. As in *SimTower*, they represent that ideal of having everything required for quality of life within the same building.

In *Civilization: Call to Power*, the Arcologies Advance allows you to have the power to build huge vertical environments. Indeed, as a reward for doing so, you lose four points of unhappiness because the overcrowded conditions usually associated with urbanization have been diminished. Everyone feels like they have living room within the culture of the Arcology.

```
FUEL CELLS                    ARCOLOGIES
[w/ SUPERCONDUCTOR]   ----->  (Arcologies)
(Aqua-Filter)
(Eco-Transit)
```

HINT: By the time you are ready to acquire the Arcologies Advance, it is very likely that you'll be head-to-head in a war with your prime rival, or involved in the Alien Synthesis version of the Space Race with a rival. Either way, you'll need to be watching your Happiness quotient because even losing one city at this point could set you back further than you expect. The Arcologies Advance is perfect for watching that aspect, no matter how you play the game.

# Asteroid Mining

## Flight 9

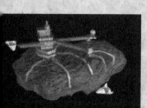

Another of the longterm dreams of mankind is to exploit the resources of the solar system. And where better to do that than in an asteroid belt, where you don't have to worry about things like friction and gravity?

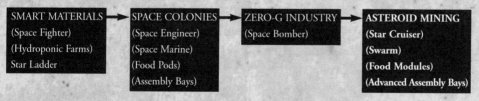

```
SMART MATERIALS        SPACE COLONIES        ZERO-G INDUSTRY       ASTEROID MINING
(Space Fighter)   -->  (Space Engineer)  --> (Space Bomber)   -->  (Star Cruiser)
(Hydroponic Farms)     (Space Marine)                              (Swarm)
Star Ladder            (Food Pods)                                 (Food Modules)
                       (Assembly Bays)                             (Advanced Assembly Bays)
```

HINT: If you're Alien-bound, fine. If not, the units are pretty expensive, and the game's not going to last long enough for you to benefit from those Food Modules and Assembly Bays.

# Astronomy

## Physical Science 2

 In the ancient world, observation of the constellations led to a better understanding of the rhythms of nature. As astral observation became more regular, humankind began to place more confidence in the idea of the constellations actually influencing everyday life. Naturally, this meant that any overt phenomena which hadn't been or was only rarely observed became a sinister omen for what was to come. In this way, astrological interpretation and astronomical observation advanced side-by-side through much of humankind's early history.

In Babylon, the constellations were pictured as celestial beings who actively impacted individual lives. The Greeks, with their cultural tendency toward creating order and taxonomy, managed to catalog the sky into the familiar twelve signs of the Zodiac. Later, Ptolemy influenced the astrological observers more toward astronomy than astrology. Yet, the break wasn't entirely clean. Ptolemy's *Tetrabiblos* had two sections (books) that were purely astrological. Yet he pushed for precise mathematical calculations and devised the geographical method of listing latitude and longitude.

Eventually, Copernicus, followed by Galileo and Kepler, proved the concept of a solar system orbiting the sun, and the modern science of astronomy was born. Astronomy is important in the history of the physical sciences because it served as one of mankind's first intuitive leaps in trying to describe the work of unseen forces at great distances and their effects on everyday life.

In *Civilization: Call to Power*, the Astronomy Advance is much more tied to the idea of agricultural cycles and religious ritual than it is to the later advances in navigation and scientific investigation. However, it is a necessary stepping-stone toward further advancement along the Physical Science technological branch and should not be ignored. Particularly, should you be an empire-builder as opposed to conqueror in playing style, you'll want to gain the Astronomy Advance early in order to be able to construct the Stonehenge Wonder and reduce your Food production requirements.

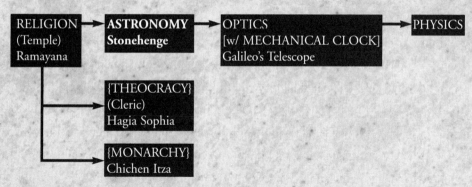

RELIGION → **ASTRONOMY** → OPTICS → PHYSICS
(Temple)     **Stonehenge**     [w/ MECHANICAL CLOCK]
Ramayana                        Galileo's Telescope

{THEOCRACY}
(Cleric)
Hagia Sophia

{MONARCHY}
Chichen Itza

**HINT:** The Astronomy Advance is a key one for the empire-building player. You will want to get the Advance in order to immediately start building the Stonehenge Wonder. Food production can be a nightmare in the early portion of the game before you've had time to build up your Public Works funds and start developing fields. If you are a conqueror in playing style, you will probably want to push forward on both the Aggressive War and Defensive War branches before gaining Astronomy.

# Banking

## Economy 3

Though there is evidence of lending or usury in the ancient world, modern banking derives its name and tradition from the glory days of Florence, Italy. In 14th century Florence, certain businessmen made a habit of sitting on a bench (*banco*) in the center of the town as they made out letters of credit to Traders in order to keep the Florentine import and export business fluid. Because of the bench where they sat, these moneylenders came to be known as *bancherii*, from which we get our modern word, "banker." It is believed that these bancherii flourished well enough to develop 80 different banking houses by the beginning of the 15th century.

By the 17th century, many countries had established national banks to assist the government with capitalization and to assist in steering monetary policy. As these banks were able to inject capital into the economy, goods increased and the economy accelerated. When the economy heated up too much, inflation would result and the national banks would have to pull currency out of the economy by refusing to lend as much.

In *Civilization: Call to Power*, the Banking Advance allows you to build the Bank Improvement in each city. This, in turn, adds 50-percent to Gold production in the host city and allows you to assign citizens as Merchants in order to improve Gold production still further.

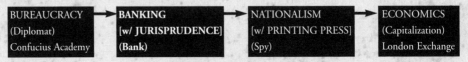

| BUREAUCRACY | BANKING | NATIONALISM | ECONOMICS |
|---|---|---|---|
| (Diplomat) | [w/ JURISPRUDENCE] | [w/ PRINTING PRESS] | (Capitalization) |
| Confucius Academy | (Bank) | (Spy) | London Exchange |

HINT: As observed with regard to the Trade Advance, conquerors will want to wait until later to acquire this Advance. Empire-builders, of course, will want to move forward on the Banking Advance at an early point in your civilization's history.

# Bronze-Working

## Defensive War 1

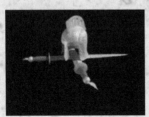

Imagine weapons made of copper or tin. Not very satisfactory, are they? They would have been too soft to hold a satisfactory edge. Early civilizations soon realized that they could make a harder metal by combining copper and tin. At various times in human history, the alloy has featured as little as two-thirds copper ore to one-third tin. At other times, the mixture has been closer to 95-percent copper and 5-percent tin. Archaeologists speculate that the difference was more one of the availability of the ore than of any awareness of an optimum mixture. In the classical era, zinc was added to the mixture in order to add longevity to monumental sculptures.

As with the advent of Agriculture, Bronze-working began in different geographical locales at different times. In the Middle East, for example, sites from the Bronze Age have been dated to 3000 BC. In China, the earliest Bronze Age sites date to circa 1800 BC. This is likely to have been the case because of the lack of copper and tin ores to be found in China, as opposed to the ready availability in much of the Near East. In all civilizations, the result is the same. Bronze tools and weapons proved to be less expensive to forge and longer lasting than the metals which preceded the versatile alloy. So, bronze became a valuable commodity.

Since bronze was such a versatile metal, it appears to have been used in several early civilizations for monetary coinage. Some empire building games from the past have had a direct link from Bronze-Working to Trade and currency, but this ignores the use of animals for barter and the earlier use of copper for coinage. *Civilization: Call to Power* foregoes a direct link from Bronze-Working to the Economic branch, but the odds are that Trade will appear as an option to research at around the same time as you are ready to research or have just completed Bronze-Working.

In *Civilization: Call to Power*, the primary result of gaining Bronze-Working is the capability of building Phalanx units (see Chapter 2). Early in the game, we recommend garrisoning your cities with Phalanx units and putting them into Sleep mode until such time as the enemy is in proximity. Later, as your enemy grows stronger, you'll want to upgrade your garrisons.

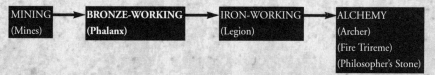

MINING (Mines) → **BRONZE-WORKING (Phalanx)** → IRON-WORKING (Legion) → ALCHEMY (Archer) (Fire Trireme) (Philosopher's Stone)

HINT: As in history, Bronze-Working should be an early consideration for any civilization. In *Call to Power*, you want this Advance in order to build a Phalanx for every city you control. Since the artificial opponents usually use Phalanx units (or Warriors) as their offensive units early in the game, you can almost always defeat them with one Phalanx unit fortified within the city.

# Bureaucracy

## Economics 2

Without an administrative system, it was necessary for kings like Sargon I and Naram-Sin to concentrate vast armies at one locale and incur tremendous expenses to feed them or to constantly send these armies on campaign in order that they could forage and plunder in order to survive. Sargon, according to McNeil in *The Rise of the*

*West*, bragged in an inscription that 5,400 men "ate with him daily." By the time of Hammurabi, writing and accountancy allowed the ruler to decentralize his armed forces to several locales in order to spread the costs and minimize the abuses and inefficiencies of having large bands of military men living by plunder. McNeil suggests that Naram Sin may have begun this process when he supplanted local rulers and priests with his own relatives, essentially a practical nepotism. He sees this as the beginning of a royal bureaucracy, which beget an infrastructure of judges, tax collectors, and garrison commanders who communicated by written order.

This example suggests that far from being the bane which we see Bureaucracy today, the proliferation of officialdom accelerated efficiency and allowed for flexibility in both the defensive and economic systems. In *Civilization: Call to Power*, the Bureaucracy Advance is placed along the Economic technology strand because the keeping of records not only allowed the monarch to accumulate more wealth through tribute and taxation, but because the written transactions allowed for more precision in terms of Trade. *Call to Power* also simulates the dissemination of knowledge inherent in a Bureaucracy by allowing construction of the Confucius Academy after Bureaucracy is possible. Also, since many of the early texts which we have excavated in the Ancient Near East include treaties (often called covenants), and many of these had an Economic component, *Call to Power* allows the construction of the Diplomat units.

Diplomat units are extremely efficient as basic intelligence gathering units and with regard to special divisive attacks. Naturally, they are also vital toward establishing relationships with rival civilizations by building Embassies. You will want to have this capacity as soon as possible.

| TRADE | BUREAUCRACY | BANKING | NATIONALISM |
|---|---|---|---|
| (Caravan) | **(Diplomat)** | [w/ JURISPRUDENCE] | [w/ PRINTING PRESS] |
| | **Confucius Academy** | (Bank) | (Spy) |

HINT: It is vital to gain the Bureaucracy Advance as soon as possible. Not only does it allow you to build the Confucius Academy Wonder, but it also allows you one of the most versatile units in the game, the Diplomat. The list of dirty tricks available to the Diplomat is to be found elsewhere, but even the vital prospect of communicating with other civilizations is dependent upon being able to build this unit. Build the Diplomat and keep your opponents off balance.

# Cannon Making

## Defensive War 5

Early Cannon tended to explode a lot at the very worst time. So, when quality Cannon became available, they were a profitable source of income for a lot of European countries. But since you really can't carry on a full-bore arms deal in *Call to Power*, we suggest you look for other ways of making money.

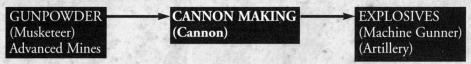

GUNPOWDER
(Musketeer)
Advanced Mines
→ **CANNON MAKING**
**(Cannon)**
→ EXPLOSIVES
(Machine Gunner)
(Artillery)

HINT: Cannon are the first of the more offensive weapons in the Defensive War branch, but they're not as good as Artillery. Unless you're in the middle of a siege war campaign, there are easier ways to get to Nuke technology.

# Cavalry Tactics

## Aggressive War 4

This Advance combines the mobility and mass of the Knight with the firepower of Gunpowder. Cavalry Tactics moves you into the period of Imperialism, and gives you the best unit for offense until the Tank. If you need to know more, read Chapters 3 and 4—preferably before you try any "Charge of the Light Brigade" stunts.

STIRRUP
(Knight)

GUNPOWDER
*Advanced Mines*

**CAVALRY TACTICS**
[w/ MASS PRODUCTION]
**(Cavalry)**
→ TANK WARFARE
(Tank)

HINT: Don't make this too tough a decision. If you want to conquer the world, research this. If not, you should be racing down the road to Electricity.

# Chemistry

## Medicine 2

 Chemistry is grounded in Alchemy. The Greeks and Romans experimented on their patients by trial and error by prescribing one chemical after another until they got the desired results. Graeco-Roman alchemists were able to cure some illnesses, preserve or improve wines, preserve foods, supplement diets, and develop an efficient black glaze for their pottery. As noted in the discussion of Alchemy, the primary focus of medieval alchemists was to make gold from lead, but they also had reasonable successes in medicine and primitive chemistry.

Modern chemistry really began to accelerate when John Dalton performed his experiments with various gases (1766-1844), building upon Isaac Newton's *Principia* and R. G. Boscovich's (1711-1787) concept of point-centers within the fundamental construction of matter. Obviously Boscovich's theories heavily influenced Dalton's development of atomic theory. Later, the Russian chemist, Mendeleyev, noticed that if chemicals were arranged in the order of increasing atomic weight, they could be arranged systematically, as similar characteristics occurred periodically. From this research, came the Periodic Table of the Elements.

Toward the beginning of the 19th century, Michael Faraday created the first known compounds of chlorine and carbon. From this research, he was eventually able to create a steel alloy and a high quality optical glass, which enabled further experiments with polarized light. Although Chemistry has impacted numerous fields through the centuries (Medicine, the advancement of explosives, and the development of synthetic materials), *Civilization: Call to Power* restricts the Advance to the Medicine branch of the technology tree.

MEDICINE [w/ OPTICS] Hospital → **CHEMISTRY** → PHARMACEUTICALS (Drug Store) Contraception → GENETICS (Infector) Genome Project

HINT: The Chemistry Advance doesn't immediately buy you any advantage, but the Medicine branch of the technology tree is absolutely vital for empire-builders who wish to win with the Alien Synthesis Project victory condition. The Advance is obviously a step on the rung toward higher Happiness through creating the Contraception Wonder and toward the very important Genome Project Wonder. So, Chemistry is moderately high on the empire-builder's priority list. Would-be conquerors will eventually want this Advance in order to build the Infector unit with its Special Attacks, but this will not be your highest priority.

# Classical Education

## Economics 4

The legacy of Rome's unification of most of the known world was a classical foundation that was preserved in Latin. Latin, the language of the classics, became the *de facto* vernacular of the learned classes. Even after every nation, indeed every section of each nation, had their own idiom, the learned classes spoke and read in Latin. As universities were formed, even the most menial conversations were conducted in Latin. For example, Boorstin tells in *The Discoverers* how the University of Paris required even requests to the lector and responses to upper class hazing to be conducted in Latin without one word of French.

As a result, the classical education came to be divided into two courses of study. The basic course of study, the *trivium*, focused entirely on grammar, rhetoric, and logic; all conducted in Latin. Once one had mastered the *trivium*, it was possible to move on to the *quadrivium*, where one received an "advanced" degree in arithmetic, geometry, astronomy, and music. As medieval universities expanded their influence, the *trivium* and *quadrivium* became universal standards for the literate classes.

The advantage of this classical tradition was that it created an international intellectual elite that could disseminate information easily in both written and oral form. The disadvantage of the classical tradition was that it created a greater gulf between the common people who spoke the vernacular or "profane" language and the elite who spoke in Latin. In *Civilization: Call to Power*, the main advantage of the Classical Education Advance is that it allows the establishment of a University Improvement. Reflective of the easy dissemination of information, the University Improvement gives a 50-percent boost in Science production.

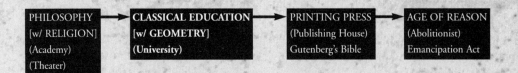

| PHILOSOPHY [w/ RELIGION] (Academy) (Theater) | → | **CLASSICAL EDUCATION [w/ GEOMETRY] (University)** | → | PRINTING PRESS (Publishing House) Gutenberg's Bible | → | AGE OF REASON (Abolitionist) Emancipation Act |

HINT: Players who prefer building empires to conquering those of others will find the Classical Education Advance to be a vital stop on the way to an accelerated program of Advances. By allowing the building of a University Improvement and moving toward the Printing Press Advance, this Advance puts you in a great position for garnering new Advances. Conquerors may wish to place this Advance farther down the line unless they need to get the Age of Reason Advance in order to remove a slave-holding rival from a position of power and efficiency.

# Cloaking

## Flight 10

One of Terry's favorite television programs when he was a young gamer was a *Star Trek* episode, "Balance of Terror." In it, a group of Romulans breaks a 100-year-old treaty and crosses the Neutral Zone. While their craft is slow and seemingly outdated, they have a secret weapon: a Cloaking device, which renders them invisible to the sophisticated sensors of the Enterprise. (The Romulans also have a commander who is a dead ringer for Spock's dad, but that's another of those cosmic anomalies we don't have time to dwell on here.)

The *Star Trek* episode played out like a high-tech version of a WWII Submarine vs. Destroyer battle, and you can get much the same feeling when trying to find a Cloaked unit in a game of *Call to Power*. The Cloaking Advance gives you the Phantom unit, which makes a Stealth Aircraft look as if it needs training wheels. This late in the game, Cloaking is well worth a look, regardless of your peace/war philosophy.

| ZERO-G INDUSTRY<br>(Space Bomber) | → | ASTEROID MINING<br>(Star Cruiser)<br>(Swarm)<br>(Food Modules)<br>(Advanced Assembly Bays) | → | CLOAKING<br>(Phantom) |
| ALIEN ARCHEOLOGY | → | WORMHOLES<br>(Wormhole Probe)<br>(Wormhole Sensor) | → | CLOAKING<br>(Phantom) |

**HINT:** Okay, if the game's still going, it's unlikely that you're close to winning via military means. So, take a Phantom or two—forget the cost at this point—and sneak them inside the enemy's defensive perimeter around the Wormhole. Better yet, if you control the Wormhole, hide two or three Phantoms around likely avenues of approach; all they have to do is slow the enemy long enough for you to win.

# Communism

## Mechanical Discoveries 5B

As observed in the summary of government types in Chapter 4, Communism was supposed to be merely a provisional state designed to facilitate the transition from a downtrodden mass of exploited workers to a classless utopia where all material possessions would be held in common. Since humanity is inherently selfish, a totalitarian regime was necessary in order to re-educate the minds, redistribute the wealth, and reorganize the structure of society.

As noted in the governmental chapter, Communism in *Call to Power* is represented as a form of government that exchanges individual freedom for efficiency. It assumes that the central planning mechanism of a totalitarian regime can be very efficient in the short run, but forces you to pay the price in Pollution. By using the 1.75x multiplier for Production and 2x multiplier for Science, you can develop your industrial base rather quickly. The Communism Advance allows you to switch your governmental type to Communism.

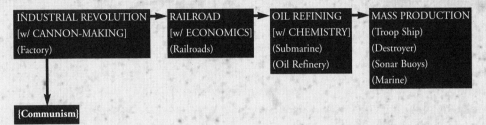

INDUSTRIAL REVOLUTION
[w/ CANNON-MAKING]
(Factory)

→ RAILROAD
[w/ ECONOMICS]
(Railroads)

→ OIL REFINING
[w/ CHEMISTRY]
(Submarine)
(Oil Refinery)

→ MASS PRODUCTION
(Troop Ship)
(Destroyer)
(Sonar Buoys)
(Marine)

{Communism}

HINT: When your empire begins to reach a medium size, Communism is the form of government that is most efficient for a quick industrial boost in Production. There is a price to be paid in increased Pollution and diminished Gold production, however.

# Advanced Composites

## Flight 5

Advanced polymers and plastics were key ingredients in the advanced technologies of the late 20th century. The Advanced Composites Advance in *Civilization: Call to Power* is used to mirror the fabricated materials that made possible portions of the stealth technology used in the United States during the Gulf War and beyond.

The Advanced Composites were resistant to temperature variation and radar detection, allowing pilots to configure an electronic profile around the plane and confuse the enemy.

In *Call to Power*, the Advanced Composites Advance allows you to build the Stealth Bomber Improvement in order to strike enemy cities without warning, and the Space Plane in order to transport military units through space and back to the earth.

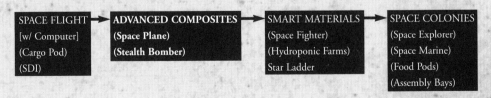

SPACE FLIGHT
[w/ Computer]
(Cargo Pod)
(SDI)

→ **ADVANCED COMPOSITES**
**(Space Plane)**
**(Stealth Bomber)**

→ SMART MATERIALS
(Space Fighter)
(Hydroponic Farms)
Star Ladder

→ SPACE COLONIES
(Space Explorer)
(Space Marine)
(Food Pods)
(Assembly Bays)

HINT: Whether you're going for the Alien Synthesis Project ending or the victory condition where you conquer the world, the Advanced Composites Advance is an important step in the right direction. If you're going for the complex endgame regarding alien life, you're going to need the capabilities that come later along the Flight branch of the technology tree. If you're ready to conquer, you're going to want special military units like the Stealth Bomber available with Advanced Composites, as well as the Space Fighter and Space Marine to come later along the Flight branch.

# Computer

## Electricity 2

Beginning with the ABC or Atanasoff-Berry-Computer, digital computing has changed the face of our world. When the U.S. Army called for a more robust version of the ABC, John W. Mauchly and J. Presper Eckert, Jr. developed the ENIAC at a cost of less than one-half million dollars. The ENIAC had only approximately 5K of memory and required 18,000 vacuum tubes and 6,000 switches to manage that 5K. Eventually, Mauchly and Eckert produced the famous UNIVAC computer of the 1950s and competitively forced IBM into the mainframe computer market.

Since that era, it's been the story of miniaturization. Computers have gotten progressively smaller and faster until we now have laptops that are light years beyond the ENIACs and UNIVACs of a few decades ago. In *Civilization: Call to Power*, the Computer Advance leads to the development of Computer Center Improvements reminiscent of the early mainframes. Fortunately, the Computer Centers add one Science point per Population number in the host city and grant an immediate 50-percent boost overall to Science production. The Computer Advance also leads to development of the Internet Wonder, expeditious dissemination of information that can lead to around ten foreign Advances per Age coming to your civilization.

| ELECTRICITY | COMPUTER | SUPERCONDUCTOR | UNIFIED PHYSICS |
|---|---|---|---|
| Edison's Lab | **(Computer Center)** | [w/ SPACE FLIGHT] | (Forcefield) |
| | **The Internet** | (Rail Launcher) | National Shield |
| | | (Maglevs) | |

HINT: Get the Computer Advance and immediately start constructing the Internet. Those ten Advances per year can almost guarantee you parity with any other civilization through the crucial part of the game. Plus, the Science bonus associated with the Computer Center Improvement doesn't hurt at all.

# Conservation

## Cultural Advancement 7

As you near the end of the Cultural line, strongly consider Conservation. Not only does it give you the ability to erect Recycling Plants and lower your Pollution, it also lets you move to Ecotopia, which is a very versatile endgame government.

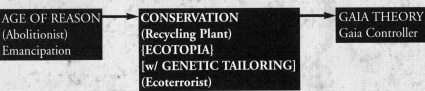

| AGE OF REASON | → | CONSERVATION | → | GAIA THEORY |
|---|---|---|---|---|
| (Abolitionist) | | (Recycling Plant) | | Gaia Controller |
| Emancipation | | {ECOTOPIA} | | |
| | | [w/ GENETIC TAILORING] | | |
| | | (Ecoterrorist) | | |

HINT: Whether you go for Ecotopia or the Gaia Controller, Conservation is a happy situation for the peaceful nation. And an Alexander player who has gone this far down the Cultural path might as well finish the job and go for Ecotopia and the Ecoterrorist unit.

# Corporate Republic

## Economics 8B

As electronic banking and instant currency conversion intersect with such phenomena as the unification of the European economy and currency, such fictional forms of government as the Corporate Republic seem more and more possible. The underlying theory of the Corporate Republic is that traditional tariffs and protectionism will give way to new mega-corporations that will move beyond the boundaries of traditional multinational corporations. These virtual countries, run by data transmission from an orbital network, are a libertarian's dream.

Naturally, the Corporate Republic Advance enables you to select a Corporate Republic form of government. For more details, see Chapter 4.

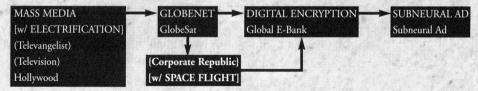

| MASS MEDIA<br>[w/ ELECTRIFICATION]<br>(Televangelist)<br>(Television)<br>Hollywood | → | GLOBENET<br>GlobeSat | → | DIGITAL ENCRYPTION<br>Global E-Bank | → | SUBNEURAL AD<br>Subneural Ad |
| --- | --- | --- | --- | --- | --- | --- |
| | | {Corporate Republic}<br>[w/ SPACE FLIGHT] | | | | |

**HINT:** The Corporate Republic is superior to Democracy, Monarchy, Republic, Theocracy, and Tyranny in terms of its impact on your fiscal (Gold) and industrial (Production) status. It is an ideal governmental form for improving your economic position or getting ready to produce military units.

# Corporation

## Economy 6

The current concept of the Corporation, as suggested in the discussion of the London Stock Exchange Wonder, came about as a result of the British crown chartering certain privileged merchants to engage in business as "one body corporate." Indeed, the entire colonial period that followed and the establishment of financial institutions, such as the London Stock Exchange, had a great flurry of speculative corporate ventures.

In the U.S., the 19th century brought about a multitude of corporations. During this period, New York enacted a statute that enabled individuals to incorporate, and many of the companies involved with the building of the Transcontinental Railroad were incorporated in order to float stock offerings. This was the era in which many of the integral corporations in the U.S. economy of that day were incorporated: American Can, International Harvester, U.S. Rubber, and U.S. Steel.

*Civilization: Call to Power*'s Corporate Branch unit could easily be known as the Franchise. Within the game's structure, the Corporate Branch has the right to franchise Production. This siphons Production from the target city to the "Home Office" of the Corporation or Corporate Branch. Once the Corporate Branch unit is in place, your opponent will have to train a Lawyer to sue you and remove the franchise.

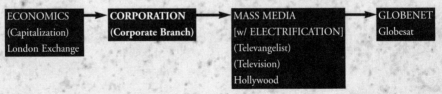

| ECONOMICS (Capitalization) London Exchange | → | CORPORATION (Corporate Branch) | → | MASS MEDIA [w/ ELECTRIFICATION] (Televangelist) (Television) Hollywood | → | GLOBENET Globesat |

HINT: Anytime you can siphon Production from your enemies, it can be a helpful thing. Empire-builders will want to use the special offensive attack provided by the Corporate Branch unit as soon as they build to this point. Conquerors will finally see something they like along the Economics branch when they reach this point.

# Cryonics

## Medicine 7

Cryogenics is a theory based on 20th century discoveries of organic flesh preserved in ice for long periods of time with no appreciable decay. As a result, some scientists believed that if a living person were quick-frozen, the person would stay alive over a long period of time until said person could be thawed out. They speculated that in the case of potentially terminal diseases, they would be able to quick-freeze the patients and keep them alive until a cure for the disease was found.

Although proof of such speculation does not exist in the present day, *Civilization: Call to Power* posits a time when Cryogenics will work. In *Call to Power*, building the House of Freezing Improvement enables Theocracies to gain five Happiness points. This is because those citizens can eat their cake and have it, too. They can, theoretically, experience the near-death realities of the afterlife while not giving up their option on life in the present world.

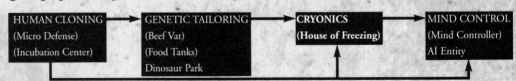

| HUMAN CLONING (Micro Defense) (Incubation Center) | → | GENETIC TAILORING (Beef Vat) (Food Tanks) Dinosaur Park | → | CRYONICS (House of Freezing) | → | MIND CONTROL (Mind Controller) AI Entity |

**HINT:** Like the form of preservation itself, Cryonics remains to be tested. If you're low on Happiness, by all means pick up this Advance and move on toward Mind Control. If you're not low on Happiness, find another Advance. This one can wait.

# Democracy

## Cultural Advancement 6B

The Democracy Advance in *Civilization: Call to Power* enables you to change your form of government into a Democracy. As observed in Chapter 4, Democracy is based on the ancient Greek ideal, but did not reach its modern form until the revolutionary philosophy of the Age of Reason, combined with the revolutions surrounding this shift in thought (primarily, the American and French revolutions). In *Call to Power*, the freedom of speech and thought implicit in a Democracy doubles Science production over that of the basic Tyranny form of government and adds a 25-percent boost in both Gold and Production. It enables a 70-percent expenditure in Science production. The only downside to Democracy is the resulting unhappiness when you need to prosecute a war.

In addition to improving the efficiency of government and economy, the Democracy Advance allows for the introduction of the Lawyer unit. Lawyer units can File Injunctions against target cities and always be successful at a cost of 300 gold. These filings can either stop all production in a given city for one turn or keep the city from completing any one item within a given turn. For 500 gold, Lawyers can sue either other Lawyers or the Corporate Branches of other civilizations. These suits always succeed and always destroy the targeted unit. Lawyers also serve to provide good intelligence on covert actions from rival Corporate Branches and Televangelists.

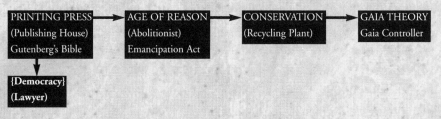

PRINTING PRESS (Publishing House) Gutenberg's Bible → AGE OF REASON (Abolitionist) Emancipation Act → CONSERVATION (Recycling Plant) → GAIA THEORY Gaia Controller

{Democracy} (Lawyer)

HINT: Everyone can benefit from Democracy in order to improve efficiency. The general exception would be the Alexander-style conqueror who isn't able to sustain a hit to his civilization's overall Happiness quotient. Even Alexander-style players can benefit from the legal assaults of Lawyers, however, if they are playing against a civilization that is doing exceedingly well along the Economics branch. Players who prefer to build empires to conquering those of others will find the Printing Press to be a useful Advance. It provides two methods of increasing your Science production upon its completion. Building either the Gutenberg's Bible Wonder or the Publishing House Improvement allows you to experience a multiplier effect that will be vital to staying ahead in the race for Wonders. If you are primarily a conqueror, though, the Printing Press is more of a luxury than a priority to your game plan.

# Digital Encryption

## Economics 9

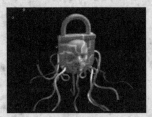

It's funny that just as digital encryption is becoming an issue in the real world, we find that the ironclad protection technology still hasn't been ironed out hundreds of years in the future. Code breaking is a time-honored profession, however, just like espionage, and it makes sense that the struggle for control of information, the digital currency of the future, would continue.

| MASS MEDIA [w/ ELECTRIFICATION] (Televangelist) (Television) Hollywood | → | GLOBENET GlobeSat | → | **DIGITAL ENCRYPTION** **Global E-Bank** | → | SUBNEURAL AD (Subneural Ad) ESP Center |

HINT: This endgame trail is not as productive as others are. However, you may find that you need the Global E-Bank in order to pump up your Gold supply. Obviously, this is also an important step toward constructing the ESP Center, potentially a viable addition to both your intelligence capability and your defensive posture (see Chapter 8).

# Domestication of Animals

## Aggressive War 2

As observed in the section on the Agriculture Advance, the Domestication Advance reflects the events occurring in the Neolithic Period, dating roughly from 9000 BC to 5500 BC. In Jarmo, on the border of Iraq and Iran, Neolithic ruins reflect a society where goats, pigs, and sheep were used for food. Even as early as 6000 BC, there is evidence of domesticated dogs. Later, evidence of cave-paintings in Europe reflect the use of oxen to pull plows, even though the plows were apparently made of wood and have not survived to the present day. Of course, the technology tree for *Civilization: Call to Power* reflects the reality that the domestication of horses followed soon enough and allowed for both scouts and mounted archers.

The immediate effect of Domestication was that it allowed man to breed his food instead of hunting it. This ensured both an ample supply and, as mankind learned basic breeding techniques, it ensured a higher quality of meat, milk, eggs, wool, and leather. In *The Rise of the West*, McNeill suggests that as two different types of society (Agricultural and Pastoral) began to live side-by-side in the Middle East, trading the surplus from Farmer to Herdsman and vice-versa became commonplace. Of course, the tension between herdsman and farmer is also reflected from the scriptural story of Cain and Abel through the accounts of 19th century range wars between cattlemen and farmers.

*Civilization: Call to Power* reflects both functions of domestication: the pastoral and the commercial. With regard to the pastoral nature of the Domestication Advance, *Call to Power* allows you to follow the Advance by building the Mounted Archer unit, a reflection of humankind's first major transportation advance with the domestication of horses. The superior movement rate over Warrior or Phalanx units make them ideal for doing early reconnaissance, and they are at least as effective as a Warrior when engaged in combat.

With regard to the commercial nature of Domestication, the Advance allows your civilization to begin building the Marketplace Improvements in each city. The Marketplace Improvement reflects that interface between pastoral and agrarian civilization which allowed both the farmers and herdsmen to trade their surpluses, but it also suggests the advance in transportation from humankind learning to ride asses, camels, and horses. Cities that are not under direct threat should consider gaining the Domestication Advance in order to be able to build the Marketplace Improvement and gain the immediate 50-percent boost in income per turn.

| AGRICULTURE | DOMESTICATION | STIRRUP | CAVALRY TACTICS |
|---|---|---|---|
| (Granary) | (Mounted Archer) | (Knight) | (Cavalry) |
| *Farms* | (Marketplace) | | |

HINT: When playing in a Large world, you need to get the Domestication Advance early so that you can build a Mounted Archer unit and get a jump on finding your enemies and the best resources before your rival civilizations can. When playing in a Large world, a Mounted Archer should probably be your first military unit; just don't build too many (see Chapters 2 and 3.)

# Economics

## Economics 5

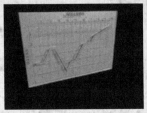

Economics is the social science concerned with the material aspects of human welfare. The basic issue of Economics revolves around scarcity. Humankind has an unlimited desire for goods and, of course, there are limited human and natural resources available for the formation of goods. The challenge of Economics is to determine the answers to such questions as how to use and organize the limited resources available to produce and provide the maximum goods for the most people. Economics policy also determines to whom and in what amounts the wealth created from the production and sale of those goods shall be distributed.

In *Civilization: Call to Power*, the Economics Advance represents the rise of a rigorous capitalism during the expansion of the industrial nations. This is reflected in the Capitalization Improvement, which generates additional Gold for a city, and the London Stock Exchange Wonder. Though we do wonder why Economics is the fifth technology in its own branch of research...

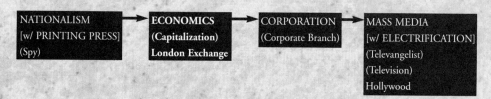

| NATIONALISM [w/ PRINTING PRESS] (Spy) | → | ECONOMICS (Capitalization) London Exchange | → | CORPORATION (Corporate Branch) | → | MASS MEDIA [w/ ELECTRIFICATION] (Televangelist) (Television) Hollywood |

**HINT:** Naturally, the increases in Gold production associated with both Capitalization and the formation of the London Stock Exchange Wonder is a positive for gamers who prefer building to conquering. As observed with regard to the Trade Advance, however, conquerors will not have to put this branch of the technology tree on their front burners.

# Ecotopia

## Cultural Advancement 7B

The Ecotopia Advance in *Civilization: Call to Power* allows you to set up this fictitious governmental form. As a governmental form, Ecotopia is pro-environment in an activist manner and pro-scientific research in order to protect the environment. As a backlash against corporate abuses of the environment in the late 21st century, environmentally conscious peoples formed the Ecotopia.

The Ecotopian form of government is extremely friendly to scientific research with a 2.5x modifier. Also, since the Ecotopian form of government arose out of a violent reaction to the corporate rape of the environment, Ecotopia is an ideal government for those who wish to prosecute an efficient war. It is particularly effective when you wish to attack heavy polluters, especially since the Ecoterrorist unit can conduct a number of special attacks.

Ecoterrorist units can conduct hits on target cities in order to create unhappiness. These units have a 50-percent chance of success in these actions and create five points of unhappiness if they are successful. Ecoterrorists can also perform nano-attacks against enemy cities. The nano-attack destroys all Improvements within the target city and has a 10-percent chance of doing collateral damage to the target's Trading partners by "infecting" them. Nano-attacks have a 25-percent chance of success. If the Ecoterrorist fails, however, there is also a 25-percent chance of his being apprehended and eliminated.

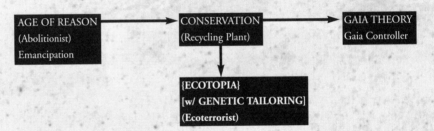

```
AGE OF REASON  ──────►  CONSERVATION  ──────►  GAIA THEORY
(Abolitionist)          (Recycling Plant)       Gaia Controller
Emancipation                  │
                              ▼
                        {ECOTOPIA}
                        [w/ GENETIC TAILORING]
                        (Ecoterrorist)
```

**HINT:** Acquiring the Ecotopia Advance is desirable for any player. Conquerors will be delighted with the special attack abilities of the Ecoterrorist unit. Builders will be delighted with the extra efficiency in Science production.

# Electricity

## Electricity 1

Most everyone has an apocryphal image in his or her mind of Benjamin Franklin standing out in the rain trying to "catch lightning" with a kite and a metal key. We're convinced that anyone important enough to be on the $100 bill had more sense than that, but it's a good story nonetheless. In more down-to-earth terms, Electricity deals with the controlled flow of electrons, which sounds simple enough.

And in fact, electrical usage has become such a simple, accepted part of our lives that it's hard to imagine the hysteria with which it was greeted more than a century ago. People were convinced that Electricity would burn down entire towns, and that anyone who walked near a power line risked being instantly struck dead from the "unnatural aura" being transmitted. Adding to this hysteria were the fuel oil and gaslight merchants who saw their way of life being threatened. They conveniently forgot, of course, that their technology, when it was originally adopted, had inconvenienced others as well.

Electricity has always been a pivotal Advance in *Civilization*, and *Call to Power* is no exception, giving this discovery its own branch on the technology tree. While the immediate effects, such as building Edison's Lab, are excellent, they pale to the long-term benefits, from Wonders and City Improvements to an impressive array of crossover technologies farther down the Electricity branch.

RAILROAD [w/ ECONOMICS] *Railroad* → **ELECTRICITY** Edison's Lab → COMPUTER Internet *Computer Center*

**HINT:** Whoever gets to Electricity first, whether warlike or peaceful, expansionist or isolationist, has a definite edge on the competition. Electricity should *always* be your first Advance that you research after Railroad, unless you are desperate for a navy of Battleships (Steel) or Submarines (Oil Refining).

# Electrification

## Construction 6

Electrification is the widespread application of Electricity in *Call to Power*. It has few good civilian or military effects to warrant the research time you spend to get it.

PERSPECTIVE [w/ BANKING] (Cathedral) → **ELECTRIFICATION** [w/ ELECTRICITY] (Movie Palace) (Listening Post) → FUEL CELLS [w/ SUPER CONDUCTOR] (Aqua Filter) (Eco-Transit)

**HINT:** This is a road that basically leads to nowhere, unless you are desperate for Fuel Cells. You can reach Arcologies through other branches, which makes this branch one to prune so that your others might bear research fruit. If you desire the greater vision range of Listening Posts, consider building the GlobeSat Wonder.

# Engineering

## Construction 4

In *Civilization II*, there really wasn't much of a debate about researching Construction; at least not if you wanted larger cities, because the population limit of eight was absolute until you built an Aqueduct. Engineering, however, was another story, because its main claim to fame was giving you the chance to build the King Richard's Crusade Wonder, which doubled your production in a single city.

Well, Richard is gone in *Call to Power*, but Engineering does offer Aqueducts as a carrot to replace him, along with the Coliseum and the Forbidden City Wonder. All things considered, it's a pretty compelling package for an expanding empire, at least in the short term.

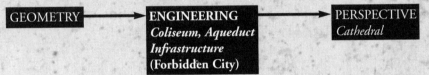

| GEOMETRY | → | **ENGINEERING**<br>*Coliseum, Aqueduct*<br>*Infrastructure*<br>**(Forbidden City)** | → | PERSPECTIVE<br>*Cathedral* |

HINT: After you gain Engineering, the next Advances down this path are Perspective, which only offers the Cathedral and Electrification, which is a long way off. Don't get caught in a technological cul-de-sac: Make certain after you gain Engineering that you move quickly to another line of research. Otherwise, you'll need more than the Forbidden City to help you stay in the game.

# Explosives

## Defensive War 6, Pre-Flight 2

It's ironic that the Chinese used the principles of explosives for fireworks hundreds of years before the Europeans started making firearms. But warriors and assassins caught up quickly. In the warring states of Italy during the Renaissance, bombings were for a while as popular as poisonings for getting rid of rivals.

Eventually, however, more civilian uses for explosives were found. The West, for example, would have stayed wild for a lot longer in the United States without explosives to blast through hills and mountains so that railroads could run from one coast to another. Those uses fail to show up in *Call to Power*, however, and we suggest that the peaceful leader can pass this by for a while, at least until some conqueror sets his sights on this fairly quick path to Nukes.

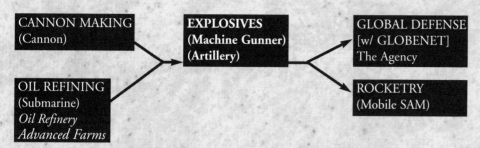

**HINT:** If you haven't yet found the path to nuclear technology, Explosives can get you there in a hurry through Rocketry, regardless of whether you've test-flown at Kitty Hawk. You also gain the most offensive of the Defensive War weapons with the advent of Artillery, plus a versatile counter-puncher with the Machine Gunner.

Paranoid peaceniks that have already made it pretty far down the Economics path can set their sights firmly on The Agency. More sober leaders should concentrate on Economic or Electrical Advances instead.

# Fascism

## *Economics 5B*

As described in Chapter 4, Fascism is a totalitarian regime that asserts the right of the state over the individual for the greater good of the nation. Fascism involves the nationalization of industry and total control of the press. In *Civilization: Call to Power*, as in actual history, Fascism utilizes Nationalism as a tool in gaining control of the military and the economy. Fascism usually promises a restoration of lost glory and the promise of military conquest and expansionism.

In *Call to Power*, Fascism is an extremely efficient form of government. It doesn't accrue Gold as fast as Democracy, but the Science modifier is equivalent to Democracy's and, reflective of national planning, Production is slightly superior. Further, not only is Fascism a solid governmental style for prosecuting warfare, but it allows the construction of the Fascist unit, the *Call to Power* equivalent of one of the original brownshirts. The Fascists have a 16-point attack value and defend at 8. Every Alexander should have one. Unfortunately, should you decide to change governments, you won't be able to keep such a fanatic around. Only Fascism allows Fascists.

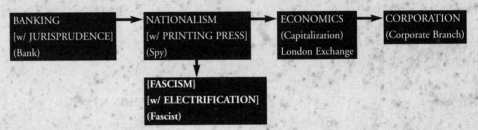

BANKING
[w/ JURISPRUDENCE]
(Bank)

→

NATIONALISM
[w/ PRINTING PRESS]
(Spy)

→

ECONOMICS
(Capitalization)
London Exchange

→

CORPORATION
(Corporate Branch)

↓

{FASCISM}
[w/ ELECTRIFICATION]
(Fascist)

HINT: Fascism is the ideal governmental form for prosecuting a war prior to the advent of Ecotopia. There are no major disadvantages for the conqueror, unless you happen to build so many Fascist units that you take a significant force reduction when you change to Ecotopia or a more advanced government later in the game.

# Fuel Cells

## Construction 7

Fuel Cells are an enhancement to existing technology, like the batteries in your cell phone, or a battery-operated automobile. Even so, the Advance doesn't benefit you unless you're a polluter.

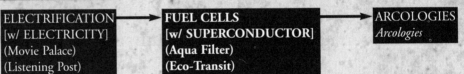

ELECTRIFICATION
[w/ ELECTRICITY]
(Movie Palace)
(Listening Post)

→

FUEL CELLS
[w/ SUPERCONDUCTOR]
(Aqua Filter)
(Eco-Transit)

→

ARCOLOGIES
*Arcologies*

HINT: Again, you can reach Arcologies through other branches. Unless you are a real polluter, think twice before spending the time here.

# Fusion

## Physical Science 6

Another recurring theme in *Call to Power* is the examination of atomic energy and how it is used. Twenty years ago in the U.S., Atomic Fusion was supposed to be the answer to all our energy needs. The question was hotly debated and wound its way into popular culture, including, of all things, a Dick Tracy nationally syndicated comic strip.

Many other nations, on the other hand, use atomic power safely. France, for example, is a much more efficient country because of its extensive use of atomic power, some of which is Fusion-based.

*Civilization: Call to Power* seems to take the tack that technology will solve everything—one way or another. In addition to the Fusion Plant (an Improvement over the Nuclear Plant), Fusion ushers in the era of Really Big, Nasty Tanks, the Leviathan and Fusion Tank.

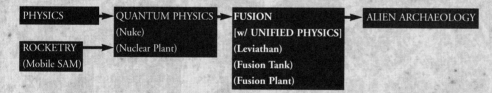

HINT: Eventually, the MAD Defense will run dry due to someone building the Nanite Defuser. So, you need to beef up your conventional forces. We tend to not like the Leviathan for offense; it's soooooo slow. If you're convinced you don't need new tanks, Fusion still offers a straight path to Alien Archaeology, so start putting those atoms through their paces!

# Future Flight 1 through 4

## Futuristic Advances

The only reason to build these is to boost your Civ score at the end of the game. Don't bother.

# Gaia Theory

## Cultural Advances 8

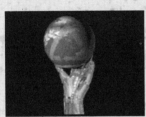

As discussed in the section covering the Gaia Controller Wonder, Gaia Theory is based upon Dr. James Lovelock's theory that the Earth is alive, a growing organism. In one publication, Lovelock described the Earth as being like a California redwood. He observed that just as the redwood is mostly dead, but is still alive along the circumference of the tree, the Earth is mostly dead but is alive in some places. The life of the Earth is best shown in the self-regulating dynamism of the atmosphere.

For example, there is 21-percent Oxygen in the Earth's atmosphere and a trace of Methane at 1.5 parts per million. Since both gases react when illuminated by sunlight (and one can easily calculate the rate at which they do react), we know that keeping those two gases at the same level requires a flux of 1,000 megatons of Methane per year because that is how much is oxidized. At the same time, the Oxygen level changes by 4,000 megatons per year because this is how much it takes to oxidize the Methane. Since there is no known chemical reaction that would create these quantities of gas each year, Lovelock postulates that there is a process ongoing at the Earth's surface that assembles loose molecules and directs them proportionately to Methane and Oxygen molecules. In this sense, the Earth "breathes."

*Civilization: Call to Power* gives you a unique opportunity to acquire the Gaia Theory Advance and then use it to build the Gaia Controller Wonder. The

Wonder enables you to put your planet back in order in the closing moments of the game by effectively ending the threat of global disaster and boosting your own Food production by 25-percent.

| CONSERVATION (Recycling Plant) | → | GAIA THEORY Gaia Controller |
| --- | --- | --- |

HINT: The Gaia Theory Advance is a great one. It allows you to eliminate the threat of global disaster (although some Alexander-type conquerors won't want to help their neighbors in this fashion) and gain a 25-percent Food production boost at the same time. This late in the game (Diamond Age), anything that can help eliminate residual Pollution is welcome.

# Genetic Tailoring

## Medicine 6

The Genetic Tailoring Advance is a refined discipline based on the Human Cloning Advance. The discipline involves DNA-splicing and enables the production of genetically enhanced Food sources within the game context. For discussions on the idea of cloning and/or genetic engineering, please read the section covering the Dinosaur Park Wonder.

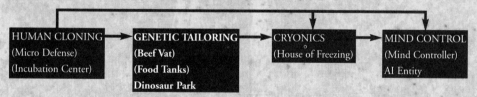

| HUMAN CLONING (Micro Defense) (Incubation Center) | → | GENETIC TAILORING (Beef Vat) (Food Tanks) Dinosaur Park | → | CRYONICS (House of Freezing) | → | MIND CONTROL (Mind Controller) AI Entity |
| --- | --- | --- | --- | --- | --- | --- |

HINT: The Genetic Tailoring Advance is nearly perfect for Empire-builders. It not only Advances you along the Medicine branch of knowledge, but it offers two ways to solve Food production problems and one way to triple your Trade revenue. Establishing this Advance should be automatic. If you are a conqueror, you should consider your Food production situation. If you're on or near the edge of what you need to take care of your civilization, build the Genetic Tailoring advance right away. If not, there are certainly other priorities.

# Genetics

## Medicine 3

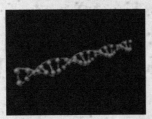

Genetic study has already advanced to a point where Mendel never could have dreamed. Aside from the Genome Project, this is a good Advance for counter-punching empires due to the insidious Infector unit.

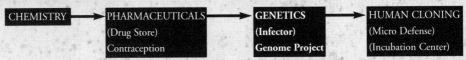

| CHEMISTRY | PHARMACEUTICALS<br>(Drug Store)<br>Contraception | **GENETICS**<br>**(Infector)**<br>**Genome Project** | HUMAN CLONING<br>(Micro Defense)<br>(Incubation Center) |

**HINT:** Now you know why you bothered with Chemistry.

# Geometry

## Construction 3, Pre-Cultural Advancement 1

Whereas Algebra (especially in its higher forms) is often said to represent abstract mathematics, Geometry personifies the concrete application of the art. Yet the fundamental basis for Geometry is the single point, which is something that we cannot clearly define. It seems unfortunately appropriate, then, that in *Call to Power*, Geometry can be a confusing Advance.

Geometry, you see, gives you *nothing*. Yet it lays directly on the path to one of the best all-around Advances in the early part of the game, Engineering. If you have any thoughts about building either the Forbidden City or Aqueducts for the continued growth of your cities, you seem to have little choice in the matter.

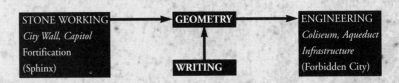

| STONE WORKING<br>*City Wall, Capitol*<br>Fortification<br>(Sphinx) | **GEOMETRY** | ENGINEERING<br>*Coliseum, Aqueduct*<br>*Infrastructure*<br>(Forbidden City) |
| | **WRITING** | |

**HINT:** The fast-growing, expansionist society will have little choice but to do the homework here. However, if you aren't interested in the Forbidden City, and you can get by without Aqueducts for a while, consider waiting to research Geometry, especially if you are an Alexander-style player. You can always Trade one of your lesser War technologies for Geometry a little later on, especially if you build the Philosopher's Stone Wonder (see Chapter 7).

# Global Defense

## Defensive War 7

 Similar to the forming of the North Atlantic Treaty Organization (NATO) and Southeast Asian Treaty Organization (SEATO) in the middle of the 20th century, the Global Defense Advance suggests the combining of intelligence-gathering capabilities and military potential of several nations for the purpose of mutual defense. In *Civilization: Call to Power*, however, the Global Defense initiative has the telecommunications and computing power of a global computer network, GlobeNet, at its disposal and builds one intelligence agency for the entire treaty organization. This is rather different than NATO and SEATO, where the U.S. has multiple intelligence-gathering organizations and most of its allies have at least one.

The Global Defense Advance is the last one in the Defensive War branch of the technology tree. The main purpose for gaining the Global Defense Advance in *Call to Power* is, of course, to construct The Agency Wonder. For a more detailed description of the history and advantages of The Agency, please see the discussion in the alphabetical listing of Wonders.

```
EXPLOSIVES          →    GLOBAL DEFENSE
(Machine Gunner)         [w/ GLOBENET]
(Artillery)              The Agency
```

**HINT:** If you didn't construct the GlobeSat Wonder, you're definitely going to need The Agency Wonder. The Agency Wonder provides the equivalent of a Spy unit in every city of your civilization, and you no longer have to send Spy units out to do your bidding. This saves both time and Gold. No matter what style of play you use, you need this Wonder if you don't have GlobeSat. If a rival has already built The Agency Wonder, however, don't bother with this Advance at all.

# GlobeNet

## Economics 8

It shouldn't come as a surprise to anyone in the age of the Internet and the World Wide Web that one of the near-future Advances postulated in *Civilization: Call to Power* is the GlobeNet Advance. GlobeNet is the result of yet more connectivity throughout the world. By gaining this Advance, you get the opportunity to build the GlobeSat Wonder, a satellite imaging system that enables your civilization to see the entire world at a glance.

If you're slightly skeptical of this system emerging, consider this. Iridium is the code name for a multi-national project that would link a ring of satellites around the globe for purposes of telecommunications. Though actual work on this system has not yet begun, it demonstrates the philosophical hope for such a system. As for using this new equivalent to an advanced Internet for purposes of spying on one's rivals, note that even today, one can get BDA (Bombing Damage Assessment) film footage of military operations on the World Wide Web (if one knows where to look).

| MASS MEDIA [w/ ELECTRIFICATION] (Televangelist) (Television) Hollywood | → | GLOBENET GlobeSat | → | DIGITAL ENCRYPTION Global E-Bank | → | SUBNEURAL AD (Subneural Ad) |

HINT: Because of the ability to build the GlobeSat Wonder (with its phenomenal intelligence-gathering capacity), the GlobeNet Advance is absolutely vital. If you can get this Advance first, it gives you a tremendous advantage in both offensive and defensive planning and preparedness. Unfortunately, once the GlobeSat Wonder has been constructed, the GlobeNet Advance becomes a very boring step toward Digital Encryption and Subneural Ad, two high-ranking Economic Advances for empire-building players.

# Gunpowder

## Defensive War 4, Pre-Aggressive War 4

Gunpowder doesn't give you any economic benefit. This Advance does, however, feature one of the few units that survives relatively unscathed from *Civilization II*, the Musketeer. These early gun enthusiasts can not only stand up to a Knight when fortified, they also perform double duty on the battlefield, serving equally well on the back row or the front row in multiple-unit combat (see Chapter 3).

ALCHEMY
(Archer)
(Fire Trireme)
Philosopher's Stone

**GUNPOWDER**
**(Musketeer)**

CANNON MAKING
(Cannon)

CAVALRY TACTICS
(Cavalry)

HINT: Everybody needs a Musketeer or three, and not just because our wives think they're cute. If you haven't already started to replace your older units, such as Legions, you don't have much of a choice now—regardless of whether your style is offensive or defensive.

# Hull Making

## Sea 3

Hull Making in *Call to Power* doesn't give you a lot immediately, other than Longships. Unless you are threatened by Piracy or looking to build island cities, you should think twice about researching this Advance—there are plenty of more rewarding Advances and Wonders to be had near the end of the Ancient era.

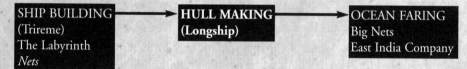

SHIP BUILDING
(Trireme)
The Labyrinth
*Nets*

**HULL MAKING**
**(Longship)**

OCEAN FARING
Big Nets
East India Company

HINT: Hull Making, and the Longships it gives you, are much more important on very large worlds, where opponents are far away; and on small worlds, where expansion space is at a premium. Longships can also give you a surprise edge in multiplayer games. But the next Sea Advance, Ocean Faring, while enticing, is not always as close as you think (it's over the edge into the Renaissance era).

# Human Cloning

## Medicine 5

As observed in the discussion of the Dinosaur Park Wonder, there has been quite a bit of speculation about the possibility of cloning since frog hearts were constructed from genetic material in the early 1970s. To reiterate that discussion, many scientists believed that human cloning would be beneficial because it would: a) enable development of ideal genetic prototypes; b) allow potential parents to avoid dysgenic possibilities in their offspring; c) allow for the creation of back-up organs and interchangeable parts between similar genetic constructs (particularly valuable in dangerous team projects like space exploration); and d) create the possibility of intimate communication (i.e., less misunderstanding) between persons of like genetic construction (particularly ending the generational gap between parents and offspring).

These are the goals of *Civilization: Call to Power*'s Genome Project Wonder, which precedes the Human Cloning Advance. With the Micro Defense (enabling you to protect yourself against both an enemy's Nano-Attack or Infect City assault) and the Incubation Center (with its 25-percent boost to Production due to genetically superior humans), it appears that *Call to Power* has allowed you to achieve this ideal.

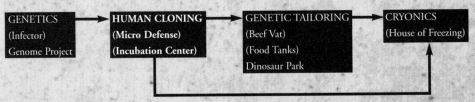

GENETICS
(Infector)
Genome Project
→
**HUMAN CLONING**
**(Micro Defense)**
**(Incubation Center)**
→
GENETIC TAILORING
(Beef Vat)
(Food Tanks)
Dinosaur Park
→
CRYONICS
(House of Freezing)

HINT: Human Cloning is particularly vital to Empire-builders. Not only does it allow you to increase production by 25-percent, but it also helps with providing a tricky defense for your cities should any of your rivals gain the ability to Nano-Attack or Infect City. Conquerors should seriously consider acquiring this Advance in order to gain the Micro Defense, but this Advance mainly benefits the defensive player who spends more time building than destroying.

# Industrial Revolution

## Mechanical Discoveries 4

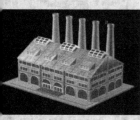 The Industrial Revolution is that phase of the 19th century when new inventions began to be applied to industry in such a way that Production was increased and the amount of Labor necessary to provide said Production was reduced. It was a time when men began to harness steam power to looms, spinning wheels, water pumps, and printing presses, as well as develop steam locomotives and automobiles. The dramatic increase in Production brought about a massive revolution that swept through Germany, Japan, Russia, and the United States by the end of the century.

On March 11, 1811, Britain received clear word that the workers who had been laid off as a result of improved efficiency gained by these new inventions were not going to stand aside quietly. In a little town called Arnold, outside Nottingham, the unemployed former knitters (called "stockingers") broke into a factory and destroyed the wooden frames of the machines, rendering them useless. The leader of the group was a man named Ned Lud, and this movement was to continue to grow under the new name, the Luddites.

Whether as a result of labor violence or the problems associated with prosecuting a foreign war with France, England didn't follow up on the technological Advances as much as the Germans and Americans, who continued with experimentation and expansion for almost another half-century past the original ferment in England.

The Industrial Revolution Advance in *Civilization: Call to Power* allows you to build the Factory Improvement with no risk of a Luddite-style labor rebellion. Upon completing a Factory, you gain a 25-percent Production boost and get the opportunity to designate some of the workforce in each city with a Factory as skilled Laborers. In turn, the Laborer specialists increase your Production.

| MACHINE TOOLS (Ship of the Line) | → | **INDUSTRIAL REVOLUTION [w/ CANNON-MAKING] (Factory)** | → | RAILROAD [w/ ECONOMICS] (Railroads) | → | OIL REFINING [w/ CHEMISTRY] (Submarine) (Oil Refinery) |

HINT: Conqueror-style players will want to get the Industrial Revolution Advance because it not only improves Production rates, but is also a step on the road to the faster movement rates when they complete Railroads. Empire-builders will simply want this Advance in order to increase Production in the aggregate (with the 25-percent Factory boost) and the addition of Laborer specialists. This is a great Advance to earn when you feel like you're falling behind other civilizations in Production.

# Iron Working

## Defensive War 2

Nomad tribes in areas north of the ancient Greeks evidently had iron weapons more than 100 years before they were widely used in Europe, but they seemed to lack a leader with the vision to get the most out of their technological edge. In *Call to Power*, Iron Working gives you Legions, but they aren't anything to make you want to trash Gaul with, either. Use this Advance as a stepping stone to better things, and don't put too much of your ego into having the biggest Short Sword on the block.

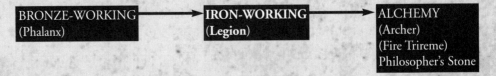

| BRONZE-WORKING (Phalanx) | → | **IRON-WORKING (Legion)** | → | ALCHEMY (Archer) (Fire Trireme) Philosopher's Stone |

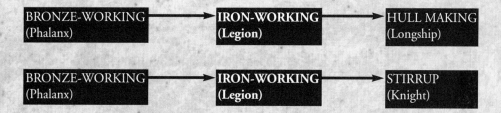

| BRONZE-WORKING (Phalanx) | → | **IRON-WORKING (Legion)** | → | HULL MAKING (Longship) |

| BRONZE-WORKING (Phalanx) | → | **IRON-WORKING (Legion)** | → | STIRRUP (Knight) |

HINT: While the Legion does provide some offensive punch, if you're really expecting a protracted offensive war, you should build Samurai instead, or move to the Stirrup, which features the Knight, the best all-around unit in the Ancient world. Would-be admirals may now move on to the Longship as well.

Still, for any player, the real reason to research Iron Working is to get quickly to Alchemy and the Philosopher's Stone Wonder (see Chapter 7).

# Jet Propulsion

## Flight 3

Whether you are going for the "Alien win" or just trying to conquer the world, this is an important stepping stone to either end.

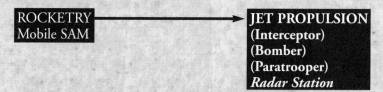

| ROCKETRY Mobile SAM | → | **JET PROPULSION (Interceptor) (Bomber) (Paratrooper)** *Radar Station* |

HINT: Strategic Air, tactical defensive air, and Insertion troops—what are you waiting for?

# Jurisprudence

## Cultural Advancement 2

Once Writing became more widespread, two simultaneous phenomena began to develop, the codification of laws and the proliferation of bureaucracy. Initially, power rested in the person of the local authority; the chief, circle of elders, or king. As centralization of power continued, there needed to be some way for the king's commands to be executed in locales where the king was not present. Around the end of the Third Millennium BC, a grandson of Sargon I named Naram Sin extended his power with a peculiar brand of nepotism. He merely replaced the local rulers and authorities with his relatives. After the collapse of his empire, the Third Dynasty of Ur (ca. 2050-1950 BC) expanded that policy by naming royal relatives to priestly office (hence, making the temple lands part of the royal income and the king's law divine in one smooth motion). The earliest collection of laws from this period would be the Laws of Eshnunna, relating to an area near Baghdad. So, by the time of Hammurabi (18th century BC), the administrative needs of a major empire required both a system of bureaucracy with accounting and reports, as well as a codified system of laws—the Code of Hammurabi.

In *Civilization: Call to Power*, the Jurisprudence Advance represents the codification and institutionalization of legal structures. Once you achieve the Jurisprudence Advance, you gain the capacity to build a Courthouse, reducing crime in your city by 50-percent, or a Samurai, a valuable military unit that represents the warrior code of Japan in the feudal era. Both of these Improvements represent some slight anachronisms. Jurisprudence as a science of laws existed centuries before either the Courthouse or Samurai institutions existed. Early courts probably took place among the elders at the city gate or the marketplace for generic disputes, and at the ruler's palace for more significant tribunals. The Samurai tradition is best associated with the feudal era of Oda Nobunaga and the warlord Hideyoshi (16th century AD). The inclusion of these Improvements at this juncture on the technology tree point toward far-ranging influences more than immediate developments. More importantly for game purposes, you'll need to gain Jurisprudence to move toward Philosophy. Citizens have a tendency to become unhappy from time to time, and the Academy and Theater buildings reduce their frustration levels tremendously.

| WRITING | → | JURISPRUDENCE<br>(Courthouse)<br>(Samurai) | → | PHILOSOPHY<br>[w/ RELIGION]<br>(Academy)<br>(Theater) | → | CLASSICAL EDUCATION<br>[w/ GEOMETRY]<br>(University) |
|---|---|---|---|---|---|---|

**HINT:** Jurisprudence is a fairly important early buy because Samurai units cost less to build than Knights and move you past the Phalanx threshold in attack and defense. Picking up Jurisprudence early also gives you a step toward getting Philosophy early and being able to have more options for dealing with the Happiness quotient. A quick buy of a Theater can certainly reduce the chances of a riot.

# Life Extension

## Electricity 6

Everybody wants to live forever. At least in the world of *Call to Power*, immortals won't have time to get bored…

| UNIFIED PHYSICS<br>(Forcefield)<br>National Shield | → | NEURAL INTERFACE<br>*Bio Memory Chip*<br>(Cyber Ninja)<br>Sensorium | → | LIFE EXTENSION<br>*Body Exchange*<br>Immunity Project | → | VIRTUAL DEMOCRACY<br>Egalitarian Act |
|---|---|---|---|---|---|---|

**HINT:** In addition to the Immunity Project Wonder, Life Extension opens the door to Virtual Democracy, one of the best endgame governments. Plus, it causes a lot less stress for your potential allies than when you are running your empire under an Ecotopia.

# Machine Tools

## Mechanical 3

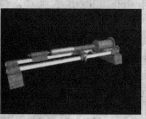

Machine tools are the door to the Industrial Revolution, and a precursor to Mass Production. Moreover, they give you the Ship of the Line, the first Naval vessel worth investing in. As such, it is an easy choice to research for the empire builder or conqueror alike.

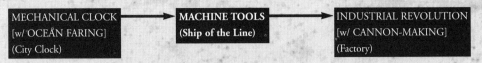

| MECHANICAL CLOCK [w/ OCEAN FARING] (City Clock) | → | MACHINE TOOLS (Ship of the Line) | → | INDUSTRIAL REVOLUTION [w/ CANNON-MAKING] (Factory) |

**HINT:** We understand that not every player will be as enamored of Ships of the Line as we are. Still, Machine Tools are a necessity, both for the empire-builder trying to reach Railroad and Electricity, as well as the Alexander-style leader lusting after the military units of Oil Refining, Mass Production, and Robotics.

# Mass Media

## Economics 7

When a modern man thinks of the term, "media," he immediately turns to Marshall McLuhan, the prophet of media. McLuhan understood that media is more than technology and more than content. He recognized it as a life-changing, indeed system-changing, process. McLuhan believed that all media consists of active metaphors by which human beings are able to extend themselves into new ideas and forms. He also recognized that the use of technology to expand and extend these new metaphors amounted to a social surgery without antiseptics. Media is so powerful that we don't know what kinds of infection they might inject into the social body.

Such reasoning is why it is appropriate that *Civilization: Call to Power* allows you to build such powerful examples of Mass Media upon completing the Advance. The Televangelist has an extremely powerful talent for extracting money from foreign cities and fomenting unhappiness around your enemies. This reflects both the commercial nature of Television and its ability to change cultural perceptions. Further, Television allows you to accrue an additional five Gold per Population point in the host cities. Finally, as observed in the discussion of the Hollywood Wonder, it allows you to extract even more from those cities that have the Television Improvement due to leveraging old film content onto the airwaves.

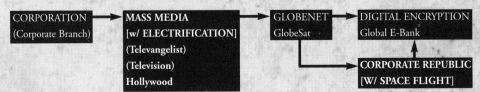

| CORPORATION (Corporate Branch) | → | MASS MEDIA [w/ ELECTRIFICATION] (Televangelist) (Television) Hollywood | → | GLOBENET GlobeSat | → | DIGITAL ENCRYPTION Global E-Bank |
| | | | | | | ↓ |
| | | | | | | CORPORATE REPUBLIC [W/ SPACE FLIGHT] |

**HINT:** Because of the offensive potential of the Televangelist and the fundraising abilities of the unit, the Improvement, and the Wonder, the Mass Media Advance is useful for any player at any time. Although some may think *Call to Power*'s take on the Mass Media is cynical, with its emphasis on getting Gold from viewers, the truth is that advertising-driven media are very mercenary. Gain this Advance whenever you need new profit centers for your civilization. If you have a surplus of Gold, you probably don't need it.

# Mass Production

## Mechanical Discoveries 7

 Mass Production is a technology based on the concept of specialized labor leading to increased efficiency. In Adam Smith's *The Wealth of Nations*, the economist/philosopher describes a primitive pin (nail) manufacturer. He elucidated how the division of labor was such that one man would pull the wire off the spool, another would straighten the wire, another would cut it, another would sharpen the point, and yet another would grind the top to make a head. He cited that two teams of five, ten men, could make 48,000 pins per day whereas, as individuals, they probably would have averaged only around 20 pins apiece per day. This may be an exaggeration, but it points out the strength of division of labor in terms of mass production.

The economy attributed to Mass Production is even more enhanced when you add the process of interchangeable parts. By using templates and molds to ensure identical shapes and functionality, skilled laborers are able to manufacture the basic parts of a mechanism while less-skilled laborers may be hired to assemble those parts. Perhaps, the most famous use of Mass Production was Henry Ford's use of the assembly line to manufacture Model T Fords. Originally, these cars were so standardized that Ford is oft quoted as saying, "You can have any color you want, as long as it's black."

In *Civilization: Call to Power*, Mass Production is associated with the Modern Age and the industrialization of nations for war. Since the Advance allows for the construction of Troop Ships, Destroyers, Sonar Buoys, and Marine units, it is a vital Advance for the Alexander-type conqueror players. The Troop Ship is an extremely efficient form of conveyance, allowing the transportation of up to five military units. The downside is that it has no offensive capacity and must be protected by escort ships like the Destroyers, small all-around fighters that are primarily used for escort duty, and Submarine searches. Marine units are fairly well-balanced at this juncture in the game with an assault value of 12 and a defense value of eight. The good news on Marines is that they are not tied to any one governmental ideology. Sonar Buoys are Tile Improvements that assist you in being passively aware of enemy fleet movements.

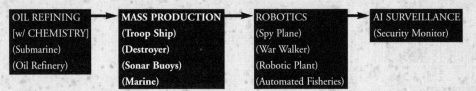

| OIL REFINING [w/ CHEMISTRY] (Submarine) (Oil Refinery) | **MASS PRODUCTION** **(Troop Ship)** **(Destroyer)** **(Sonar Buoys)** **(Marine)** | ROBOTICS (Spy Plane) (War Walker) (Robotic Plant) (Automated Fisheries) | AI SURVEILLANCE (Security Monitor) |

HINT: The Mass Production Advance opens all sorts of doors for the Alexander-style player. Not only is it an important intermediary step toward the powerful Spy Plane and War Walker to be constructed under Robotics, but it offers a wide variety of useful units in its own right. The Destroyer unit is versatile, and the Marine unit is fairly well-balanced for this stage of the game. Only elite Special Forces like the Fascist or Plasmatica units are really stronger at this point. Even empire-builder gamers will want this Advance, since it is an intermediary step toward the efficiencies of the Robotic Plant and Automated Fisheries under the Robotics Advance. Mass Production should be a high priority at any time for all players, especially for conqueror-style gamers.

# Mechanical Clock

## Mechanical Discoveries 2, Pre-Cultural Advancement 6

The word for clock comes from the Middle Dutch word, *glocke*. The word means "bell" and reflects the origin of mechanical clocks within their religious usage. The first recorded clocks in Europe are the so-called *horologia excitatoria*. Apparently, one monk would have such a clock in his cell and it would sound a small bell when it was time for devotions. This would awaken the monk and he would, in turn, go and manually sound the large bell which summoned the entire monastery to prayer.

Obviously, these clerical clocks were built to sound the hours of devotion. By the end of the 14th century, municipal clocks in town halls and church clocks were sounding out all of the hours equally. This enabled a 24-hour mindset to begin to prevail. In the Middle Ages, secondary wheels were added to the main wheels within the clockworks of the tower so that figures could perform as the clocks struck the hours. The clocks weren't any more accurate than they had been, but they were certainly more impressive.

The City Clock Improvement in *Civilization: Call to Power* is based on this history. Just as the clocks at the end of the 14th century moved humankind toward a consciousness of 24-hour days, as well as exact hours and minutes, so does the City Clock. As a result, Gold production is stimulated to reflect the more accurate working hours being monitored by employers.

| AGRICULTURAL REVOLUTION | MECHANICAL CLOCK | MACHINE TOOLS | INDUSTRIAL REVOLUTION |
|---|---|---|---|
| (Pikeman) | [w/ OCEAN FARING] | (Ship of the Line) | [w/ CANNON-MAKING] |
| (Mill) | (City Clock) | (Factory) | |

> HINT: Even though the Mechanical Clock Advance only allows construction of the City Clock Improvement, all players should want to get the Advance as a high priority. For the conqueror, Mechanical Clock is a stepping-stone toward the offensive units which can be created with Oil Refining and Mass Production. For the empire-builder, Gold production is instantly stimulated and more valuable Advances follow on the Mechanical Discoveries branch of the technology tree. It also allows you to get to the Age of Reason through the back door.

# Medicine

## Medicine 1

While the famed Ancient Greek physician Hippocrates would have been disappointed, there are some good gameplay reasons for Medicine to debut so late in the game, not the least of which is the Infector unit. Historically, there have been more significant developments in Medicine in the past 100 years than in the previous 1,000, maybe even the last 10,000 before that. Medicine thus appropriately debuts just on the blurred edge between the Renaissance and the Modern eras, and brings with it a burst of new technologies. There are a number of wide-ranging Wonders and technologies down the Medicinal path that will appeal greatly to the empire-builder, if not the conqueror.

CLASSICAL EDUCATION [w/ GEOMETRY] (University) → **MEDICINE** [w/ OPTICS] *Hospital* → CHEMISTRY

**HINT:** Medicine looks like a really boring path when you begin, especially for the conqueror, who can reach the AI Entity and ESP Wonders by crossing over from other branches of research. But for the empire-builder, the Contraception, Genome Project, and Dinosaur Park offer a lot of cash and Happiness down the road, at a time when you can generally put them to good use.

And the Hospital, with its minus-three to counteract the effects of over-crowding, is a welcome sight for any player, regardless of playing style.

# Mind Control

## Medicine 8

Robert Heinlein once wrote, "A fakir can be tolerated, but an authentic soothsayer should be shot on sight. Cassandra didn't get half the kicking around she deserved (in the *Iliad* by Homer)."

If Telepaths were for real in the next century, why would anyone trust them? One of the reasons that language was invented was to give some distance in communication between two individuals; that distance is short-circuited when someone can read your every thought.

But when the technology is on your side, things are of course different. Our advice is that Mind Control is a fact of life in the *Civilization: Call to Power* future, and you might as well get used to it—and take advantage of it.

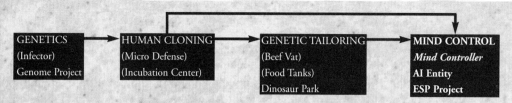

| GENETICS | HUMAN CLONING | GENETIC TAILORING | MIND CONTROL |
|---|---|---|---|
| (Infector) | (Micro Defense) | (Beef Vat) | *Mind Controller* |
| Genome Project | (Incubation Center) | (Food Tanks) | **AI Entity** |
| | | Dinosaur Park | **ESP Project** |

**HINT:** Mind Controllers are fine, but rather than plunk down production and gold for one in every city, consider building the AI Entity instead (check out our caveats in Chapter 7 first). Empire builders should probably cement their lead by protecting themselves from war with the ESP Project. Best of all would be if you could build both Wonders. But then, if you're that far ahead, you're probably going to win anyway.

# Mining

## Construction 1, Pre-Defensive War 1

Even with the advent of high-tech plastics, most people still feel more comfortable with steel bodies for their automobiles and aluminum construction for the aircraft in which they fly. We prize old brass bedposts and shiny new stainless eating utensils, we drool over the chrome on a vintage Harley-Davidson motorcycle, and refuse to give up our perfectly-seasoned cast-iron cornbread skillets. We use quartz crystals in our digital watches, and buy our loved ones diamonds and emeralds for special occasions.

In fact, metals and stones, both precious and common, are so deeply rooted in our culture that it's hard to conceive of the Advance of world civilization, much less any kind of a reasonable standard of life, without them. Yet, it's possible that you can begin a game of *Call to Power* without the basic means to get at these literally fundamental building blocks of society—you have to first discover Mining.

Generally speaking, you have a 90-percent chance of starting the game with Mining (see Chapter 1). If you don't get Mining, you have little choice but to research it, especially on higher difficulty levels, where the computer players are virtually guaranteed to have it at the start. Although the only immediate effect of Mining is to let you build mines, that's not to be sneezed at, even if your workers have to toil away in a dusty mine shaft. Moreover, Mining leads to Stone Working and Bronze Working, crucial technologies in the early part of the game.

According to the terrain type, Mining a square gives you either +5, +10, or +15 production, and +5 gold (where applicable). Keep in mind that you can't mine certain types of terrain, such as Forests. Only if your first few cities are surrounded by Forests (unlikely), should you pass on immediately researching Mining.

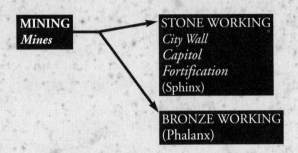

**MINING**
*Mines*

**STONE WORKING**
*City Wall*
*Capitol*
*Fortification*
(Sphinx)

**BRONZE WORKING**
(Phalanx)

**HINT:** Mining is a must for success. In fact, if you already have Toolworking, you should make Mining your first research choice. After you start reaping the benefits of mines, you'll have more resources to work toward other Advances and to afford military units to defend your empire, as Mining leads directly to Bronze Working and the Phalanx unit.

# Monarchy

## Physical Science 2B

As observed in Chapter Five, Monarchy dates back to the river valley civilizations of the Tigris-Euphrates Valley. There, the warrior cultures of the conquering rulers accepted a de facto "divine right" in the minds of the conquered peoples and used it to centralize their kingdoms. Evidence of weaponry and the evolution in construction of city walls to become more and more effective in defense help us to understand the shift to monarchy under this warrior caste. Interestingly enough, the same kind of shift does not appear to have taken place in the Indus Valley. There, the priestly influence seems to have been limited to religious and social authority used to help cities survive the destructive onslaughts of nature (particularly flooding). Weaponry and armor do not figure in excavations from the earliest eras, and yet the urban layouts and physical evidence suggest a highly centralized society.

So, historical evidence leads us to realize that Monarchy is the most efficient government for the early stages of human organization. For example, though the Hebrew Scripture suggests an amphictyonic league comprised of twelve tribes with no centralized leader, we see that this idealized government had broken down by the 10th century BC when King Saul was anointed king.

In *Civilization: Call to Power,* unlike earlier games in the *Civilization* series, you will notice that the Advances representing the theory of a form of government are all side roads on the technology tree. They are useful in allowing you to institute new and more efficient forms of government to meet your needs, but you do not have to acquire all forms of government in order to succeed. In general, these theoretical Advances enable you to build the occasional special unit and Wonder, but they are not required stops along the technology tree. In addition to allowing you to establish Monarchy, the most efficient early government (due to the 25-percent bonus in Science and Production), the Monarchy Advance enables you to build the Chichen Itza Wonder, described in the alphabetical listing of Wonders. You will want to be able to move past Monarchy as soon as possible, however, because the 50-percent limit in investment for Science is too constraining.

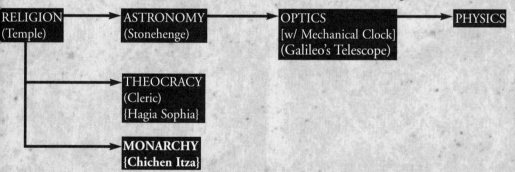

HINT: Monarchy is a nice Advance to pick up because it allows you to accept a boost in Production and Science. It is also a useful government from which to conduct war. If you want to build instead of conquer, however, you are better off picking up the Theocracy Advance at this stage in the game, because you get the same bonus in Science and Production, plus a bonus in Gold and an increased opportunity to invest in Science.

# Nano-Assembly

## Mechanical 10

 The theory of a nano-assembler is that a small, programmable protein machine will take a large molecule (sometimes called the "workpiece") and maneuver it within a solution containing organic solvents and dissolved substances such that the protein machine can attach specific molecules against the workpiece in exact locales. By so combining molecules together, a cellular bonding takes place in which anything could feasibly be built. Some picture this as a construction process analogous to what enzymes do in chemical solutions. Enzymes, such as carbonic anhydrase, can process almost one million molecules per second. Assuming the existence of such nano-assemblers, the assumption is that they could construct more than one million molecules per second and construct anything, anywhere, at an incredibly rapid pace.

Of course, such theory is based upon some other principles; AI sophistication and the size of the construction to be built.

The AI sophistication depends upon analogies to human neurons and a neural approach to human intelligence. Eventually, the miniaturization and development of bio-aware computers would theoretically allow such a protein-based computer as the nano-assemblers posited by today's most theoretical scientists. As for the size of the construction, many conceptual scientists see the idea as being similar to the construction of a large building. The iron grid of the framework is built first and elevator/crane technology on the inside of the framework. Tools and construction materials are routed upward and outward throughout the gridwork of the building from these elevators and cranes. In like manner, scientists perceive the vascular system of plants and animals. Raw materials would be routed through the vascular systems of the nano-constructions by the nano-assemblers. Imagine, if you will, a vehicle taking shape in a huge vat. As raw materials are dumped into the organic solution with the nano-assemblers, a white liquid delineates the incredible rise in activity. Then, the viewer would see first the framework arising, and then the exterior and interior taking shape as new materials are added and the protein programming moves the nano-assemblers to other tasks.

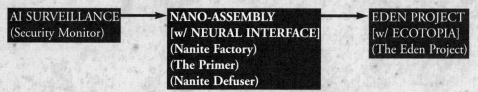

In *Call to Power*, Nano-Assembly is the penultimate Advance on the Mechanical Discoveries branch of the tree. It is a Diamond Age Advance that accelerates production of vital units to meet individual crises by allowing construction of: the Nanite Factory (letting you "Rush Buy" anything for 1 gold per Population); the Primer Wonder (which doubles the effects of all specialist citizens); and Nanite Defuser (ends threat of nuclear war by eliminating nuclear weapons). It can easily be a significant Advance for turning the tide of history at a late point in the game. Don't wait too late to pick up this Advance.

| AI SURVEILLANCE<br>(Security Monitor) | → | NANO-ASSEMBLY<br>[w/ NEURAL INTERFACE]<br>(Nanite Factory)<br>(The Primer)<br>(Nanite Defuser) | → | EDEN PROJECT<br>[w/ ECOTOPIA]<br>(The Eden Project) |
|---|---|---|---|---|

HINT: Pick up the Nano-Assembly Advance as soon as you can. It will enable you to build a Nanite Factory, and that one Improvement should be sufficient to stave off any pending invasions by simply allowing you to out-produce any armies or special forces that your enemy may send at you. This is a great Advance. If you can build both the Nanite Factory and the Primer Wonder, no one at all should be able to out-produce you.

# Nationalism

## Economics 4

Nationalism is a recurring phenomenon in which feelings of national pride and patriotism overshadow local and, at times, religious differences. Nationalism enabled centralized governments to command vast numbers of people and resources with rapid logistics of movement due to a central allegiance based on the ritual and faith of national patriotism. By AD 1500, this centralization was primarily reflected in two ways: a diplomatic force and a professional army.

With this in mind, it should not be surprising that Nationalism recurred in various periods. The Romanticism of the 18th century was reflected in theories of cultural nationalism, such as Johann von Herder's idea of the Volksgeist or "folk spirit." The importance of this theory cannot be overstated when one considers how an

Adolf Hitler of the modern era would evoke the folk traditions of his people in order to mobilize the German population prior to World War II. Further, it should not be surprising that the Industrial Revolution, with its increased efficiencies, brought about a renewal of Nationalism.

Unlike the philosophy of Montesquieu, Nationalism was primarily an instrument to divide "us" from "them" and allow both the prosecution of an efficient war and the aggrandizing of war booty. Montesquieu eloquently expressed the humanitarian dilemma when confronted with rampant Nationalism. He suggested in his *Pensee* that if he were to know something useful to France that would be disastrous to a neighboring country, he would not reveal it to his leaders because, "I am a man before I am a Frenchman, or (better still) because I am necessarily a man, and only by chance a Frenchman." In *Civilization: Call to Power*, Monesquieu's sentiment does not rule because attainment of the Nationalism Advance allows you to build a Spy unit. As you will notice in the "Dirty Tricks" section of Chapter 4, Spy units can inflict havoc in a number of different ways, from intelligence gathering through espionage to covert actions.

| BANKING [w/ JURISPRUDENCE] (Bank) | → | NATIONALISM [w/ PRINTING PRESS] (Spy) | → | ECONOMICS (Capitalization) London Stock Exchange | → | CORPORATION (Corporate Branch) |

> **HINT:** Since Nationalism allows the recruitment of Spy units, it is valuable for every style of player. Not only do the Spy units provide valuable intelligence as to the strength of your opponents, but they also allow for an amazing array of Special Attacks as the game progresses. Nationalism should become a top priority for every style of player, no matter when this late Renaissance Age Advance becomes available to you.

# Neural Interface

## Electricity 5

In the fiction of William Gibson and others, humans can communicate directly with AI personalities. If the thought of that gives you the creeps, it's supposed to.

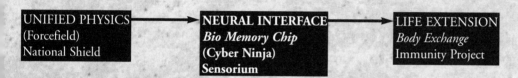

UNIFIED PHYSICS
(Forcefield)
National Shield
→
**NEURAL INTERFACE**
*Bio Memory Chip*
(Cyber Ninja)
**Sensorium**
→
LIFE EXTENSION
*Body Exchange*
Immunity Project

**HINT:** The Sensorium and Immunity Project make a terrific one-two punch if you can pull it off. Check out a more detailed discussion of these Wonders in Chapter 7.

# Ocean Faring

## Sea 4

If Ocean Faring gave you a Ship of the Line or even a super-Longboat, we'd be more in favor of researching it. But who ever heard of Ocean Faring with no real ocean-worthy ships?

HULL MAKING
(Longship)
→
**OCEAN FARING**
*Big Nets*
**East India Company**
→
STEEL
(Battleship)

**HINT:** If you have a lot of coastal cities, you'll benefit from Big Nets. We don't think this is worth it for the East India Company, except maybe during multiplay (see Chapters 7 and 9). You'll have to research this eventually to get Steel, but those sexy gray Battleships are a long way away at this point in the game—wait a while.

# Oil Refining

## Mechanical Discoveries 6

Millions of years after they walked the earth, the dinosaurs still rule the world. Only this time, it's from everyone's gas tanks. Crude oil yields gasoline, kerosene, natural gas, and polymers of all types. And while *Call to Power* doesn't include Plastics as an Advance, the game does recognize the production values of petroleum by letting you construct an Oil Refinery in each of your cities. Then again, it also recognizes the high pollution levels of these facilities as well. The advanced farms, we assume, are due to the power that the combustion engine gave to the farmer in the form of automated farm equipment. Conquerors and peace-loving empires alike will benefit from the sneaky Sub, which can really do some damage before the discovery of Mass Production and Destroyers.

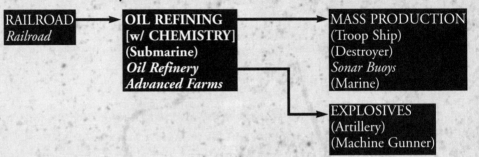

| RAILROAD | OIL REFINING | MASS PRODUCTION |
| *Railroad* | [w/ CHEMISTRY] | (Troop Ship) |
| | (Submarine) | (Destroyer) |
| | *Oil Refinery* | *Sonar Buoys* |
| | *Advanced Farms* | (Marine) |

EXPLOSIVES
(Artillery)
(Machine Gunner)

HINT: If you want to get to the treasures of Mass Production and Robotics, there's no turning back now!

# Optics

## Physical Science 3

It's ironic that *Call to Power* requires the Religion Advance as a prerequisite to acquiring the Optics Advance, since there was considerable religious objection to the study of Optics during the Middle Ages. The religious authorities took as literal the ascription of "light" to both Jesus and God and taught that experimentation with light was tantamount to performing a chemistry experiment on the elements of the Eucharist. Even those who were not so devout suggested that experiments with lenses, mirrors, prisms, and reflectors created visual lies (*deceptiones visus*).

Fortunately, Galileo's experiments with the telescope and Robert Hooke's *Micrographia*, a study of light and color that moved toward the development of the microscope, helped lead to additional advances, such as the use of magnifying lenses to ascertain the quality of commercial cloth and Antoni van Leeuwenhoek's (1623-1723) discovery of bacteria. Even so, Hooke and Leeuwenhoek were subjected to ridicule in the popular literature and even the scholarly societies of the time.

Since advances in Optics led to both discovery of the world without (telescope) and the world within (microscope), *Call to Power* uses the Optics Advance to allow the development of Galileo's Telescope and as a prerequisite for the Medicine Advance. Although this Advance is extremely worthwhile in pushing forward your civilization's development, it doesn't really reflect the contribution of Optics in many areas of life: personal vision, assessment of economic quality, lighting, and safety.

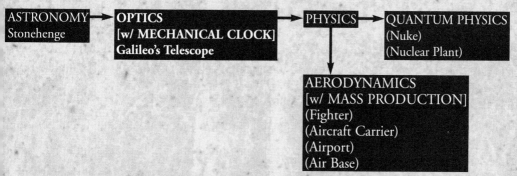

HINT: The primary reason for developing the Optics Advance is to gain the 200-percent boost to Science production through constructing Galileo's Telescope. If you are ahead of your rivals or find yourself moving along contentedly in Science Production, it is probably better to move another direction in the short term and only gain this when you're ready to move on to the Medicine branch of the technology tree. If other civilizations are outpacing you, however, you'll need to get this Advance and Wonder as soon as possible.

# Perspective

## Construction 5

Reflective of humankind's liberation from the tyranny of tradition was the rediscovery of Perspective during the late 14th and early 15th century AD. In the Middle Ages, the use of linear perspective in art had fallen out of favor. Like Plato of classical tradition who had denigrated the use of Perspective as a "trick," many classical scholars and artists had insisted that the use of the technique was less than ideal. They believed that images should be presented as they were and not to be diminished because of distance and appearances.

A major influence in the rediscovery was Filippo Brunelleschi, the designer of the famous cathedral in Florence. Ironically, Brunelleschi's architectural contribution was to return to the classic work of Vitruvius, restoring classical dimension to architectural design. Yet, he determined to build a grand dome for the Florentine cathedral and did so with innovative construction of a dome within a dome and a cellular network of supports (not to mention the new styles of cranes he developed for moving materials to high places along its framework).

Later, Brunelleschi experimented with a wooden frame and flat mirror in order to draw, in linear perspective, the baptistery that stood in the piazza opposite the Florentine cathedral. By looking through a small hole in his panel and examining the scene as reflected in the mirror, he was able to fix the right point of vision to realistically paint the scene. The resulting Perspective sketches influenced an entire school of Florentine painters (such as Alberti and Masaccio), but more importantly, freed thinkers to combine the practicalities of Science with the vision of Art. Such a combination had a powerful influence on everyday life.

In *Civilization: Call to Power*, gaining the Perspective Advance enables you to build the Cathedral Improvement. The Cathedral Improvement memorializes the contributions of visionaries, such as Brunelleschi, and celebrates the freeing of humankind from legacies of literalism. On average, civilizations gain three Happiness points for building a Cathedral, but Theocracies benefit the most (+5 Happiness points), and Communist governments the least (+1 Happiness point).

| ENGINEERING | → | PERSPECTIVE | → | ELECTRIFICATION | → | FUEL CELLS |
|---|---|---|---|---|---|---|
| (Coliseum) | | **[w/ BANKING]** | | [w/ ELECTRICITY] | | [w/ SUPERCONDUCTOR] |
| (Aqueduct) | | **(Cathedral)** | | (Movie Palace) | | (Aqua Filter) |
| (Infrastructure) | | | | (Listening Post) | | (Eco-Transit) |
| Forbidden City | | | | | | |

**HINT:** The Perspective Advance doesn't seem like it carries you very far, but it can be an integral part of your strategy when you are hurting for Happiness points. The conqueror-style player may want to switch government form to a Theocracy and build a Cathedral in order to prosecute an offensive war more effectively with low risk of rebellion and rioting on the home front. The empire-building player will only prioritize this Advance when Happiness is at a low because Production is high and you're using a maximum amount of labor with few Entertainers.

# Pharmaceuticals

## Medicine 3

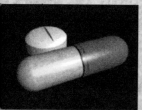

Pharmaceuticals are an offshoot of advanced Chemistry. Whereas early doctors used combinations of herbs and minerals to attempt to heal their patients by trial and error, Pharmaceutical laboratories are designed to create particular drugs for specific results. Once a specific result has been achieved in lab animals, the Pharmaceutical laboratory duplicates the chemical constituency of the drug and initiates a testing program that will eventually, with Food and Drug Administration approval, be tested on human beings.

During the last half of the 20th century, the advancement of Pharmaceuticals was enough that many diseases were wiped out and some, like Epilepsy, were controlled. Pharmaceuticals enable humans to resist bacterial influences and, at times, fight symptoms of infection or disease, like fevers. In *Call to Power*, the Pharmaceuticals Advance is mostly valuable for increasing Production (since healthier workers are able to work more hours) and gaining the Contraception Wonder. The latter increases Happiness throughout your civilization, since it allows the joy of sex without at least one of the associated fears.

CHEMISTRY → PHARMACEUTICALS (Drug Store) Contraception → GENETICS (Infector) Genome Project → HUMAN CLONING (Micro Defense) (Incubation Center)

HINT: Empire-builders should prioritize the Pharmaceutical Advance. Not only does it allow you to increase Production by 25-percent, but it also helps with the ever-elusive Happiness quotient. Plus, it is yet another step on the branch toward the knowledge necessary to eventually succeed with the Alien Synthesis Project. Conquerors may opt to keep Pharmaceuticals as a low priority since the Infector unit, which comes with the next Advance on the path, is the only temptation to be found in acquiring this particular Advance in a hurry.

# Philosophy

## Cultural Advancement 3

When in college, Terry was subjected to the old adage, now a joke, that all Philosophy after Plato consisted of mere footnotes to his work (Plato's work, not Terry's, Johnny hastens to add). Then Terry read Jean-Paul Sartre, and wondered if the joke was on him. Afterward, he changed his major to English...

Philosophy has always been a key element in *Civilization*, because it granted the first civilization to discover it a free Advance. Philosophy was also the first of the pivotal discoveries in *Civilization II*, as it led to a wide range of technologies.

In *Call to Power*, Philosophy has been reigned in considerably, but it's still a good way to branch out from Religion and Physical Science. Plus, there are the Gutenberg's Bible and Emancipation Act Wonders to consider, especially for the peaceful empire-builder.

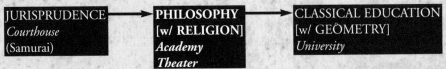

JURISPRUDENCE *Courthouse* (Samurai) → PHILOSOPHY [w/ RELIGION] *Academy* *Theater* → CLASSICAL EDUCATION [w/ GEOMETRY] *University*

**HINT:** If, like Plato, you wish to build a Utopia, you'll want to go far down this peaceful branch of research, right through Classical Education (and the University) to the Age of Reason. Would-be conquerors can likely pass on this until they've cornered the Cavalry market.

# Physics

## Physical Science 4, Pre-Cultural Advancement 6, Pre-Economics 5, Pre-Flight 1

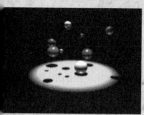

Yes, we know: For all its ballyhooed prominence in history, this marks another of those damnable discoveries that gives you nothing immediately. But unlike Geometry, the new science of Physics opens up everything from the promise of Flight to Nukes and beyond. The modern era beckons and Physics can propel you right into it— hopefully before your competitors get there!

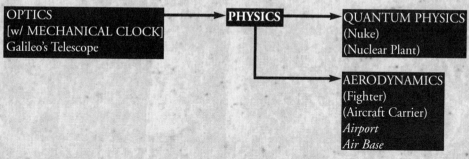

OPTICS
[w/ MECHANICAL CLOCK]
Galileo's Telescope

PHYSICS

QUANTUM PHYSICS
(Nuke)
(Nuclear Plant)

AERODYNAMICS
(Fighter)
(Aircraft Carrier)
*Airport*
*Air Base*

**HINT:** If it's Nukes you desire, don't wait for an apple to fall on your head. It's unlikely, but possible, that you could split the atom well before 1940 with a little luck (in one game, on an easier difficulty level, we managed it in the 19th century). Peaceful societies can benefit as well from the peace of mind they will get from SDI, as well as the additional research paths that now present themselves. Regardless of your playing style, Sir Isaac Newton's ghost will frown upon you if you pass up a chance to research Physics as soon as possible.

# Printing Press

## Cultural Advancement 5

 In China, block printing was common during the eighth or ninth century, and movable type was used as early as the eleventh century. Yet its introduction into the western world was considerably slower. For example, the Qumran community from which we get some of the oldest extant biblical texts, seems to have had copy rooms where one leader would read from the existing text and copyists would write down the phrases as they were dictated. This had the effect of mass production, but was much more expensive in manpower than the movable type of later years. It also had the added disadvantage of occasionally allowing errors of hearing to be inserted into the texts.

In the monasteries of Europe, particularly Ireland, there is evidence that monks would often copy the texts as individuals, with ornate illustration added to establish their individual identities. However, there is still some evidence for readers and transcribers in the European tradition. Considering the relative scarcity of parchment at a reasonable price, it was probably just as well that those in the west continued to copy by hand. Labor was still the most inexpensive part of the equation.

When the Printing Press was adopted, however, it became an important agent of social change through the dissemination of knowledge because it enabled more individuals (and eventually, even masses of people) to be able to read about important advances. The rapid increase in the number of copies of each volume also allowed for the ongoing preservation of knowledge by ensuring that more books would survive. In *Civilization: Call to Power*, this power to the masses is reflected in the ability to create the Gutenberg's Bible Wonder. This gives a ten-percent boost to Science to reflect rapid flow of information and resists Convert City attacks by reducing the reliance of the masses upon the professional Clergy. It also allows you to build the Publishing House Improvement, which gives a 25-percent boost to Science.

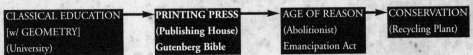

| CLASSICAL EDUCATION [w/ GEOMETRY] (University) | → | PRINTING PRESS (Publishing House) Gutenberg Bible | → | AGE OF REASON (Abolitionist) Emancipation Act | → | CONSERVATION (Recycling Plant) |

HINT: Players who prefer building empires to conquering those of others will find the Printing Press to be a useful Advance. It provides two methods of increasing your Science production upon its completion. Building either the Gutenberg's Bible Wonder or the Publishing House Improvement allows you to experience a multiplier effect that will be vital to staying ahead in the race for Wonders. If you are primarily a conqueror, though, the Printing Press is more of a luxury than a priority to your game plan.

# Quantum Physics

## Physical Science 5

Whereas the physics of relativity deal with matter on a large scale and the cosmic relationships of space-time, Quantum Physics is based upon a quantum theory that deals with the elementary particles of matter. Quantum field theory categorizes something like 200 different varieties of elementary particles of matter. Mathematically, the calculations in Quantum Physics are so complex that even elementary particles with extremely minute energy and mass will yield infinite results without going through mathematical gyrations, such as subtracting infinite terms from each other.

*Civilization: Call to Power* uses the Quantum Physics Advance to point the way to more efficient use of atomic energy. After gaining this Advance, you can build nuclear weapons (Nukes) and a Nuclear Plant to boost your Production by 50-percent while reducing your Pollution index by the same 50-percent. Hence, the Quantum Physics Advance has something for everyone. A powerful weapon enhances the war machine of the conqueror, and a non-polluting boost in Production enhances the industrial complex of the empire-builder.

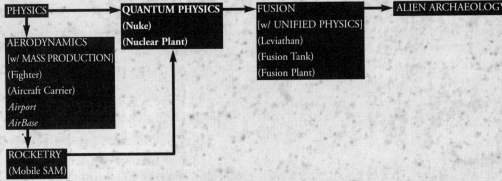

```
PHYSICS ──────────► QUANTUM PHYSICS ──► FUSION ───────────► ALIEN ARCHAEOLOGY
                    (Nuke)               [w/ UNIFIED PHYSICS]
AERODYNAMICS                             (Leviathan)
[w/ MASS PRODUCTION]  (Nuclear Plant)    (Fusion Tank)
(Fighter)                                (Fusion Plant)
(Aircraft Carrier)
Airport
AirBase

ROCKETRY
(Mobile SAM)
```

**HINT:** Quantum Physics is an ideal Advance to get before your rivals. As in real life, there is a definite advantage to having a nuclear capacity. Conquerors should build Nukes and use them, as well as take advantage of the simultaneous Production boost and Pollution reduction. Empire-builders should grab the nuclear capability for the Production/Pollution advantage, but keep the Nuke option as an ace in the hole for a nuclear standoff against your aggressor rivals. Though the MAD defense (Mutually Assured Destruction) approach only involves trade-offs of cities rather than of entire civilizations, it is useful to have a Nuke in your arsenal (see Chapter 3 for more).

# Railroad

## Mechanical Discoveries 5

At the beginning of the 19th century (1804), Richard Trevithick used the first steam locomotive to pull a coal train along the Pendarren Tramroad in Wales. Almost a decade later, James Fenton invented the spring-loaded safety valve (1812), which enabled regular commercial steam locomotive service to begin pulling coal trains in Middleton. In 1813, Christopher Blackett built the Puffing Billy and Wylam Dilly in order to haul coal from Wylam Colliery near Newcastle. The first railway company to handle public traffic was the Stockton and Darlington Railway, formed in 1821. By 1827, the phenomenon had moved to the United States, as the Commonwealth of Maryland granted a charter to the eventual founders of the Baltimore & Ohio Railroad. In turn the B&O ordered their first engine, the Best Friend of Charleston, in 1830. By 1850, the railroad fever had moved on to Australia.

The history of railroading is the story of industry. It is an efficient means of transporting large loads of heavy equipment and materials or perishable commodities. Since the railroads were the dominant form of distribution during the Industrial Revolution and the economic expansion of the late 19th century, those railroad magnates who figured out how to control the monopolistic railroads could make and break farmers, cattlemen, and industrialists by means of schedules and fare structures. Hence, the unscrupulous railroad magnates became popularly known as "robber barons."

In *Civilization: Call to Power*, the Railroad Advance merely enables you to build Railroad Tile Improvements. Since, however, said railroads enable you to move at five times your basic movement rate, grabbing this Advance is well worthwhile for both those of economic and military mindset. If you are an Alexander, you'll want it to move troops. If you're an empire-builder, you'll need the Railroad Advance to increase efficiency.

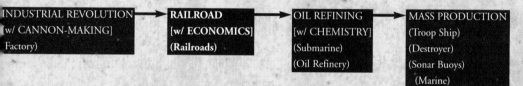

| INDUSTRIAL REVOLUTION [w/ CANNON-MAKING] (Factory) | → | RAILROAD **[w/ ECONOMICS]** **(Railroads)** | → | OIL REFINING [w/ CHEMISTRY] (Submarine) (Oil Refinery) | → | MASS PRODUCTION (Troop Ship) (Destroyer) (Sonar Buoys) (Marine) |

**HINT:** Since building Railroads enables you to increase your movement to five times the normal rate, this is an extremely good Advance for any gamer to earn. For those who prefer to conquer, it not only provides immediate efficiency in troop movements, but also moves you toward complete dominance of the sea through earning Oil Refining and Mass Production and enabling you to build the fleets available from those Advances. For the empire-builder, you simply cannot resist the increased efficiency in moving units from trouble spot to trouble spot (see the Mobile Defense discussion in Chapter 3 for more).

# Religion

## Physical Science 1

Although it is possible to look at Religion as a great divider of mankind, due to the number of sectarian wars perpetrated in the name of true believers through the millennia, Religion is also a great unifier for humankind. In the earliest, primitive societies, Religion answered the questions of "Why?," and served to bond individuals and later tribes together. It formed a foundational structure of belief that could then be translated into the "What?" This can most readily be seen in Mesopotamia, where the religious l eaders were able to unify a significant segment of society around "divine laws" for irrigation and storage. The religious leaders told the people what to do, and underscored this with divine authority as the answer to "Why?" Even as conquerors would enter the picture, they would often be seen as the anointed or chosen one of the gods because the "What?" of their victory translated into divine rationale for their victory.

Even in the Neolithic ages that preceded the unified societies of Mesopotamia, there is physical evidence of people who believed in an "afterlife" in which the dead would need much the same items with which they dealt in everyday life. Whether at pre-Israelite Jericho or in later Egyptian religion, we see evidence of individuals buried with the tools and possessions with which they lived. This reflects the propensity of Religion to provide consolation and hope in the midst of anomie and death. By tying the familiar to the unfamiliar, peoples were able to move past their fear and cope with life.

In addition, Religion had a tendency to preserve the traditions of various peoples. Though revisionism would sometimes occur as one faith fell out of favor, priests tended to be conservative enough to retain the basic mythologies, traditions, and laws of their people. This enabled primitive humankind to begin to piece together some meaning in the incessant change of life.

In *Call to Power*, Religion is the first Advance on the Physical Science branch of the technology tree. This is because the designers perceive Religion as not only canonizing the traditions, mythologies, and laws of various peoples, but as being the first to introduce rigorous methodologies to the understanding of life. Such a rigorous methodology, a parallel development to rituals, enabled humankind to ask both "What?" and "Why?" questions of the world around them. Whereas prior installments in the *Civilization* series minimized the contribution of Religion, *Call to Power* places it in an early and honored position.

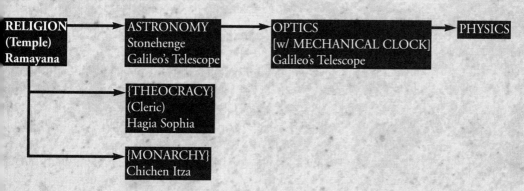

RELIGION
(Temple)
Ramayana
→ ASTRONOMY
Stonehenge
Galileo's Telescope
→ OPTICS
[w/ MECHANICAL CLOCK]
Galileo's Telescope
→ PHYSICS

→ {THEOCRACY}
(Cleric)
Hagia Sophia

→ {MONARCHY}
Chichen Itza

**HINT:** Not only will you need the Religion Advance in order to get started on the Physical Sciences branch of the technology tree, but you will also need it in order to make the first change from your inefficient Tyranny into a more efficient form of government. Both Monarchy and Theocracy are more efficient than Tyranny. Further, we find it advisable to build Temples wherever any discontent appears in your civilization. Unhappiness can really hurt you at inappropriate times.

# Republic

## Economics 3B

The Republic Advance allows you to change to the Republic form of government, which represents the ideal of Plato. This Republic, it should be noted, is a lot different in *Call to Power* from the government typically represented by the *Civilization* series. For more, see Chapter 4.

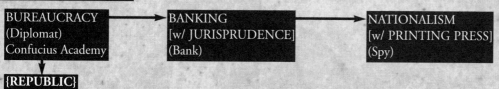

BUREAUCRACY
(Diplomat)
Confucius Academy
→ BANKING
[w/ JURISPRUDENCE]
(Bank)
→ NATIONALISM
[w/ PRINTING PRESS]
(Spy)

{REPUBLIC}

**HINT:** The best all-around government in the early and mid-game, well worth the little "side trip" down the research tree if you're peaceful. Since the Republic doesn't have the military penalties that it did in prior versions of *Civilization*, it's a good choice for a conqueror as well, which makes sense, given that Rome was a Republic...

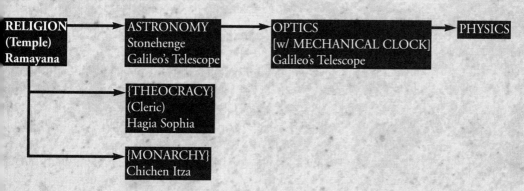

# Robotics

## Mechanical 8, Crossover Medicine 5

Robots have been around since the short story "Robot" was serialized in the 1920s. It became an icon of science fiction through such films as *Forbidden Planet*, and the writing of Isaac Asimov, particularly his concept of the Three Laws of Robotics, which were designed to help and serve humankind.

*Call to Power* looks at this Advance more cynically than the good Doctor: Robotics is a treasure trove of war units and the production facilities to get you rolling into the endgame.

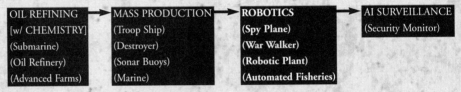

| OIL REFINING | MASS PRODUCTION | ROBOTICS | AI SURVEILLANCE |
|---|---|---|---|
| [w/ CHEMISTRY] | (Troop Ship) | (Spy Plane) | (Security Monitor) |
| (Submarine) | (Destroyer) | (War Walker) | |
| (Oil Refinery) | (Sonar Buoys) | (Robotic Plant) | |
| (Advanced Farms) | (Marine) | (Automated Fisheries) | |

HINT: Alexander-style leaders should waste no time getting to Robotics. Peaceful players can benefit to an extent, but are better off spending their research elsewhere.

# Rocketry

## Flight 2, Crossover Physical Science 5

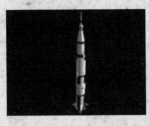

Long before rockets landed men on the moon, they were used in combat. With unguided rockets, fighters could take out slow bombers, and both the Germans and Russians used Rocket Artillery on the Eastern Front during WWII. Rocket technology came into its own, however, when the Germans launched the V-1 "Buzz Bomb" at England during 1943 from bases across the Channel in France. Though the V-1 was of little actual military value, suffering from a terrible lack of accuracy, its successor, the V-2, was a sophisticated missile that, like

German jet fighters, potentially could have affected the outcome of WWII. Fortunately for the rest of the world, they weren't built in sufficient numbers. *Call to Power* focuses solely on the military aspects of the Rocket, albeit giving equal time to defense (SAM) and offense (Nuke, with Quantum Physics).

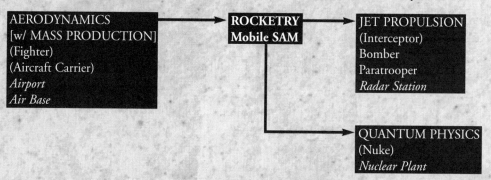

AERODYNAMICS
[w/ MASS PRODUCTION]
(Fighter)
(Aircraft Carrier)
*Airport*
*Air Base*

ROCKETRY
**Mobile SAM**

JET PROPULSION
(Interceptor)
Bomber
Paratrooper
*Radar Station*

QUANTUM PHYSICS
(Nuke)
*Nuclear Plant*

HINT: If you plan an invasion of your enemy's country, it's a tough call at this point whether to go for Paratroopers, but we always go for Nukes first; they take longer to build than conventional weapons. If you time it right, your Nukes should be just getting into the silos just as you're rolling out the Bombers and Paratroopers. If you're worried about defense, you can go for Interceptors, but they aren't going to be much help against Nukes (check out Chapter 3 for our MAD defense strategy).

# Sea Colonies

## Sea 6

With so much of the Earth's surface covered by water, it is no wonder that humankind has often dreamed of the possibilities inherent in creating an underwater colony, a fully functional Atlantis. As one of *Civilization: Call to Power's* science-fiction Advances, Sea Colonies allow you to fulfill that dream. Once you acquire the Advance, you can create the Sea Engineer unit to build your colony, a Stealth Submarine to protect the colony, an Undersea Mine to supplement the Production of the colony, and Undersea Tunnels to speed up movement within your colony and between other colonies.

The Sea Colonies Advance allows you to open up the entire planet to your colonizing influence. Indeed, you'll notice that the structure of a Sea Colony is quite similar to that of a Space Colony. Many of the same Advances in technology, from pressurization containment to creation of biospheres, are required in either type of colony.

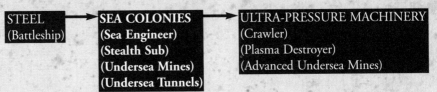

| STEEL | SEA COLONIES | ULTRA-PRESSURE MACHINERY |
|-------|--------------|--------------------------|
| (Battleship) | (Sea Engineer) | (Crawler) |
| | (Stealth Sub) | (Plasma Destroyer) |
| | (Undersea Mines) | (Advanced Undersea Mines) |
| | (Undersea Tunnels) | |

**HINT:** If you're an Alexander-style player, you'll find that control of the sea is vital and that acquiring this Advance is yet another important step in doing so. Plus, you'll enjoy having the Stealth Submarine at your disposal, allowing you to transport up to four Nukes without anyone detecting you. If you're an empire-builder in playing style, you need this Advance in order to continue maximizing the resources at your disposal and exploiting them in your economy.

# Ship Building

## Sea 2

Ship Building doesn't lead to technology riches, at least not for a long while. But it does give you the opportunity to grow your empire quickly if you build a lot of coastal cities. We don't like to place much of our empire's efforts into Public Works in the early part of the game, but the costs for nets give you a more than reasonable return on your investment. That alone is enough to highly recommend this Advance.

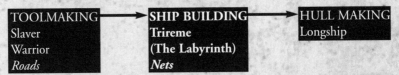

| TOOLMAKING | SHIP BUILDING | HULL MAKING |
|------------|---------------|-------------|
| Slaver | Trireme | Longship |
| Warrior | (The Labyrinth) | |
| *Roads* | *Nets* | |

**HINT:** Even if you aren't interested in the Labyrinth and the additional income it brings, you should toss your net into the water. On large maps, Triremes are a good investment, just in case one of your competitors starts closer to your empire than usual.

# Smart Materials

## Flight 6

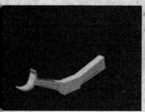

Like piezo-electric crystals, which generate their own electrical fields, the Smart Materials postulated in *Civilization: Call to Power* are dynamic compounds that adjust to their environments. In the *Call to Power* fiction, the Smart Materials are controlled by a microprocessor and can be adjusted to repair stress cracks, reduce weight, or form resistance. As a result, the raw materials represented in this Advance are ideal for construction of space-faring vehicles, such as the Space Fighter, which gives you a global strike capacity. This Advance also yields technology for space constructions, such as the shielding for Hydroponic Farms, which boosts your Food production, and the structure of the Star Ladder, essentially an elevator into space.

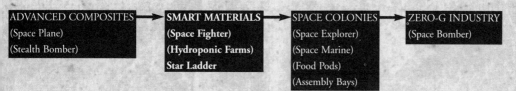

| ADVANCED COMPOSITES | SMART MATERIALS | SPACE COLONIES | ZERO-G INDUSTRY |
|---|---|---|---|
| (Space Plane) | **(Space Fighter)** | (Space Explorer) | (Space Bomber) |
| (Stealth Bomber) | **(Hydroponic Farms)** | (Space Marine) | |
| | **Star Ladder** | (Food Pods) | |
| | | (Assembly Bays) | |

HINT: The Smart Materials Advance is necessary for any style of player. By adding Food production via the Hydroponic Farms Improvement, you can either continue to build your population or you can more effectively prosecute warfare. If you're interested in the latter, the long-range capacity of the Space Fighter is definitely worth your while.

# Space Colonies

## Flight 7

One of the long-term dreams of humankind has been the colonization of Space. To the L5 Society, building Space Colonies meant colonizing other planets, possibly terraforming them and developing off-planet industries in order to capitalize further Space exploration.

In *Civilization: Call to Power*, the Space Colonies Advance allows the building of Space Colonies. Similar to the Sea Colonies, these bastions of exploration are built by the Space Engineer unit and protected by the Space Marine unit. The Space Colony is self-supporting by virtue of the construction capability of the Assembly Bays Tile Improvement and fed by the Food Pods Tile Improvement.

Since the Space Marine has an assault value of 24 and a defense value of 20, the protection mentioned earlier is formidable indeed. Add to the high assault value the fact that the Space Marine can actually attack from ships without having to land on an intermediary square, and you have a very valuable (but expensive) military unit.

So, like the Sea Colonies Advance, the Space Colonies Advance has something to offer for every style of player. Conquerors will enjoy the higher quality of the Space-borne units, if not their exorbitant costs, while empire-builders will relish opening up yet another part of their cosmos for building, managing, harvesting, and exploiting.

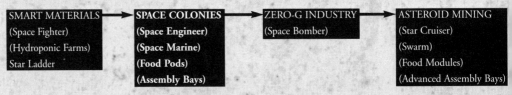

| SMART MATERIALS | SPACE COLONIES | ZERO-G INDUSTRY | ASTEROID MINING |
|---|---|---|---|
| (Space Fighter) | (Space Engineer) | (Space Bomber) | (Star Cruiser) |
| (Hydroponic Farms) | (Space Marine) | | (Swarm) |
| Star Ladder | (Food Pods) | | (Food Modules) |
| | (Assembly Bays) | | (Advanced Assembly Bays) |

HINT: Gamers going for the Alien Synthesis Project will definitely need to follow this technological branch. The bonus Food and Production via the Tile Improvements won't hurt at this stage, nor will the Space Marine's defense. Conquerors may lust after the combat efficiency of the Space Marines and other special units along the Flight path, but will need to keep keenly aware of the cost-to-performance ratio.

# Space Flight

## Flight 4

In *Call to Power*, this is a few years more advanced than our current real-life technology. Except for the SDI, which remains very controversial today, this Advance makes a lot of sense.

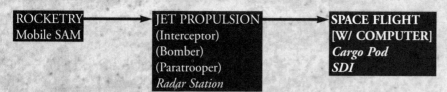

| ROCKETRY<br>Mobile SAM | → | JET PROPULSION<br>(Interceptor)<br>(Bomber)<br>(Paratrooper)<br>*Radar Station* | → | SPACE FLIGHT<br>[W/ COMPUTER]<br>*Cargo Pod*<br>*SDI* |

**HINT:** While you're blitzing up the Flight path, make sure that you already have the Computer Advance well in hand (even if you have to give up some military or Tech to get it), or else your plan will never get off the runway, as it were.

# Steel

## Sea 5

Steel is basically carbonized iron. When heated at extremely high temperatures and rapidly cooled, it can keep a very sharp edge. Steel has a variety of uses in all aspects of life due to its strength and durability. Nevertheless, the "mystery of steel" generally refers to its use in bladed weapons. From the legend of *Excalibur* buried in a stone for King Arthur, to the very real tales of Samurai *katana* blades capable of removing a man's head with a single stroke, swords of Steel have become an indelible part of our culture.

In *Call to Power*, Steel is portrayed not with a blade, but with that ultimate floating weapon, the Battleship (which we like a lot, see Chapters 2 and 3). Thus, Steel is the first Sea Advance that we can recommend pretty much without reservation.

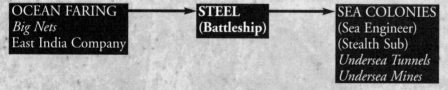

| OCEAN FARING<br>*Big Nets*<br>East India Company | → | STEEL<br>(Battleship) | → | SEA COLONIES<br>(Sea Engineer)<br>(Stealth Sub)<br>*Undersea Tunnels*<br>*Undersea Mines* |

**HINT:** If you are going to contest the seas (in our mind, a pretty good idea by this time in the game), you'll need Battleships. Of course, the next Advance down the Sea branch is so far away that Steel is practically a dead-end Advance for much of the game.

# Stirrup

## Aggressive War 3

For those of us raised on Hollywood movies, where every Roman Centurion or Greek Warrior had a British accent, we fail to realize how difficult it was for horsemen in the Ancient world to fight. With the notable exception of Stanley Kubrick's *Spartacus*, most of these films show mounted warriors disdainfully and effectively slashing at hapless foot soldiers in a scene right out of the Crusades. Problem is, when Rome, Carthage, and Macedonia, *et al*, did most of their "partying" around the Mediterranean, none of their mounted troops had any idea what a Stirrup was. This meant that they couldn't grip the horse particularly well. And controlling their mount well enough to change direction and re-charge?— Forget it.

The invention and use of the Stirrup was one of the great innovations in warfare, as revolutionary in its own way as gunpowder and fighter aircraft would be later. From light horsemen to armored Knights, the mounted warrior would rule the battlefield for hundreds of years. If that sounds like something you'd like to test out on your enemies, be our guest. Just make sure he hasn't jumped past you to Cavalry.

DOMESTICATION (Mounted Archer) *Marketplace* → STIRRUP **(Knight)** → CAVALRY TACTICS (Cavalry)

HINT: Knights are critical for all empires, not just warmongering ones. Check out our tips on Mobile Defense in Chapter 3, and research the Stirrup as early as possible.

# Stone Working

## Construction 2

We've rhapsodized about precious stones (see *Mining*, this chapter), so we'll focus here on the gameplay aspects of this Advance.

*Call to Power* gives this timeless craft its due. Stone Making gives you the most practical benefits per research amount spent of almost any Advance in the game. The ability to build City Walls, which increase your defense by +4 for each unit inside the walls, means that you can manage for a much longer period of time with just Phalanx units. This leaves you more resources to research and to build Wonders of the World.

Speaking of Wonders, Stone Working allows you to build the Sphinx, which reduces your Military Readiness costs by 75-percent. This is a huge benefit if you need to fight a war, whether offensive or defensive, because it lets your forces stay ready practically all of the time at an affordable rate.

We don't recommend that you build Capitols very often, because you should take the time when the game begins to build your initial Capitol at the most advantageous site possible. Still, it's nice to know that if moving your Capitol to a central location in your empire can improve the Happiness of far-flung cities, it's possible (and cheaper than building a Granary, for example) to do so.

More long-range benefits of Stone Working include jump-starting your civilization on the road to Engineering, which lets you build the Aqueduct Improvement, a must as your cities enter adolescence. In short, if you don't build this Advance early on, you'll find yourself "shooting bricks" later.

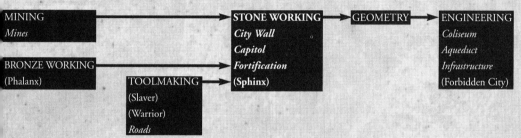

**HINT:** Especially if you are near potential enemies, Stone Working is essential. It gives you the ability to construct City Walls and the Sphinx Wonder, a fabulous offensive/defensive military punch in the early part of the game. Unless you are desperate for the Happiness that Religion brings, consider Stone Working early on, and move toward Engineering (but see our notes on *Geometry* elsewhere in this chapter).

# Subneural Ad

## Economics 10

Nearly everyone has heard about the experiments at drive-in theaters during the late 1950s when subliminal subtitles were played in various films using a tachistoscope so that viewers could neither consciously see nor read the subtitles. These subtitles suggested that it was the appropriate time to buy popcorn or get a soft drink. As a result, snack bars experienced a measurable surge in volume and, eventually, the government was forced to outlaw such subliminal seduction.

In *Civilization: Call to Power*, the Subneural Ad Advance goes a step further. In this case, subliminal suggestions can be transmitted directly to the subject's brain. The subject is not likely to be aware of the transmission, but the subliminal advertisement will definitely bring about results. In the game's fiction, the Subneural Ad is a potent offensive weapon that advertises non-existent products in the cities of rival civilizations. By doing so, the victims are possessed of a lust for these non-existent products and find themselves frustrated and unsatisfied. So, the unhappiness quotient of the target city is increased. For further covert action, the Subneural Ad can also set up a Franchise in an opposing city in order to drain Production in the same way that the Corporate Branch unit does.

| MASS MEDIA [w/ELECTRIFIATION] (Televangelist) (Television) Hollywood | → | GLOBENET GlobeSat | → | DIGITAL ENCRYPTION Global E-Bank | → | SUBNEURAL A (Subneural Ad) ESP Center |

HINT: Both gamers who play as conquerors and empire-builders need to find ways to negate their opponents from time to time. The Subneural Ad Advance enables you to force a Production hit on your enemies and make sure that they have problems with unhappiness. Bringing down the Happiness level of a city makes it easier to conquer in the long run because it will either force the enemy to make adjustments in the labor force or to create new and expensive Improvements to make the citizens content once again. Such maneuvers should weaken the enemy prior to your anticipated invasion. As an added bonus, the Subneural Ad advance allows you to build the ESP Project and improve your defensive capacity (see Chapter 9). However, this is balanced by the somewhat negative factor that it makes all of your Corporate Branches obsolete.

# Superconductor
## Electricity 3

A Superconductor is a substance that has practically no resistance to electricity at temperatures near absolute zero. Since any transfer of energy involves some loss of efficiency, the incredibly lower resistance of a Superconductor means a lot more energy that can be focused on an application.

| ELECTRICITY | COMPUTER | SUPERCONDUCTOR | UNIFIED PHYSICS |
|---|---|---|---|
| Edison's Lab | (Computer Center) | [w/ SPACE FLIGHT] | (Forcefield) |
| | The Internet | (Rail Launcher) | National Shield |
| | | (Maglevs) | |

HINT: Your Mobile Defense (See Chapter 3) will be much improved by the fast movement along Maglevs, and this puts you closer to the National Shield. More aggressive players, however, will appreciate being one step closer to the Cyber Ninja.

# Tank Warfare
## Offensive War 5

The Tank marks the end of the line for the traditional Offensive War unit. Until they become obsolete in the endgame, it never hurts to have a few Tanks in your armed forces. Most of the good late-game units either lack the Tank's mobility, such as the Leviathan, or you can only use them with a particular form of government (Plasmatica, Ecoterrorist, and so forth). So, the Tank gives you a little military flexibility as you move into the Genetic, and maybe even the Diamond age—not bad for a unit that had its historical debut in WWI.

CAVALRY TACTICS (Cavalry) → TANK WARFARE (Tank)

HINT: It's about the most straightforward decision you'll make during the game. We like tanks for Mobile Defense, regardless of whether we're fighting a war. Buy 'em, polish 'em, love 'em.

# Technocracy

## Mechanical Discoveries 9B

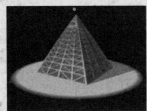

In *Call to Power's* form of government called Techocracy, the technologically elite have enslaved the less-enlightened masses by means of coercion and generous use of pharmaceuticals. In short, for all but the technological elite, the quality of life has significantly declined while basic Production and Science production have doubled and Gold production has achieved a 50-percent boost.

In addition to the Production bonuses provided by the Technocracy Advance, forming a Technocracy allows you to build an elite unit armed with plasma cannons. The Plasmatica unit has attack strength of 15, plus defense strength of 15. This makes her nearly the equal of the Fascist unit in attack strength, but clearly superior in defense.

ROBOTICS
(Spy Plane)
(War Walker)
(Robotic Plant)
(Automated Fisheries)

AI SURVEILLANCE
(Security Monitor)

{TECHNOCRACY}
(Plasmatica)

MIND CONTROL
(Mind Controller)
AI Entity

NANO-ASSEMBLY
[w/ NEURAL INTERFACE]
(Nanite Factory)
The Primer
Nanite Defuser

EDEN PROJECT
[w/ ECOTOPIA]
The Eden Project

HINT: If you need to pump up Production, Technocracy is definitely the form of government to use. Plus, if you are an empire-builder who needs stronger defense units, you can't beat the Plasmatica as a freestanding military unit. Alexander-style players may prefer the Fascist, but others will want the better-balanced Plasmatica.

# Theocracy

## Physical Science 2B

A Theocracy is a central, unified government that purports to be under the direct command of the dominant deity within a civilization. It is a government in which the laws are codified directly from scriptural precedent (regardless of which scripture takes precedence in a given culture), and human authority is tied directly into the imprimatur of the priesthood or clergy. As a result, Theocracy tends to breed its own brand of nationalism with regard to believing that "God" (in whatever form the culture perceives the dominant deity) is on the side, and nearly exclusively so, of the ruling religious hegemony. This central belief that "God" is on the side of the believing civilization tends to lead to both homogeneity in culture and an extreme intolerance toward other faiths and lifestyles.

As a result, Theocracies tend to be legalistic with very little internal dissension and extremely formidable with regard to prosecuting a holy war or jihad. This is why the Theocracy form of government in *Civilization: Call to Power* offers a 25-percent boost in Production, Gold, and Science with little repercussions in Happiness when going to war. It reflects the idea of an entire civilization rallying to prove that they are the best, the blessed of the controlling deity.

Theocracies in history include, of course, the Israelite Kingdom. The ancient Israelites practiced Holy War in order to win battles against allegedly stronger neighbors. By adhering to appropriate strictures, God was said to have intervened on their side (witness the triumphs of King David and the overwhelming defeat of Midian by Gideon). Whenever they disobeyed God, such as when the Israelites attempted to take Ai immediately after Jericho and without awaiting God's instructions, they were soundly defeated.

A modern example of a Theocracy would be the nation of Iran. No Iranian leader ever lost his job for losing a war. The entire population is willing to sacrifice in lives and quality of life in order to try for the eventual victory. The minor defeats of the present are because Allah wills it.

Any conqueror worth his salt in *Call to Power* will opt for the Theocracy form of government as soon as it becomes available. Not only are the Production, Gold, and Science bonuses worthwhile, but the Cleric unit has some diabolical special attacks (See the section on "Dirty Tricks" in Chapter 3). Combined with the Hagia Sophia Wonder, the Cleric can practically milk a rival civilization dry by merely invoking a "tithe."

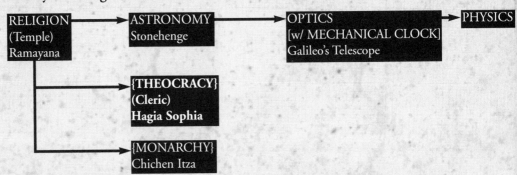

RELIGION (Temple) Ramayana → ASTRONOMY Stonehenge → OPTICS [w/ MECHANICAL CLOCK] Galileo's Telescope → PHYSICS

{THEOCRACY} (Cleric) Hagia Sophia

{MONARCHY} Chichen Itza

**HINT:** The Theocracy Advance opens many doors. Not only does it provide for a more efficient government than do Tyranny and Monarchy, but it allows you to build one of the most versatile special force units in the game, the Cleric. Clerics can foment dissension and generate income for the Theocracy. Alexander-style conquerors should gain this Advance at an early point in the game in order to glean extra efficiency, income, and covert strike capability.

# Toolmaking

## Sea 1, Pre-Defensive War 1, Crossover to Construction 2

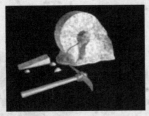

It's been proven beyond any reasonable doubt that higher primates, such as gorillas and chimpanzees, can communicate in sign language, and it's even been argued that they can employ rudimentary tools. Nevertheless, Toolmaking as an applied craft is still considered one of the primary

things that sets humans above the animals. Consider dolphins, which, although they might be on a par with humans in terms of raw intelligence, lack the capability to shape their environment through the use of tools.

Toolmaking covers a lot of ground throughout history, and could thus be the opening Advance in almost any category of research. But, for whatever reason (we assume because all the other slots were filled with things like Agriculture), Toolmaking in *Call to Power* constitutes the first Advance down the lanes of sea travel and technology. In terms of practical use during play, however, the tech category matters little. True to its versatile nature, Toolmaking opens up crossover avenues to Stone Working and Bronze Working, in addition to a direct path to Ship Building (Triremes) and Hull Making (Longboats).

Toolmaking also allows you to build Roads, which aren't as beneficial in *Call to Power* as in *Civilization II* because they confer no trade benefit. Still, they are vital to connecting the cities of your empire, particularly if you wish to keep a compact, mobile fighting force for defense (see Chapter 3).

With the Slaver and Warrior units now at your disposal, you have the chance to try a riskier strategy: Use Warriors units to defend against Barbarians, and Slavers to explore and to enslave your enemies. For more details, see Chapter 5.

Eventually, however, you'll want to move on to Phalanxes for more traditional defense, and to the benefits of City Walls. Don't get so caught up on this traditional path, however, that you neglect to develop your abilities on the seas. Quite often, untouched, hospitable islands are well within reach of even the primitive Trireme, and Longboats (two Sea Advances hence) really expand the overseas range of your empire.

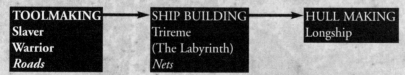

| **TOOLMAKING** | SHIP BUILDING | HULL MAKING |
|---|---|---|
| **Slaver** | Trireme | Longship |
| **Warrior** | (The Labyrinth) | |
| *Roads* | *Nets* | |

HINT: Whatever research path you choose to follow, the best thing is that it's hard to go wrong with Toolmaking. If by some rare chance you don't begin the game with this crucial Advance, you should research it first thing—no exceptions. Then, if you're into making money for your artisanship, go for Ship Building and the Labyrinth Wonder (though we suggest first taking the crossover path to Bronze Working for defense).

# Trade

## Economics 1, Crossover Mechanical 1

The origins of Trade can be illustrated by the market economy in the ancient Middle East. The basic level was primarily local Trade between simple craftsmen and peasants. At a slightly higher level were the artisans and traders from the bigger towns in a given area. These artisans and traders served landowners, priests, and royal officials by supplying them with finished goods of local manufacture and relatively rare luxuries from afar as they became available in provincial Trade. Finally, there were a few urban centers with relatively sophisticated manufacturing capacity which engaged in Trade relationships throughout the known world.

The urban centers of Mesopotamia were connected to each other and to seaports by Caravan routes. The domestication of the camel allowed Caravans to move overland across the desert instead of circumnavigating the shorelines of the Arabian Peninsula. In addition, the Sea Peoples (probably the Cretans) navigated the Mediterranean and cross-pollinated the goods and cultures around the Mediterranean shores.

In *Civilization: Call to Power*, the Trade advance celebrates the domestication of the camel and the importance of Caravans by enabling you to build Caravan units upon the completion of the Advance. Naturally, having Caravan units allows you to create a Trade Route between two of your own cities or between one of your cities and a foreign one. See Chapter 2 for information on the various Goods available for Trade.

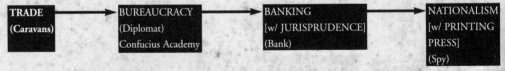

| TRADE (Caravans) | → | BUREAUCRACY (Diplomat) Confucius Academy | → | BANKING [w/ JURISPRUDENCE] (Bank) | → | NATIONALISM [w/ PRINTING PRESS] (Spy) |

**HINT:** If your goal in *Call to Power* is simply to conquer, put Trade fairly far down in your queue. If your goal is to build a large empire, you'll want to earn this Advance relatively quickly. For the conqueror, there isn't a lot of value on this branch of research until you get to Nationalism. For the empire-builder, there is a valuable unit or Improvement at every step.

Plus, Trade can give you an early jump toward Mechanical Discoveries through the Agricultural Revolution. Just remember that the program does apply some randomness concerning which new Advances you are offered next. Far-off Advances, especially ones that could jump you into another era, usually show up later in the research queue.

# Ultra-Pressure Machinery

## Sea 7

 The final advance in the Sea branch of the technology tree is Ultra-Pressure Machinery. This advanced technology, designed to withstand the pressure found many fathoms beneath the waves, is extremely useful in building Production and enhancing your military position. Ultra-Pressure Machinery enables the construction of Advanced Undersea Mines. These modernized mines double the value of the original Undersea Mines. Gold production jumps from 5 per turn to 10; and ordinary Production doubles to 30/40/50, depending on the terrain.

Militarists will enjoy the new units available upon the completion of this Advance. The Plasma Destroyer has an assault value of 30 and defensive value of 15. Anywhere on the ocean, the Plasma Destroyer has the capacity to Bombard enemy units without fear of counter-attack. Also, the Crawler is essentially a "stealth" invasion vehicle that holds up to five units.

[ 173 ]

| SEA COLONIES | ULTRA-PRESSURE MACHINERY |
|---|---|
| (Sea Engineer) | (Crawler) |
| (Stealth Sub) | (Plasma-Destroyer) |
| (Undersea Mines) | (Advanced Undersea Mines) |
| (Undersea Tunnels) | |

HINT: At this point in the game, you either know what you need to catch up with or pass other civilizations—or not. The Advanced Undersea Mines can be helpful in both Gold and Production if you are within striking range of your rival civilizations. If not, you might want to opt for the Plasma Destroyer and try to take out a considerable number of opposing units by using its heavy attack value. If you need to make up ground, this is a good Advance.

# Unified Physics

## Electricity 4

In the search for a "Theory of Everything," Unified Physics tries to reconcile classic Physics with Quantum Mechanics, among other things. Good luck, we say.

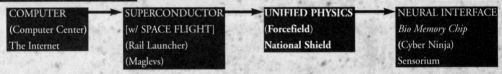

| COMPUTER | SUPERCONDUCTOR | UNIFIED PHYSICS | NEURAL INTERFACE |
|---|---|---|---|
| (Computer Center) | [w/ SPACE FLIGHT] | **(Forcefield)** | *Bio Memory Chip* |
| The Internet | (Rail Launcher) | **National Shield** | (Cyber Ninja) |
| | (Maglevs) | | Sensorium |

**HINT:** Unless you're seriously into defense, the main claim to fame of Unified Physics is that it gets you closer to 1) the Sensorium wonder, and 2) the Immunity Chip.

# Virtual Democracy

## Electricity 7

Virtual Democracy is an idealized futuristic version of pure democracy. The "one person-one vote" ethos is handled via a virtual assemblage of the entire population, and Nano-technology allows for almost unlimited food and clothing. Because the virtual citizens of the Virtual Democracy are comfortable with the ever-evolving version of cyberspace in this Brave New World, this is the form of government where Science advances the fastest. So, Virtual Democracy is absolutely vital for those gamers headed for the Wormhole Sensor and Alien Synthesis Project ending.

Virtual Democracy also lets you create the Egalitarian Act Wonder. By eliminating all discrimination and poverty, you can actually use this Wonder to recruit any foreign cities facing revolt into your own civilization.

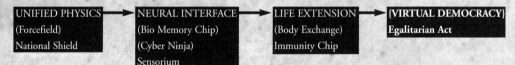

| UNIFIED PHYSICS | NEURAL INTERFACE | LIFE EXTENSION | {VIRTUAL DEMOCRACY} |
|---|---|---|---|
| (Forcefield) | (Bio Memory Chip) | (Body Exchange) | **Egalitarian Act** |
| National Shield | (Cyber Ninja) | Immunity Chip | |
| | Sensorium | | |

> HINT: Virtual Democracy is obviously the ideal form of government for those who wish to build their economies and civilizations to win the ultra-scientific Alien Synthesis Project endgame. Although the Science production is attractive, it doesn't recommend itself to the Alexander-style player.

# Wormholes

## Flight 8, Crossover Flight 10

Wormholes, of course, refer to singularities, which we cannot completely explain with our current understanding of Physics. The thesis in *Civilization: Call to Power* is that the alien civilization uncovered through the Alien Archaeology Advance came through the Wormhole. Therefore, the only way to locate the alien civilization is to find the wormhole, send a probe through the wormhole, capture alien DNA, and use some additional Advances to duplicate the alien and artificially create a new alien child to influence the future of civilization.

As noted in the discussion of the Wormhole Sensor Wonder, you are unlikely to win under Alien Synthesis Project conditions without getting the Wormholes Advance and Wonder. The civilization that builds the Wormhole Sensor gets a five-turn head-start to exploit the Wormhole before the other civilizations can locate it.

| ALIEN ARCHAEOLOGY | WORMHOLES | CLOAKING |
|---|---|---|
| | (Wormhole Probe) | (Phantom) |
| | (Wormhole Sensor) | |

> HINT: Conquerors need not apply. Of course, if you've allowed a rival civilization to survive this long, you'd better nab the Wormhole Advance and beat your opponent to the Wormhole, hadn't you? After all, if it's

possible for you to win with the Alien Synthesis Option, it's possible for them. As for empire-builders, this is the moment you've been waiting for. Don't wait a second. Get the Advance, build the Wonder, take the head start, and hope you don't have a setback in the laboratory.

# Writing

## Cultural Advancement 1

 The earliest forms of writing appear to be symbolic accountancy. Archaeological sites in the Middle East have confirmed this again and again. Many of the earliest libraries consist of tablets and broken pieces of pottery that indicate names (or symbols representing names) and inventory of wine, sheep, and grain taken in tribute, tithe, or tax. Many of these tablets were pictographic and later shifted to an alphabetic or phonetic representation. Such evidence suggests that writing was used initially to keep temple accounts. Later, rare personal contracts are recorded. The temple accounts shifted to royal accounts as the religious hierarchy lost ground to warrior kings who could unite multiple city-states and demand tribute.

In ancient Ugarit, a city in what is now Lebanon, the alphabet consisted of 32 characters presented in cuneiform fashion. This means that the characters were combinations of wedge-shaped impressions on clay tablets. Early Phoenician and Hebrew alphabets consisted of 20-30 character symbols. These *alephs* and *beths* eventually became the alphas and betas of Ancient Greece. From the names of these letters, we get the term, *alphabet*.

Writing materials appear to vary according to the location. In Egypt and China, where reeds were plentiful, papyrus became the chosen medium. In Mesopotamia, clay tablets were used first. Later, after the use of ink became more predominant, broken shards of pottery were used for recordkeeping. Regardless of materials used, writing enabled records and accomplishments to be recorded for posterity. Writing also allowed the inception of bureaucracy, because writing enabled messengers to take written instructions from official representative to official representative.

In *Civilization: Call to Power*, the Writing Advance is the first on the Cultural Advance branch of the technology tree. It does not allow the building of any special units or Improvements, but it opens the door toward Jurisprudence.

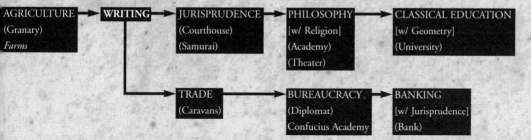

Writing is an important crossover technology that serves as a prerequisite for both Geometry and Trade. Naturally, Geometry is important on the Construction Advance branch, and the Trade is the first building block on the Economic Advance branch.

| AGRICULTURE | → | WRITING | → | JURISPRUDENCE | → | PHILOSOPHY | → | CLASSICAL EDUCATION |
|---|---|---|---|---|---|---|---|---|
| (Granary) | | | | (Courthouse) | | [w/ Religion] | | [w/ Geometry] |
| *Farms* | | | | (Samurai) | | (Academy) | | (University) |
| | | | | | | (Theater) | | |

| | TRADE | → | BUREAUCRACY | → | BANKING |
|---|---|---|---|---|---|
| | (Caravans) | | (Diplomat) | | [w/ Jurisprudence] |
| | | | Confucius Academy | | (Bank) |

HINT: Writing should be an early priority. However, we still stress that you should probably get the Bronze-Working Advance (for Phalanxes) first—especially if you're playing in a smaller world or where there are lots of rival civilizations.

# Zero-G Industry

# Flight 8

Imagine being able to construct huge aerospace vehicles without having to deal with gravitational effects. Such has been the dream of industrialists ever since humankind safely put men in Space for the first time. In *Civilization: Call to Power*, the Zero-G Industry Advance is preliminary to enabling you to build the Space Bomber unit with its range of 50 and ability to Bombard from Space.

| SPACE COLONIES | → | ZERO-G INDUSTRY | → | ASTEROID MINING | → | CLOAKING |
|---|---|---|---|---|---|---|
| (Space Engineer) | | (Space Bomber) | | (Star Cruiser) | | (Phantom) |
| (Space Marine) | | | | (Swarm) | | |
| (Food Pods) | | | | (Food Modules) | | |
| (Assembly Bays) | | | | (Advanced Assembly Bays) | | |

HINT: As tempting as the Space Bomber with its near-limitless range may be, gamers should check out the 300-point support cost before building it. That's one expensive hunk of hardware.

# Concerning the
# Wonders of the World

## What They Are, What They Do, and Why They Make *Civilization: Call to Power* So Wonderful

Imagine, if you can, a world without the Sphinx. The great empire of ancient Egypt may be dust now, but this wonderful monolith still stirs in us a desire to know the mysteries of the Pharaohs in a way that the treasures of King Tut cannot. Part of it is the structure's sheer size, and the fact that, thousands of years before modern technology, the Egyptian people erected a monument to their great civilization with little more than the sweat of their backs and a fierce determination to finish the job. That the Sphinx still exists today, and that it is exotic, featuring the body of a big cat and the head of a man, makes it only that much more enticing to us.

Perusing books and photos with pictures of the great works of humanity is fun. And there's nothing like visiting the Louvre to gaze upon the Mona Lisa, or to actually smell the inside of the Washington Monument, and to touch its walls. But few people can travel everywhere to see every great work ever made. Moreover, some of the greatest achievements throughout history have been less about structures than ideas: The Magna Carta, The Gettyburg Address, and The Declaration of Independence, to name only a few. Therefore, viewing the parchment on which these ideas are founded has a certain weight, but doesn't necessarily put you in the mindset of

President Lincoln in 1862, for example. Finally, many great works, such as the Great Library of Alexandria, have been lost to us through the follies of history.

This is where a game like *Civilization: Call to Power* comes in. It lets you reshape history in your own image, to understand why the Labyrinth brought trade to its owner from all over the Mediterranean. When you complete the Emancipation Wonder, you don't just call for freedom as an abstract concept, you actually free all slaves in all empires—pretty heady stuff for a computer game.

You can further the advance of knowledge by building Galileo's Telescope and Thomas Edison's Laboratory, open up embassies throughout the land by finding the Philosopher's Stone, or even close all embassies by holing up in your Forbidden City. The advantage of doing all of these things, even the more fanciful things, such as discovering ESP and creating AI entities to rule society, is that you see exactly how and why things happen as you progress in the game. And unlike most "history lessons," *Call to Power* is anything but dry.

What follows are our views on the Wonders of the World as seen in *Call to Power*. After we put each Wonder in historical perspective, we show you how to get there through a breakdown of the technology tree. Finally, we offer tips on how to best use each Wonder (or whether to build it at all), both for a military strategy, and for those who pursue a more political/economic strategy. History marches on, so don't dally dreaming about the Sphinx, lest your opponent builds it before you!

# The Agency

*"These men are extremely well-disciplined, and they have a history of engaging in such activities that will serve us well. They will appear spontaneous and ideologically motivated. These men carry their own cover and will not be traceable to us."*

—G. Gordon Liddy on his special teams prior to Watergate

| | |
|---|---|
| **ERA:** | Modern |
| **BRANCH OF KNOWLEDGE:** | Defensive War |
| **DEVELOPMENT:** | Global Defense + 7,200 Production Units = THE AGENCY |
| **OBSOLESCENCE:** | Alien Archaeology |
| **EFFECT:** | Gives the equivalent of one Spy unit for every city in the host civilization |

## Political/Economic Advantages

If you haven't been able to construct the GlobeSat Wonder by the time you're reaching the close of the Modern Age, you'll need The Agency Wonder. It is no accident that The Agency Wonder is located on the Defensive War branch of the technology tree. It is extremely useful for keeping the empire of the empire-building player intact. After building The Agency Wonder, you will no longer have to send Spy units cruising along your borders to see what your enemies are up to. You will simply know whenever your city faces danger as the enemy units actually approach your cities. For example, no Televangelist sneak attacks will be possible when you have The Agency. Each city will recognize the threat independently.

The Agency is a relatively inexpensive buy for this period in the late mid-game. You major choices are likely to be the aforementioned GlobeSat (a better overall purchase than The Agency), the Genome

World War II was an important time for the intelligence service. Code breakers and undercover agents saved many lives through the interception of military secrets. At the close of the war (AD 1945), President Truman worried about the concept of the military complex having control of all of the sensitive intelligence. He rightly believed that such control of information could lead to a military coup. Therefore, one of the early accomplishments of the Truman administration was to create an intelligence gathering organization that was neither beholden to the professional military or to the State Department. Originally, this organization was known as the Central Intelligence Group. Later, it became known as the Central Intelligence Agency (CIA).

During the Cold War, the CIA was an important key to the defense of the United States (as was MI-5 in the U.K.) in its constant covert maneuvering with the

Project, or the Internet. GlobeSat, since it opens to you the entire world map and shows you where units are, is far more valuable than The Agency, which serves as pure defense. The Genome Project may be more attractive than The Agency if you're lagging behind in production and need that boost. The Internet Wonder is also a superior buy when you're lagging behind your rivals on the technology tree. The gain of ten new Wonders per age (an average) could be absolutely vital to your defense.

During the latter part of the Modern Age, The Agency Wonder can provide significant piece of mind for the empire-builder who doesn't own the GlobeSat wonder. If security is uppermost in your mind and GlobeSat is not available, there is no question about The Agency being your highest priority unless, as previously noted, you have a production or advancement of knowledge gap that is more vital to fill.

Soviet Union's KGB. Awareness of the existence of international spies (sometimes called, "spooks") brought about the spy phenomenon of the '60s, complete with James Bond, The Avengers, and more. By the Nixon administration in the early '70s, however, matters had gone awry. The CIA may have bungled the attempted assassination of Cuba's Fidel Castro (possibly contributing to the assassination of President Kennedy), but they appeared to be complicit in the assassinations of several military leaders in Latin America and highly involved in spying on U.S. citizens. After the Watergate scandal had pushed Nixon from office, U.S. President Gerald Ford curtailed the authority of the CIA for domestic surveillance by executive order.

In spite of the abuses in our lifetime, there is always a need for intelligence vital to national security. In

## Military Advantages

Even an Alexander-the-Great-type player needs a defense. Yet, the chances are that you've been advancing so rapidly as the mid-game comes to a close that you didn't manage to get the GlobeSat Wonder built before your rival. Given a choice between GlobeSat and The Agency, an Alexander should always go with GlobeSat because the widespread information gleaned gives an advantage in strategic planning. Without the GlobeSat option, The Agency looks very tempting. With the Agency, you won't have to leave any Spy or Diplomat units behind your lines. Each city functions like a Spy. This frees those units to work behind enemy lines as they gather information for your next assault. You might even be able to disband some Spy units once this Wonder is in place, since you don't need

*Civilization: Call to Power*, The Agency Wonder represents a surveillance and information gathering organization which merely accumulates top-secret data on your enemies, but does not engage in any of the covert activities that forced Ford to reign in the CIA in the late '70s. Functionally, The Agency operates as though there were a Spy unit in each city. In this way, no rival can sneak up on you, but you don't have the maintenance costs associated with actually placing a Spy in each city of your civilization.

...he domestic surveillance capability any longer.

As with the empire-builder, however, you may need to opt for The Genome Project Wonder if you have any kind of production gap for which to compensate. Or you may choose the Internet Wonder if you need to catch up on

advances by stealing from, er, benefiting from the free exchange of information with your enemies.

One easy way to judge the priority of The Agency in your strategic goal is to consider how active your rival civilizations have been on your borders. If they haven't

been that active to this point, The Agency may be Cold War overkill. If, however, you are investing in a lot of units for domestic surveillance behind your lines, it's a no-brainer. Get The Agency, and get it fast.

# AI Entity

*"The human brain resembles nothing so much as a bowl of porridge."*

—Alan Turing, quoted from a BBC Radio interview

| | |
|---|---|
| **ERA:** | Diamond |
| **BRANCH OF KNOWLEDGE:** | Medicine |
| **DEVELOPMENT:** | Mind Control + 12,000 Production Units = AI ENTITY |
| **OBSOLESCENCE:** | Never |
| **EFFECT:** | Immediately quells all riots or revolts in all your cities |
| **DOWNSIDE:** | AI Entity may start a new revolution and splinter host civilization |

## Political/Economic Advantages

As the benevolent leader of a booming civilization, you really shouldn't need the AI Entity Wonder. You will have been monitoring the Happiness levels of all of your cities and managing your growth so that quality of life is not diminished. If you haven't quite managed such a lofty goal, the AI Entity can be a quick fix for a low Happiness quotient within your civilization. Just be aware that the AI Entity Wonder carries a large uncertainty factor with it. If it becomes self-aware and revolts against you, there is likely to be a schism throughout your entire civilization. Some of your cities will stick with you, but many will revolt and follow the AI leader.

In the late 1960s motion picture, *2001: A Space Odyssey*, the computer was known as HAL, an acronym formed by sliding the letters IBM back one letter in the alphabet. You can still get a chuckle out of just about anyone who has seen the film by saying, "I can't do that, Dave," a reference to the self-aware computer's decision to defy its human crew. The joke is likely to continue with a slow, sing-song version of "Bicycle Built for Two" ("Dai-sy! Dai-sy!") as a follow-up reference to the scene where the crew member disables HAL. From that day to this, HAL has been the symbol of the self-aware computer or artificial intelligence (AI). HAL was even used as a foil for Steve Jobs' keynote at Macworld in 1999. Yet, there has been comparatively little progress on authentic AI in the last decade.

Advocates for the concept of authentic artificial intelligence point to the human cerebrum as a biological analog to the computing process. The rear area

The moral of the story is that you shouldn't build the AI Entity Wonder unless you have a serious morale problem throughout your civilization. Even so, you are much better off dealing with discontent and unhappiness through manipulating entertainers, building theaters, and reducing work hours than you are considering the potentially risky AI Entity option. Even though the risk of the AI Entity breaking down and going berserk is only three-percent, you've worked far too hard for your far-flung empire to risk its dissolution unless you are absolutely forced to do so.

of the brain (occipital, parietal, and temporal lobes) function as the input section of the brain as it receives auditory, tactile, and visual data. Then, after algorithmic processing takes place, the frontal lobes take up the output mechanism. Such functionality leads some AI advocates to believe that it is possible to duplicate such a set-up in digital form.

When one looks at the way neurons function, the temptation to make a computer analog gets even stronger. Neurons are apparently cells with a negative net charge of ions within them. When neurons "fire," they apparently pass positive ions between them so that this negative net charge is temporarily interrupted (by chemical data or input) and then restored. Advocates of authentic AI believe that the use of negative ions here is analogous to an electrical charge in a computer and that the synaptic gates, which pass chemicals back and forth, are like the logic gates in the computer.

## Military Advantages

When you're constantly at war, there is inevitably a price to pay. War isn't pretty and it places an economic burden on the home front. If your citizens feel strongly enough that the war is necessary, they may suffer through rationing and shortfalls for a time. Eventually, though, they're going to become unhappy. If they become unhappy enough, you can no longer prosecute the war effectively.

In *Civ:CTP*, the AI Entity Wonder gives you the option that many a warhawk must have wanted during the Vietnam Era. Using the AI Entity Wonder, you can immediately stop any and all unrest in your entire civilization. This is an excellent option for the player who is continually at war or continually pushing productivity to the maximum in order to prepare for war. The only downside is a three-percent chance that the AI Entity will rebel and you'll end up with a

*Civilization: Call to Power* assumes that such analogs can be constructed. But it moves further into the area of science fiction, suggesting that entire civilizations can become the equivalent of wireheads (individuals accepting electrical charges in the pleasure centers of their brains). Using an embedded chip in your citizens, you will be able to control your empire's Happiness quotient through this Wonder. The disadvantage is that the AI Entity wonder might, like HAL, rebel against you.

bigger mess (along with a splintered civilization with less cities) than you started with. You are gambling a bit with this Wonder, but for the Alexander-type player, the gamble is probably worth it.

The biggest dilemma to be faced by the Alexander-style player in this early portion of the Diamond Age is to decide whether to first research the AI Entity or to fund the Eden Project. If you're dipping into the yellow in Happiness and worried that a revolution could be around the corner, you need to prioritize the AI Entity. If you're merely low in Happiness, but still in the green, consider the Eden Project first. If you have the GlobeSat Wonder, the choice is easy. See if your closest rival has more pollution than you do. If so, fund the Eden Project Wonder first and wipe out three of the rival civilization's cities. Then, you can build the AI Entity should you need it.

# Chichen Itza

*"And they built up with their bare hands/What we still can't do today."*

—Neil Young, *"Cortez the Killer"* from the *Zuma* album (banned in Spain)

| | |
|---|---|
| **ERA:** | Ancient |
| **BRANCH OF KNOWLEDGE:** | Government |
| **DEVELOPMENT:** | Monarchy + 2,160 Production Units = CHICHEN ITZA |
| **OBSOLESCENCE:** | Mass Production |
| **EFFECT:** | Eliminates crime throughout your civilization |

## Political/Economic Advantages

Crime rate in *Call to Power* is a direct result of overcrowding and unhappy people in general. With the elimination of crime, you can afford to "cheat" a little on your economy. This doesn't mean that you can risk riots, but it does mean that you can push a lot of your cities into the "yellow" on the Happiness bar. And it's those subtle differences in production, surplus food, and extra gold that give you the edge on your opponents. With Chichen Itza, you can often stay just far enough ahead of your competitors to get the Wonders and Advances you need *before* they do. These, in turn, can be used to gain other advantages over your opponents, so that you get a domino effect.

All of the great civilizations of what is now loosely called Latin America are generally given short shrift in the greater scheme of history. Part of the reason for this is that they seem to have developed very quickly early on and then stagnated as they stamped out most all of their local opposition. Unlike the Greeks, Persians, Romans, and Carthaginians, for instance, the Aztecs and Mayans had no real threats to their respective sovereignties, and thus no real reason to keep developing technology. One of the more intriguing "what ifs" of history concerns the Mongols, who supposedly considered crossing the frozen Bering Straits into North America. Would the Aztecs and Mayans have had a prayer? Only Kublai Khan knows for sure.

In any case, the Mayans seem to have had the wheel well before their Mesopotamian River valley counterparts, yet they used it for children's toys. As far as we

Of course, it's possible that your success will anger some of your most volatile competitors. So, make sure to pick one of them out and bring that nation along the garden path with you, making treaties and swapping Advances to your benefit. Since you no longer have a trade loss (or other gold loss) due to crime, make a point of pushing your newfound friend for favorable Trade Routes.

Finally, try to combine Chichen Itza, if possible, with the Confucius Academy. This incredible combo lets you spread out your empire far and wide, without any of the usual repercussions for crime and unhappiness caused by distance from your capital. True, you'll eventually have to deal with these Wonders' effects expiring, but for the next several hundred years, we think you'll find it's worth the effort.

**Chichen Itza**

can tell, they never seriously considered making war chariots, much less more modern weaponry. So, when these societies were faced with Europeans armed with gunpowder, they quickly crumbled. Of course, the fact that the Europeans brought influenza and smallpox with them didn't hurt their chances.

Even in *Civilization II*, it was very hard to win with the Aztecs, because they started at a disadvantage in terms of terrain and technology. It's nice, then, that *Call to Power* gives these neglected empires their day in the court of history, especially since all civilizations start equal, with no "handicapping" other than difficulty level.

Of course, you don't have to play the Mayans or the Aztecs to build Chichen Itza, which is one of the most original Wonders in *Call to Power*, because it

## Military Advantages

The turns, at 50 years a pop, tend to fly by in the Ancient era. Thus, you have to be selective of what Wonders to build, particularly in games at a higher difficulty level. We still insist that the Sphinx (see elsewhere this chapter) is a

higher priority for any would-be military machine. Still, it's hard to argue with the efficiency of eliminating crime throughout your civilization.

In fact, if you are between wars, the potential of

Chichen Itza is very enticing. First, cut your military spending back severely, and focus on production in your largest city. With a little luck, your neighbors will leave you alone long enough to complete the Wonder (by this time, if you've followed our advice, Barbarians shouldn't be much

ties in with crime, a new and welcome gameplay element. The ability to eliminate crime entirely by building Chichen Itza, at least until the discovery of Mass Production, is one that offers a boon for any civilization, regardless of what strategy it employs.

The idea that a civilization that practiced blood sacrifice (however otherwise civilized) should be viewed as the pinnacle of law and justice in society stretches the imagination, perhaps a bit too far. Then again, violent crime is way down in Texas since they reenacted the death penalty...

of a threat). Just to make sure, have two of your medium-sized cities convert to cranking out maximum gold, in case you have to "Rush Buy" the Wonder at the last minute.

Once you've finished erecting Chichen Itza, you will find that the amount of gold and food you save will pay for your Wonder purchase within a few turns, since even a modestly-sized empire loses up to 10-percent of its production to crime every turn. If you can manage to build Chichen Itza *and* the Sphinx, you will almost certainly have the most efficient war effort on the planet. Don't waste your military advantage: At this stage, you should try to eliminate at least one rival before the end of the Renaissance, an era you'll reach soon enough, given the pace of the game.

# Confucius Academy

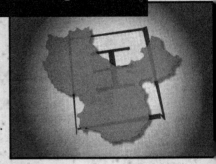

*"When the command is wrong, a son should resist his father, and a minister his august master."*

—*Confucius*, Li-Chi.

| | |
|---|---|
| **ERA:** | Ancient |
| **BRANCH OF KNOWLEDGE:** | Economics |
| **DEVELOPMENT:** | Bureaucracy + 2,160 Production Units = CONFUCIUS ACADEMY |
| **OBSOLESCENCE:** | Mass Production |
| **EFFECT:** | Eliminates all unhappiness caused by city distance from the capitol |

## Political/Economic Advantages

Whether you are an empire-builder or a conqueror, you will want to build a far-flung empire with cities all over the map. When you do build or conquer cities away from your original capitol, you will either incur significant unhappiness or significant expense in combating that unhappiness. Early on, you may be able to weather the unhappiness, but as you begin to ramp up production and start using Tile Improvements to mine the mountains, harvest the sea, and farm the plains, you won't want any kind of an anchor weighing against your future growth. Having to "hire" entertainers in order to assure adequate Happiness is counter-productive.

The Confucius Academy is an ideal second buy for those who want to focus on founding and improving their own cities rather than focusing on Trade Routes. This is because you will have to purchase entertainers, construct theaters, or build provincial capitols in order to

Toward the middle of the sixth century in China, a wise teacher known as Confucius began to teach a moral philosophy concerning duty and the so-called "Higher Man." As presented in the quotation that precedes this discussion, Confucius believed that the main duty of children and citizens was to obey their parents and the authorities. The highest authority, however, was a basic morality. Said morality was not determined by a systematic regime of rigorous logic, however. Rather, Confucius used dialogues to teach his students, much as Socrates would do at a later time. One general principle was to be sympathetic toward all men. Confucius' philosophy was extremely practical, however. When presented with the idea of returning good for evil, as with the Tao of Lao-Tzu, Confucius questioned whether one would then have to return evil for good. He quickly stated that one must return justice for evil.

reduce unhappiness without the Wonder. Any of these three solutions to the unhappiness problem will cost you where it counts—in production units. In a medium to large world, Confucius Academy is probably a better second buy than the Labyrinth because foreign trade isn't likely to be available very early on such maps. Even if trade becomes available early on, it will mean accruing gold rather than production units (and production is cheaper than having to spend your gold in a "Rush Buy" situation). In a small world, the Labyrinth is probably a better second Wonder for those who are interested in building up trade.

Naturally, if your goal is to build up your gold quickly, and you're not worried about siphoning off production units in favor of the monetary units, you can simply build the Labyrinth and not worry about unhappiness. You can always switch a common laborer over to entertainer status when you have the need. Just make sure that you're monitoring the Happiness scale of your civilization every turn. You don't want to have rioting reduce your overall growth curve.

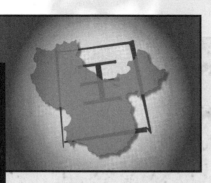

## Confucius Academy

Confucius' favorite topic was government. He believed that good government was derived from good leaders. He believed that the government should be filled with good men and regularly expunged of those who proved themselves crooked. One means of becoming crooked in Confucius' opinion was foreign influences. Confucius was a stern believer in isolationism. Another major emphasis in Confucius' thought was on manners. He believed that when manners began to decay, so would government.

After Confucius' death, a rival school called the Legalists gained ascendancy for a time. The foremost leader was a minister named Shih Huang-ti. He attempted to burn all of the Confucian literature. After a time, however, a wiser emperor found the Confucian literature which had been hidden by his disciples, and Confucianism became revered under the T'ang Dynasty.

## Military Advantages

An Alexander-type player isn't as likely to get the opportunity to build the Confucius Academy. Since Stonehenge for the food production bonus and the Sphinx for the price of war reduction are the top two priorities for the military mas-termind, the Confucius Academy is likely to have been completed by a rival civilization before it is wise for an Alexander to create it.

If the Confucius Academy is still available as your third choice, however, it will save you a lot of hassle in the long run. The Confucius Academy is particularly valuable to a conqueror in a large world. In such a case, you might consider opting for it immediately after completing either Stonehenge or the Sphinx, especially if you know that

In *Civilization: Call to Power*, the Confucius Academy builds upon Confucius' theory of good government based upon good officials. Building the Confucius Academy will immediately eliminate the unhappiness that is accumulated by distance from the capitol city. Since reducing unhappiness has a significant cost in terms of shifting workers to entertainers and having to create and maintain theaters, the Confucius Academy can save you significant amounts of gold and productivity until its obsolescence following the introduction of the Mass Production Advance.

another civilization is already fairly far along in completing the other priority Wonder, and you do not have enough gold to make a "Rush Buy." If you do have enough gold to make a "Rush Buy" (and this isn't likely at this point in the game), go for the second priority Wonder and then immediately switch to Confucius Academy upon the completion of your priority.

Just remember that the more cities you have in remote locales, the more valuable the Confucius Academy Wonder is to your strategic game plan. Also, remember that the fact that it lasts until the Mass Production Advance takes effect means that it is likely that you'll exploit this Wonder for a longer time than you'll be able to exploit the Labyrinth, with its demise after the Age of Reason Advance.

# Contraception

*"We want to have our cake and eat it too. We want to gorge ourselves at the table of an affluent society whose continued prosperity, we are told, necessitates a constantly expanding market. And sex sells anything. At the same time we want to cherish our national memories of Pilgrims and piety."*

—*Harvey Cox,* The Secular City

| | |
|---|---|
| **ERA:** | Modern |
| **BRANCH OF KNOWLEDGE:** | Medicine |
| **DEVELOPMENT:** | Pharmaceuticals + 7,200 Production Units = CONTRACEPTION |
| **OBSOLESCENCE:** | Alien Archaeology |
| **EFFECT:** | Gains 5 Happiness points for host civilization |

## Political/Economic Advantages

The major dilemma for an empire-builder as the Age of the Renaissance is coming to a close and the Modern Age is beginning will be whether to build the Edison's Laboratory Wonder or to research the Contraception Wonder. Both are extremely valuable at this point in the game and both reach obsolescence at the beginning of the Diamond Age with the Alien Archaeology Advance. It is difficult to pass up the average of ten Advances per age gained with Edison's Laboratory, but Happiness is difficult to manage at any point in the game and having

Although some Egyptian sources indicate the use of crocodile dung as an important ingredient in a birth control ointment, by far the most common form of contraception in the ancient world was the application of an herbal mixture to the labia. Aristotle describes this in his *History of Animals*. He advises women to prepare themselves with "oil of cedar, or with ointments of lead, or with frankincense, commingled with olive oil." In most of the ancient world, however, population was limited by means of exposure or induced miscarriage rather than by contraception. Much of contraceptive lore revolved around *coitus interruptus* and the rhythm method.

Eventually, condoms made from animal membranes came into existence and later still, they were made out of latex rubber. Although condoms were and are

the Contraception Wonder is a bonus. Obviously, a civilization which is well ahead of its rivals will have less need for the Edison's Laboratory Wonder and can simply create Contraception in order to allow flexibility without having to worry about the Happiness quotient. Conversely, a civilization falling behind its rivals should prioritize Edison's Laboratory.

The Contraception Wonder is extremely useful whenever it can be obtained, however. Where many buildings or improvements that enhance Happiness are merely local quality-of-life enhancers, it's always nice to be able to improve Happiness civilization-wide.

fairly effective, it was the advent of the oral contraceptive and its widespread adoption in the latter part of the 20th century that had a revolutionary impact on society.

As reflected in the quotation which precedes this discussion, the sex drive is a powerful motivator and the human animal longs to satisfy this desire. Over the centuries, both religious and social authorities have tried to control their constituents by controlling the sex drive. Perhaps the most visible was the teaching of Pope Pius XI, renewed in *Casti Connubi* on New Year's Eve of 1930. The pope declared any act of conjugal love that guarded against procreation to mean, "Those who indulge in such are branded with the guilt of a grave sin."

## Military Advantages

The Alexander-style player is faced with the same dilemma as the empire-building player. Is the Edison's Laboratory Wonder or the Contraception Wonder right for your civilization? Again, the two Wonders cost the same, reach obsolescence at the same time, and usually become available at approximately the same point in the game. Which do you choose?

If you have been using so many production units to churn out military units, you may be falling behind on the Science curve. In such a case, you'll probably want to opt for the Edison's Laboratory Wonder. The average of ten bonus Advances per age is extremely enticing and can cover a significant degree of scientific neglect. If, however, your civilization is on the brink of riots and revolution due to a low Happiness quotient,

*Civilization: Call to Power* takes seriously the desire for many to have sexual satisfaction without undue risk of bringing unwanted offspring into the world. Researching the Contraception Wonder will enable gamers to bring an instant boost of five Happiness points into their civilization. Since Happiness is a factor with which players have to be concerned throughout the game, the availability of the Contraception Wonder is welcome at any point in the game. Coming as it does in the mid-game makes it all the more valuable.

you can't research the Contraception Wonder quite soon enough. Five points of Happiness applied universally to your ever-expanding civilization can save you from building a multitude of theaters and temples. This saves gold and production units in the long run, resources which can be put to better use in conquest as you take what you want.

In general, you'll probably discover that the Contraception Wonder has more immediate impact, as it automatically changes the Happiness quotient. However, it will take longer to see the additional dividends accrue, as you won't have to build lots of theaters and temples or assign numerous Entertainers just to maintain your Happiness status-quo. Contraception is an extremely useful Wonder, but the Edison's Laboratory versus Contraception dilemma is a very real one.

# Dinosaur Park

*"In theory, if we were skilled enough at genetic engineering, we could move from any point in animal space to any other point. From any starting point, we could move through the maze in such a way as to recreate the dodo, the tyrannosaur, and trilobites."*

—*Richard Dawkins,* The Blind Watchmaker.

| | |
|---|---|
| **ERA:** | Genetic |
| **BRANCH OF KNOWLEDGE:** | Medicine |
| **DEVELOPMENT:** | Genetic Tailoring + 7,200 Production Units = DINOSAUR PARK |
| **OBSOLESCENCE:** | Cloaking |
| **EFFECT:** | Quadruples Gold  from Goods in Host City |

## Political/Economic Advantages

At first glance, you're probably going to think that the Dinosaur Park Wonder is just another Labyrinth. Fortunately, it is much more. The idea of a cultural site drawing enough tourist business that all civilizations trade with you is very similar to the Labyrinth, but the payoff is significant. A 300-percent bonus to every existing Trade Route with the Host City is a remarkable piece of low-lying fruit for an empire-builder to pick. Of course, like the lottery, you have to buy a ticket to win. If you have no Trade Routes in your Host City, you'd be a fool to waste your time with this Wonder.

So, build the Dinosaur Park as soon as you get the chance. This is one of the few times in the game where you can be

Cloning, the capacity for building a new organ or organism from the genetic material of existing cells, has been an emerging technology within our lifetime. Frog hearts were constructed from genetic material circa AD 1970, and a number of books and scientific papers began to consider the morality of cloning and genetic engineering at that time. Of course, it wasn't until much later that an entire animal, a Scottish sheep, was cloned, but that revived the controversy once again. Many scientists believed that cloning was a positive venture because it would enable development of ideal genetic prototypes (as in *Civilization: Call to Power*'s Genome Project Wonder). Secondly, it would allow potential parents to avoid dysgenic possibilities in their offspring. Also, cloning would allow for the creation of back-up organs and interchangeable parts between similar genetic constructs (particularly valuable in dangerous team projects like space exploration). Finally, cloning would create the possibility of intimate

certain that, "If you build it, they will come." Triple digit exploitation without hurting your Happiness quotient doesn't come often.

The only competing Wonder in this timeframe is likely to be the Star Ladder. Since the Star Ladder allows you to build a Space City, boost your food by 15 units, and your production capacity by five units, it's a pretty tempting choice, as well. The latter is slightly more expensive than the Dinosaur Park, however, so your choice will rest on a combination of factors, including cost and priority of gold, production, and food. Naturally, if your goal is to build up your gold quickly, the Dinosaur Park Wonder is superior. Long-range, you'll have to make a tough decision.

communication (i.e., less misunderstanding) between persons of like genetic construction (particularly ending the gender gap between parents and offspring).

Some of the difficulties with these arguments reflect the fact that limiting the gene pool to allegedly desirable traits is fine in a static environment, but not in a constantly changing world such as Earth. In imposing such limitations, it is questionable whether there would be sufficient latent variability in this "improved" gene pool to preserve humankind's (or even the animal kingdom's) inherent adaptability. In short, we might potentially design ourselves into an evolutionary cul-de-sac. Further, anyone who has observed monozygotic human twins should note that the intimate communication so engendered from sharing the same genetic material is sporadic and undependable at best.

## Military Advantages

The question of whether to build the Dinosaur Park at this stage in the game depends on your attitude toward Trade. Some Alexander-style players don't do a lot of Trade because they know they're going to be going to war with their rivals soon enough as it is. They don't want to lose the Trade Routes whenever they go to war. Rather than micro-manage their economies to allow for such a loss, they would rather focus on general production issues. If, however, you have Trade Routes in the appropriate city, by all means build the Dinosaur Park. The bump in income will fuel your war machine quite nicely. Obviously, you shouldn't bother if you don't have any or many Trade Routes in the city in question.

Regardless of the background of the cloning concept, the possibility intrigued a novelist named Michael Crichton. After writing a novel where a scientist indeed accomplishes what Dawkins suggests in the quotation that precedes this discussion, the *Jurassic Park* film brought this concept into the minds of the masses. Ironically, the crisis at the amusement park with dinosaurs *in situ* comes about because the park's environment is not static. The human variable causes havoc, which accelerates into disaster.

In *Civilization: Call to Power*, the Dinosaur Park Wonder is built in the 22nd century and is predicated on the DNA decoding accomplished during the Genome Project. Its effect is to dramatically increase the power of your Trade Routes. This makes it an extremely valuable economic Wonder.

At this point in the game, you are probably better off building the Star Ladder Wonder. The Star Ladder Wonder gives you a boost in food (always welcome) and production without interfering with the prosecution of any of your offensives. Since the Star Ladder is not tied to any relationships with rival civilizations, it gives you advantages without the disadvantages attached to the Dinosaur Park boost. Of course, as with any Wonder, it may be to your advantage to construct the Dinosaur Park simply to deprive a rival with several Trade Routes from benefiting from it. Offense is, as your know, often the best defense.

# East India Company

*"Trading rights were obtained at Surat when Thomas Best defeated a much superior Portuguese fleet in 1612... In following years the Dutch and British East India Companies established trading posts scattered along the coast. The Indians welcomed the newcomers because they envisaged an opportunity to play off the three European nations against each other."*

—R. Earnest Dupuy and Trevor. N. Dupuy, The Encyclopedia of Military History

| | |
|---|---|
| **ERA:** | Renaissance |
| **BRANCH OF KNOWLEDGE:** | Sea |
| **DEVELOPMENT:** | Ocean-Faring + 4,320 Production Units = EAST INDIA COMPANY |
| **OBSOLESCENCE:** | Mass Production |
| **EFFECT:** | Gives the civilization building it 5 Gold for each foreign overseas Trade Route; All Naval Movement by this civilization increases by 1 |

## Political/Economic Advantages

Don't get us wrong; extra gold is always welcome. But when you consider that you have to pump the same amount of production and/or gold into this Wonder as you would into the London Stock Exchange for far less economic benefit, why bother? It's going to be difficult to get much out of this without a large number of Trade Routes, and that's a situation that invites Pirates, and inevitably, wars as well.

At one point, England was a second-rate power that narrowly escaped being a Spanish colony due to the bravery of a rather motley group of sailors, privateers, and scalawags led by Sir Francis Drake. The untimely death of Spanish naval leader Santa Cruz, and a fortuitous storm that sank the famed Spanish Armada (along with the accompanying invasion force) didn't hurt either. The fact that the British rose from this humble state to build afterwards the most far-flung empire the world had ever seen could be argued to be the greatest comeback for any nation in history.

England kept everything together with its navy, the most powerful in the world over three centuries, and to a lesser degree, its quintessentially profes-

If the East India Company were to expire a bit later, say, with Robotics, Jet Propulsion, or Computers, we could recommend building it. For now, however, the only reason would be if someone else completes the London Stock Exchange before you, and you were forced to switch to this Wonder.

## East India Company

sional, if small, army. Once control of an area was established, the British would politely, yet ruthlessly exploit the resources native to the area: tea from India, rubber from Southeast Asia, and furs and stout oak trees from the New World, among others.

The British weren't the first to do this; the Spanish, Mongols, the Romans, and even the Mayans come to mind, but Britain was the most efficient.

In *Call to Power*, the East India Company represents the synthesis of military and economic power that reached its peak in the Age of Mercantilism. It's a nice idea, but the problem is, this Wonder is

## Military Advantages

We always recommended building the Lighthouse in *Civilization II*, because it not only gave you an extra movement space at sea, it also allowed you to sail into deeper waters. Better yet, the Magellan's Expedition Wonder from *Civilization II* let you move an additional *two* spaces, and it *never* expired. So, we go from a potential *three* extra Naval Movement in *Civ II* to an additional *one* with the East India Company, and the latter expires early as well. Would-be admirals are advised to look elsewhere for a naval edge.

less effective for your economy than either Adam Smith's Trading Company from *Civilization II* or the London Stock Exchange in *Call to Power*. While we respect the British and their economic legacy, the East India Company strikes us as a case of one Wonder too many. Or more accurately, too little, too late.

And if it's economic relief for you military machine you crave, build the London Stock Exchange instead.

# Eden Project

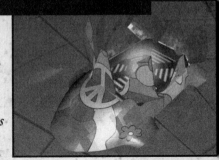

*"A chunk the size of a small country breaks off from Antarctica, as the long-frozen continent heats up."*— Michael D. Lemonick, One Big Bad Iceberg, Time, *March 20, 1995*

*"You can have any color you want, as long as it's green… 50 percent of our scientific laboratory R&D budget goes to environmental research."*

—Ford Motor Company advertisement, 1999

| | |
|---|---|
| **ERA:** | Diamond |
| **BRANCH OF KNOWLEDGE:** | Mechanical Discoveries |
| **DEVELOPMENT:** | Eden Project Advance + 8,000 Production Units = EDEN PROJECT |
| **OBSOLESCENCE:** | One-time use |
| **EFFECT:** | Converts the 3 most polluting cities on the map into parks |

## Political/Economic Advantages

If you are ahead in the game when following an economic/production strategy, it's quite possible that you have one of the three most polluting cities in the world, which makes the Eden Project a little risky. On the other hand, if you don't build it, some other civilization is almost certain to do so. Therefore, you need to make sure that you concentrate on building Recycling Plants, Eco-Transit systems, and Fusion Plants, all of which you should have discovered by this point in the game.

It's hard to read a national weekly magazine or watch the nightly news these days without some reference to the environment, whether positive or negative. Every year, Congress and the Oval Office debate the relative merits of balancing the national budget versus costly environmental protection legislation. In many areas, recycling such items as newspaper, glass, and certain types of plastics is voluntary. In some places, it's become the law of the land. Disasters such as floods are invariably big news, and a movie about a twister was one of last year's highest-grossing films.

It's fitting, then, that one of the major themes throughout every version of *Civilization* has been that of pollution and its effects on the environment.

One strategy that seems tempting, but generally doesn't work, is to try to rush the Gaia Controller Wonder before someone else completes the Eden Project. Problem is, if one of your cities is among the three most polluting, however the pollution is reduced, the pollution proportions will still be basically the same; your city will still be turned into a park, and you've wasted the time and resources on Gaia. If you are behind going into the endgame, however, this option can get you back into the game. In any case, think long and hard before you go green.

While Chapter 1 provides a pretty in-depth description of how pollution affects you, it's significant enough to repeat here that in *Civilization: Call to Power*, environmental effects are included for more than mere political correctness; they actually affect gameplay.

If the environment in *Call to Power* was doomed, and there was little you could do to change that fact, regardless of your personal feelings on the subject, you'd have to admit it wouldn't be much of a game.

## Military Advantages

If you are a fairly straightforward military commander, you are probably a little uneasy at the prospect of changing your government and building Ecoterrorists (for our tips on this and other types of Unconventional Warfare, see Chapter 3). If you pass on the Eden Project, however, you miss out on a great way to complement your conventional combat force.

Unless one of your cities is among the three most polluting in the world, the Eden Project lets you strike a blow against one, two, or maybe

Fortunately, there are several ways that you *can* positively affect the environment. Among these, the most aggressive choice you have is to change your government to an Ecotopia. In addition to using Ecoterrorists (see Chapter 3), you can build the Eden Project, which turns the three most polluting cities into lush, green parks. It's as if you've crossed Greenpeace with a group of rabid militants.

ven three of your chief rivals without having to fire a real hot (Big Polluter almost lways equals Big, Important City). Losing cities at this tage of the game gives those ivals a huge disadvantage oing into the endgame, and this could be the edge you need to win militarily.

Even if you don't win outright, the ability to create Park Rangers (only available after finishing the Eden Project) lets you send what is essentially a mobile Nanite bomb to take out enemy structures. It's guerilla warfare at its most surreal, but it's also generally very effective.

# Edison's Lab

*"The noisy, sputtering arc lamp was impractical for indoor use, but for that purpose the incandescent light bulb patented by Thomas Edison in 1880 became available in a few years and spread as swiftly as the growth of power plants permitted. In 1882 there were only 38 central power plants in the country, but before the end of the century there were over 3,000."*

—C. Vann Woodward, The Ordeal of Industrialization

*"Genius is ten percent inspiration and ninety percent perspiration."*

—*Thomas Edison*

| | |
|---|---|
| **ERA:** | Modern |
| **BRANCH OF KNOWLEDGE:** | Electricity |
| **DEVELOPMENT:** | Electricity + 7,200 Production Units = EDISON'S LAB |
| **OBSOLESCENCE:** | Alien Archaeology |
| **EFFECT:** | A chance to automatically discover every Advance you research (Averages to 10 free discoveries per age) |

## Political/Economic Advantages

For our money, Edison's Lab is one of the most critical Wonders in the entire game for a peaceful society. Every time you research an Advance, there is a chance that you will automatically discover it for free. In general, you benefit to the tune of ten free Advances per era (we've received as many as 13, which we consider a lucky number for a change). Since Edison's Lab doesn't expire until the discovery of Alien Archaeology, this can give you up to 24 Advances. In fact, if you are comfortably ahead in research, you can wait to discover Alien Archaeology, keeping the Edison's Lab Wonder active. This strategy can let you leap

Great scientists often do other things in life before their major breakthroughs occur. Albert Einstein, to name just one example, was a clerk before he rewrote the laws of physics with quantum mechanics. Thomas Edison was nowhere near the brilliant theorist that Einstein or Fermi was, and in fact, he lacked even the most basic of college degrees. But Edison was prolific and determined at his craft (he recently received a posthumous honorary degree). Eventually, Edison would become an incredibly successful inventor, garnering hundreds of patents that helped to bring the world into the 20th century at full speed.

Edison kept at his work for decades, long after most scientists would have faded. Inventing practical solutions to the problems of everyday life *was*

ahead of other Civilizations, even farther in the Flight, Medicine, Economics, and Cultural Advancement branches of research. Just think of the Wonders that you could start building long before your rivals even discover the requisite technologies!

You can also use your technological edge as a carrot, trading some of your less sensitive Tech for favorable Trade Routes or Treaties. And best of all, if you see signs that a jealous militaristic civilization is planning on coming after you, it's likely that you'll have

higher-tech units to defend yourself. Be careful that you don't get so wrapped up in the joy of research, however, that you fail to notice the sabres rattling.

Edison's life. It's been argued, for instance, that until the invention of compact disc audio technology in the 1980s (and the similar digital CD-ROM technology that lets you play games like *Call to Power*), there was very little change in the basic methods used to make sound recordings from those Edison pioneered a century ago.

For many of his successes, Edison partnered with J. Pierpont Morgan, whose wealth financed Edison's practical applications and showed the way toward the privately funded scientific ventures that would remake the world in the following decades. Their greatest success was the incandescent light bulb, which let U.S. cities work and play at night; it was essential to the growth of America in the late 19th and early 20th centuries.

## Military Advantages

At first glance, it doesn't seem that Edison's Lab would be all that beneficial to the Alexander-style leader. But shiny new military units, like any improvement, are only possible through better Tech, and this Wonder is the shortest path to new Advances. It's hard to argue with up to ten free Advances per era, especially since research is rarely given as many resources by a militaristic society as a peaceful one.

Our favorite strategy when building this Wonder is to:

1. Make peace with as many nations as possible (unless, of course, we have one on the ropes).

2. Cut military spending and focus on research.

3. Develop new weapons systems before anyone else, particularly air power.

4. Then take out as many rivals as possible before the Diamond age.

Thus, it seems entirely appropriate to us that Edison's Lab would be one of the most practical Wonders in any game of *Call to Power*. Regardless of your overall strategy, it's hard to turn down a scientific boost that usually gives you ten or more free Advances per era. What a wonderful way to honor the memory of this most American of inventors!

When used correctly, this aggressive strategy can help you to win the game almost before the endgame begins.

There are other Wonders available during this stage of the game. But Hollywood is only preferable if you need cash to carry out an expensive military campaign, and it's only effective if other civilizations obligingly build lots of television sets. The more critical dilemma comes from whether to take the research boost that Edison's Lab affords, or to go for the more immediate effects of Contraception, which gives you additional Happiness in every city. If you're doing a reasonable job of keeping your cities from rioting, then by all means go for Edison. But if you are constantly having to create entertainers and compromise your production to keep the home folks happy, then it's Contraception first, light bulbs later.

# Egalitarian Act

*"We sailed into the port of New York in July of 1918. I was on deck, miserable and seasick, an' I didn't notice everyone startin' to cheer until the fella beside me gave me a nudge. An' I looked up an' there was the most beautiful lady I ever seen in me life."*

—*Garth Ennis, Preacher: Proud Americans*

| | |
|---|---|
| **ERA:** | Diamond |
| **BRANCH OF KNOWLEDGE:** | Electricity/Virtual Democracy |
| **DEVELOPMENT:** | Virtual Democracy + 20,000 Production Units = EGALITARIAN ACT |
| **OBSOLESCENCE:** | None |
| **EFFECT:** | Causes all revolting Foreign Cities to join owner's civilization |

## Political/Economic Advantages

Used in conjunction with the Virtual Democracy form of government (which you must discover in order to build this Wonder), the Egalitarian Act can give you the economic and production cushion you need to win the endgame. Having all your citizens in every city celebrating for five straight turns is an incredible boost. During this period, make sure to maximize whatever it is you need most. Generally, we suggest that you either maximize production (to rapidly complete another Wonder), or pump up your research to get ahead of the crowd in the all-important search for the Wormhole and related technologies.

This is not to say that you should drop everything and build this Wonder. If, for example, you are in heated competition with your rivals to complete another impor-

In 1865, Union forces broke through Robert E. Lee's final defenses around Richmond, effectively bringing the American Civil War to a dramatic close. Hearing the news, Abraham Lincoln made a trip, despite the obvious danger to himself, to visit the captured Confederate capital. When General U.S. Grant asked his president what the occupying Union forces should do regarding the local populace, Lincoln replied, "Let 'em up easy, Sam. Let 'em up easy."

Of all political and social philosophies, Egalitarianism is the most difficult to achieve in the real world, as it calls for an end to all kinds of prejudice; racial, religious, lifestyle, and otherwise. Even in the United States, which considers itself the leader of the free world, it's hard for people to change their points of view, to lose the prejudices with which we are all raised.

ant late-game Wonder, such as the AI Entity or the Global E-Bank, you should consider passing on the Egalitarian Act. Likewise, if you are already comfortably ahead in the "alien space race," you'll probably finish the game before you'd be able to get the most out of the benefits of this Wonder. Keep in mind that if you should add cities to your empire from other civilizations losing them through revolt (the other major befit of the Egalitarian Act), it can seriously damage your credibility. All your neighbors know is that the city used to be theirs, and now it belongs to you, regardless of the fact you acquired it through peaceful means. This can drag you into a war you really don't want, unless you've built the ESP Center as well, in which case, the rest of the game should be smooth sailing.

So, when we view the video of the Egalitarian Act, it tends to elicit mixed emotions. On the one hand, it's easy to poke fun at the self-righteous tone, which resembles nothing so much as a public service announcement you'd probably see on late-night television. Still, the thought behind this particular Wonder is a worthy one that hearkens back to those words spoken by Lincoln to Grant so long ago; that anyone, even a defeated enemy, is worthy of being brought back within our good graces, to be accepted as an equal.

While Lincoln is best known as the Great Emancipator, in *Call to Power*, the Egalitarian Act is, in spirit at least, like the Lincoln we so admire, more so than the Emancipation Wonder is—so different than politicians of today. For all the alien DNA and Mind Control and various other science fiction trappings of the last stage of the game, this one Wonder makes it all worthwhile. It represents the chance to

## Military Advantages

The Egalitarian Act is a two-edged sword for the late-game militant. Virtual Democracy, for all its economic benefits, isn't a particularly efficient wartime government. Even so, if you really want to build this Wonder; if perhaps, another late-game Wonder

has slipped through your fingers, there are ways to use the Egalitarian Act to your advantage.

The economic benefits are just as helpful on the military side, especially since wartime governments at this stage of the

game tend to have a less than ecstatic populace. While your folks at home are positively giddy in celebration, you should launch an all-out assault at either an enemy you can eliminate, or to cripple an enemy that you consider your greatest threat. Since you only enjoy five turns of bliss, you will have to coordinate your

believe, if only within the context of a game, that the future will bring with it wisdom that can finally eliminate prejudice. In this respect, the Egalitarian Act serves as a futuristic Statue of Liberty, a beacon of light for all people.

Still, at the risk of allowing our usual cynicism to creep in, it does seem that even this Egalitarian idealism has its limits. Once you complete the Egalitarian Act, your citizens celebrate for five turns, which is certainly a big boost to your economy and the happiness of your cities. Plus, all revolting enemy cities immediately join your nation. Good stuff, to be sure, but wouldn't it be better if this golden age of enlightenment didn't have to end, at least not until the game is over?

forces to grab the most territory and destroy as many enemies as possible very quickly. After things return to normal, you are going to have to either give up the fight and return home, or risk a protracted conflict that will drain both your resources and your morale.

Another, more insidious method is go the subversive route. Using unconventional warfare, you have a very good chance of making enemy cities revolt, causing them to immediately come over to your side. However you justify this in your own mind, just be careful trying this tactic against other human players, as they tend not to see your point of view, especially late in the game.

In the end, for all of the Egalitarianism Act's worthy aspirations, the sad thing is that you can be very non-egalitarian and still win the game. After all, even Lincoln had to suspend the Writ of Habeus Corpus during the Civil War—nobody, it seems, is perfect.

# Emancipation Act

*"We all declare for liberty; but in using the same word, we do not all mean the same thing."*

—*Abraham Lincoln*, Address to the Sanitary Fair, Baltimore, MD *(April 18, 1864)*

| | |
|---|---|
| **ERA:** | Renaissance |
| **BRANCH OF KNOWLEDGE:** | Cultural Advancement |
| **DEVELOPMENT:** | Age of Reason + 5,760 Production Units = EMANCIPATION ACT |
| **OBSOLESCENCE:** | None |
| **EFFECT:** | Frees all slaves in the world. Cities with slaves in foreign civilizations (not yours) have a -3 happiness for the next 5 turns, and may suffer riots as a consequence. Riots are likely, but not inevitable if the city has ultra-happy people. |

## Political/Economic Advantages

If you are an empire-building player who prefers to play the economic-cultural side of the game's equation, the Emancipation Act wonder can be a terrific equalizer. Since it significantly weakens any slave-holding opponents, it is particularly useful to create disruption in said opponent's economy and advancement. Naturally, you won't want to build it if your civilization depends on slave labor.

Since the Emancipaton Act Wonder requires the Age of Reason as a prerequisite for its institution, it is a great Wonder to shoot for along the Cultural Advancement branch. The Age of Reason Advance itself weakens any opponent who has the Forbidden City, Labyrinth, Philosopher's Stone, Ramayana, Sphinx, or Stonehenge Wonders. It signals the maturing of the Renaissance Era and prepares your civilization for the move into the Modern Era.

On New Year's Day in 1863, President Abraham Lincoln ordered the emancipation of slaves in every portion of the United States of America. Since the Union did not recognize the legitimacy of the Confederacy, this order applied to all parts of the United States. Since the Confederacy disputed the authority of the Union in this matter, believing such to be the authority of the individual states, this action had the result of further infuriating the enemies of the President while serving as a largely symbolic action to his allies. Yet, the so-called Emancipation Proclamation proved to be a milestone that would rally troops and serve as an icon for the forces against the rebellion.

During the American Civil War, 100,000 of the slaves who were freed by the Emancipation Proclamation actually enlisted in the active military of the Union before even one year had passed from the initial

he Emancipation Act is a marvelous move if you are agging behind an opponent who uses slaves to supple- ent his or her civilization's abor force. It also guarantees hat no rival civilization will e able to use slave labor to atch up to your level of dvancement. Note, however, hat the Wonder costs twice s much as other Wonders in he time period. This is because the Emancipation Act never becomes obsolete. Once implemented, it affects all civilizations for all time. This high cost, of course, means that you will need to make sure that you are build- ing it within your city with the highest level of productiv- ity and that you will need to assign the building of defen- sive units and economic improvements to the lesser cities in your civilization. Naturally, if your opponents are not using slave labor, this Wonder is far too expensive to build and should be post- poned until it can truly impact your opponents.

order. Of these, half were armed and placed in combat ranks. As Lincoln himself noted in December of 1863, "Giving the double advantage of taking so much labor from the insurgent cause and supplying the places which otherwise must be filled with so many white men."

In *Civilization: Call to Power*, the Emancipation Act Wonder is not tied strictly to the historical action in the United States of America. It is a global act, founded upon the egalitarian principles of the Age of Reason, which precipitates action throughout the world. It immediately frees all slaves in any slaveholding civilization and potentially creates a riot situation in those cities that have slave populations. Hence, the Emancipation Act Wonder has the same dual function as that described by Lincoln. First, it reduces your enemy civilization's productivity (as well as your own, if you are using slave labor) by forcing

## Military Advantages

As observed in the main text, an offensive-minded conqueror can really utilize this Wonder to disrupt slave-holding civilizations. To take maximum advantage of this Wonder, an Alexander-like gamer should begin deploying military troops in the direction of slave-holding cities as soon as the Wonder is initiated. In this way, you may well be able to attack the target city as soon as the effects of the Wonder are invoked by the program. A city facing a riot situation or a city that has just completed its revolution is going to be much easier to conquer than a fortified city with a garrison. If you have enough units and your rival has enough slave-dependent

major cities into chaos. No matter which general strategy you are following, economic-cultural or military-conquest, it is helpful to reduce your enemy's capacity to move forward. Second, for those on the route of conquest, it means that either your enemy's ability to defend such cities will be reduced or that these cities may be so successful in throwing off the yoke of your enemy's tyranny that they form other civilizations entirely. In the case of the latter, these new civilizations will have had so little time to build up military capacity that they will be easy pickings for an advanced military state. Either way, you improve your chances.

The best feature of the Emancipation Act Wonder is that it never becomes obsolete. Once this Wonder enters the world, slavery is gone forever. This, of course, reflects the fact that once humankind has tasted the fruit of freedom, there is no return to a former life. As was the mantra in the Age of Reason, liberty is innate. So, it is in *Call to Power*.

cities, you could potentially take out a full civilization in a few short turns by using the Emancipation Act offensively.

Alert gamers will realize that using an Abolitionist unit next to a slave-holding city can generate much the same effect, but this costs 1,000 gold and is not permanent. If the rival civilization has a going slavery operation, it will be easy to start capturing slaves for use in other garrisoned cities, and this will require further effort and expenditure to accomplish what the Emancipation Act can accomplish globally and permanently. If you have only one rival slave-dependent city, use the Abolitionist unit's capability. If there are more, the Emancipation Act Wonder is well worth your while.

# ESP Center

*"I could never send my thoughts into any-body else's head. Even when the power was strongest in me, I couldn't transmit. I could only receive... So right there I was con-demned to be society's ugliest toad, the eaves-dropper, the voyeur."*

—*Robert Silverberg*, Dying Inside

| | |
|---|---|
| **ERA:** | Diamond |
| **BRANCH OF KNOWLEDGE:** | Medicine |
| **DEVELOPMENT:** | Mind Control + 14,400 Production Units = ESP CENTER |
| **OBSOLESCENCE:** | None |
| **EFFECT:** | Opens embassies in foreign civilizations even during war, and foreign civilizations have higher regard for owner. |

## Political/Economic Advantages

If you are trying to gain a victory through peaceful means, this is one of the most crucial Wonders in the game, well worth whatever you have to spend to get it. Not only does the ESP Center improve your standing with every other AI civilization, but it also prevents them (including human-controlled civilizations) from starting a war with you. If that isn't enough, it gives you permanent embassies for the remainder of the game: remember, The Forbidden City is obsolete by now (see elsewhere this chapter).

Thus, you can convert the remainder of your defense budget to research, toward your quest to find and grab the Wormhole. You'll find that setting up favorable trade routes will almost certainly be

One of the most intriguing themes in all of speculative fiction is that of telepathy, otherwise known as
extra-sensory perception, or simply ESP for short.
From old gothic horror movies and Spider-Man
comics to watching The Amazing Kreskin on the
*Tonight Show*, the idea that someone might be able to
perceive the environment with more than just the five
human senses has captured our imagination, even
though the evidence is muddled at best.

Lest you scoff too quickly, remember that hypnosis, a
valuable psychiatric tool, is based on little more than
certain cadences in the human voice. And while hypnosis has been used for more than 100 years, nobody
really knows *why* it works, much less why it doesn't
seem to work on everybody.

Even assuming that deriving the secrets of the human
mind causes a breakthrough that lets us, biochemically
or otherwise, use ESP, it stands to reason that it will

easier due to your newfound
charisma, and you can concentrate on maximizing your
production and growth.

We recommend that you
combine this Wonder with
the AI Entity, as it keeps you
form having to worry about
the happiness of your people.

It's very unlikely, especially on
higher difficulty levels, that
you'll be able to build both
the ESP Center and the
Immune Cell Project. But as
a rule, you won't have to go
to war, even through unconventional means like bio-
warfare, so you're probably
safe. Just be sure to not let

your ESP Center be taken
out by a natural disaster, or
an unnatural one, like the
Eden Project (see elsewhere
this chapter).

be many years before this "technology" has any practical application. Think about it; the experience for a potential ESPer would likely be traumatic, similar to someone blind since birth suddenly achieving sight. Specialists using ESP techniques would have to be trained to somehow shut out the cacophony of mental "voices" filling the telepath's brain.

On the other hand, if all the science fiction and horror authors were right, and there really are individuals out there who are capable of telepathy, why would they ever show themselves? Coming out of the ESP closet would almost certainly condemn them to being test subjects. In fact, they'd likely be removed from society and forced to breed more of their own kind. If released to do espionage, for example, they need never return home, because one assumes they could always evade potential captors simply by reading their thoughts. Therefore, what leader would be trusting or naïve enough to let a telepath out of his sight?

## Military Advantages

Given that, especially in a close game, it's not terribly likely that you'll be able to build both the ESP Center and the Immune Cell Project, we recommend that military-minded leaders go for the latter. However, if that option isn't available, or if despite our prediction, you actually *can* pull off building both Wonders, there are some reasons to do so.

Having everyone like you a little more sounds pretty wimpy, we realize. Nevertheless, it could allow you to sign a lasting treaty with a rival on one front (remember, no one can start wars with the holder of the ESP grail), leaving you free to crush a more dangerous opponent on the other flank. If you have tried at all to keep

All in all, it seems most likely to us that the classic ESPer would be one paranoid individual. Yet, in *Call to Power*'s altruistic future (which sometimes makes the goody-goody *Star Trek* folks seem normal), the ESP Center Wonder makes everyone like you better. It even prevents other nations from starting wars with you. Those must be really pure thoughts you're emanating, or else the ESP training is even better than advertised.

Anyway, in practical game terms, the ESP Center is a futuristic combination of *Civilization II*'s United Nations, Marco Polo's Embassy, and the Eiffel Tower, all rolled into one. The drawback is that you don't get this three-Wonders-in-one bargain until the game is 75 to 80 percent over. Trust us, it's still worth your time and money.

your reputation honorable (as we recommend in Chapter 4), you may even get the opportunity to form an alliance and crush a third party. After all, there still will be time to betray your erstwhile friend in the final turns of the endgame if you are close enough to winning via world conquest.

Finally, having free embassies everywhere is not to be taken lightly. Information is always a key to victory. And after the game's over, you can read all the minds of your enemies, and stay in control of your empire forever—ha-ha! (Okay, that's getting a little *too* paranoid, even for us).

# Forbidden City

*"Small Excess: Keeping still out of necessity. You are in a situation that requires great restraint and which can only be traversed in small steps. The solution is to trust that you do not know everything, and that trust in the power of the Unknown will safely see you through."*

—*I Ching, Hexagram Number 62*

*"Without seeing the magnificence of the royal palace, one can never sense the dignity of the emperor."*

—*T'ang Dynasty poet*

| | |
|---|---|
| **ERA:** | Ancient |
| **BRANCH OF KNOWLEDGE:** | Construction |
| **DEVELOPMENT:** | Engineering + 2,160 Production Units = FORBIDDEN CITY |
| **OBSOLESCENCE:** | Age of Reason |
| **EFFECT:** | Prevents other nations from starting wars with you; |
| | Automatically closes all foreign embassies; |
| | Earns higher regard from all other civilizations |

## Political/Economic Advantages

For those who revel in peaceful expansion, the Forbidden City is hardly as enticing as the Philosopher's Stone Wonder. Closing off foreign embassies tends to lose you profitable things like Trade Routes and exchanges of research. If you aren't careful, building the Forbidden City can play right into the hands of a rival militaristic government because it isolates you from potential allies, as well. An Alexander-style leader may use this situation to pick off other peaceful nations one by one, building his strength for the time when your Forbidden City "shield" becomes obsolete, at which time he will inevitably turn his conquering attentions to *you.*

If, however, you are doing well without the need for foreign aid, be that military or economic, you can use the Forbidden City as a short-term boost to your economy. Basically, you should stop all

Throughout history, the policy of isolationism generally doesn't bode well for a society over the long haul. Even if the Spanish hadn't brought smallpox to the New World, the Mayan and Incan empires were ripe for the plucking. Their lack of contact with other cultures had convinced them of their own superiority, and they were ill prepared to deal with strong evidence to the contrary. In this century, the United States' insistence on staying out of European politics contributed to both the start and the length of World Wars I and II. These things do go in cycles, however. One needs merely to look at this decade's American actions in the Gulf War, or the U.S. Federal Reserve's and U.S. Treasury's influence in helping to prevent a meltdown in the world economy, as recent examples of one nation's involvement on a global scale.

So, it seems curious to us that such an isolationist icon as the Forbidden City of China would be chosen

military expenditures, provided that you have your cities garrisoned against Barbarian incursions (see our recommendations in Chapter 3), and focus on research goals and building up gold reserves. When the Forbidden City Wonder is about to expire, start upgrading your defensive forces for the inevitable conflict.

One big exception to the above advice: If your research is about to thrust you into the Renaissance (less likely, but possible), ignore the Forbidden City and go for the East India Company instead, where all those foreign Trade Routes will fill your coffers with gold.

## Forbidden City

as a Wonder of the World in *Civilization: Call to Power*. Certainly the structure itself was magnificent, an opulent city-within-a-city in the heart of Beijing. The Meridian Gate alone, which forms the major entrance to the Forbidden City, was well over 100 feet tall. The Ming Dynasty was famous for its delicate construction, and the ceramics (certain Ming vases are now considered priceless) and the interior of the Forbidden City were showcases of their age, particularly the Imperial Garden, much of which survives intact today.

In game terms, the Forbidden City in *Call to Power* is an intriguing Wonder, though for most players, it won't be as effective as the Philosopher's Stone, available around the same time frame. The Forbidden City is reminiscent of the Great Wall from *Civilization II*, in that it prevents other nations from carrying on a

## Military Advantages

At this stage of the game, we recommend that your first priority should be to build the Philosopher's Stone Wonder instead, because of the advantage that an embassy in every civilization gives you. However, if you can't get that Wonder, the Forbidden City offers you an excellent alternative.

Face it, the Alexander-style leader is not all that concerned with undergoing the expense of building up potential Trade Routes only to conquer those nations and lose all that income. And while the ability to have foreign embassies is a good one due to the information you collect on your potential enemies, it's also a good policy to deny other nations similar access, and building the Forbidden City neatly accomplishes that goal by closing all foreign embassies. Plus, if another

war with your civilization. The Forbidden City does not offer, as the Great Wall once did, extra protection against Barbarians, but as we've shown in Chapter 3, you can deal with those foes fairly easily in any case. If you do decide to build the Forbidden City and isolate your civilization, keep in mind that this period of serenity will last only for a short time, as this Wonder expires more quickly than most.

civilization ripe for the plucking builds the Forbidden City, you won't be able to start wars with it until the Wonder expires during the Age of Reason. If you build the Forbidden City yourself, you deny that safety blanket to your enemies.

This brings us to the most underhanded trick you can employ with the Forbidden City. You see, no one can start wars with the owner of the Forbidden City, but there's nothing that prevents the Forbidden City *owner* from starting his own war. You can actually be quite aggressive in going after one civilization, confident that the others are forced to leave you alone, provided that they haven't already signed a Military Alliance with the civilization you are targeting. Just make sure that when you are near to completing this Wonder, you have the military force in place to take advantage of it; the Forbidden City doesn't last as long as the Sphinx.

# Gaia Controller

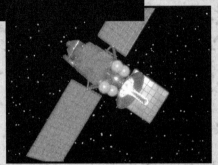

*"The observations and experiments so far made to test Gaia... have led to new discoveries, such as that the ocean algal bloom emit gases such as dimethyl sulphide that can affect the clouds and possibly the climate of the Earth."*

—James Lovelock, Preface to The SimEarth Bible

| | |
|---|---|
| **ERA:** | Diamond |
| **BRANCH OF KNOWLEDGE:** | Cultural Advancement |
| **DEVELOPMENT:** | Gaia Theory + 20,000 Production Units = GAIA CONTROLLER |
| **OBSOLESCENCE:** | None |
| **EFFECT:** | Ends threat of Global Disaster, +25% food boost to the host civilization |

## Political/Economic Advantages

Since you're predominantly focused on building your empire, as opposed to destroying that of others, constructing the Gaia Controller is a win-win situation. Not only do you avoid the hazards associated with global pollution (global warming which, in turn, causes disastrous flooding due to the melting of glaciers and ice fields), but you altruistically assist everyone else in the game world. That's probably a good thing, since many of them are likely to be your trading partners by the time this Wonder is available.

Best of all, you are the only one who gets the 25-percent food production boost from controlling the atmosphere and weather. After all, you are going to favor your fields the most, aren't you? Even as late

Gaia Theory, the scientific hypothesis that the Gaia Controller Wonder is based upon, suggests that the Earth is a system where the evolution of organisms is intricately interconnected with the evolution of the total environment. It all started during the glory days of the U.S. space program (AD 1965) when Dr. James Lovelock and Dr. Dian Hitchcock began to realize that the entire thrust of the space program's search for life in outer space was predicated upon the idea of Earth-like life. Hitchcock and Lovelock decided to find a method to detect life, even if it wasn't carbon-based. The initial tests modeled Earth's atmosphere and observed that inexplicable chemical adjustments were constantly taking place between the depletion of methane due to oxidation and the amount of oxygen depleted in the oxidizing process. Raw chemical reactions do not account for this, so he hypothesized a life principle to account for it.

In the game as the Gaia Controller Wonder becomes available, food production is at a premium. The other Wonders available during the early Diamond era or early endgame framework are solid, but food production should always be a number-one priority for empire builders who want to win economically. You can't win without human resources, and food production limits those human resources.

The only dilemma you may possibly face at this point in the game is the choice between building the Global E-Bank, taking advantage of the potential fiscal gain, and the Gaia Controller. Obviously, this will depend on whether you need food production or monetary production more at the moment of decision.

Later, Lovelock and a new partner, Andrew Watson, decided to test the Gaia hypothesis using a mathematical model. This model was called "Daisy World" and can be experienced by owners of the old *SimEarth* game on several personal computer platforms (Amiga, Macintosh, PC). Simply put, the more white daisies planted on a world, the more heat is reflected back toward the source. The increase in reflected heat brings about a cooler climate. So, black daisies grow in order to absorb the heat. Naturally, the proliferation of black daisies causes it to get warmer so that white daisies proliferate, starting the cycle again. Gaia Theory recognizes that the so-called albedo effect (amount of heat retained or reflected due to "whiteness") is only one variable in the complete living system known as Gaia (named after the classical goddess), but posits that this is a start.

## Military Advantages

You don't really want to help anyone else, do you? There are only a few good reasons for an Alexander-type player to construct the Gaia Controller. First, because your civilization is suffering from pollution, reduced production and flooding due to global warming. Second, you desperately need to pump up your food production in order to keep building military units. Or, third, because you've already zapped the biggest polluter in the world with the Eden Project.

Given the choice between constructing the Gaia Controller, the Eden Project, or the AI Entity (Wonders to be encountered in the early endgame), the latter two are likely to be your best bets. If your closest rival civilization happens to be a big polluter, it's worth building the Eden Project just to lop off three of

In *Civilization: Call to Power*, the Gaia Controller Wonder is depicted as a satellite which controls weather and atmosphere around the planet in order to reduce pollution and optimize food production. Obviously, such a contraption does not exist as of yet, and one wonders if indeed it could exist without humankind figuring some way to shift the balance back and undo the work of this scientific goddess, the Gaia Controller Wonder. Whether such an invention will ever be feasible or not, the beauty of the Gaia Controller Wonder is that it benefits everyone in general, while helping its builder the most.

his cities. If your empire is threatening to crumble from within because of a low Happiness quotient, the AI Entity looks like a stronger Wonder to choose at this point in the game. Of course, given a specific situation, a 25 percent food bonus is always welcome, and it's always satisfying to keep rival civilizations from getting such a bonus. The choice will depend on your game situation, but at 24,000 production units, you should make sure you're making the right choice. You won't have time to make up ground in the endgame if you choose poorly at this point.

# Galileo's Telescope

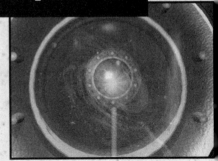

*"For the apparent irregular movement of the planets and their variable distances from the Earth, which cannot be understood as occurring in circles homocentric with the Earth, make it clear that the Earth is not the centre of their circular movements."*

—Nicolaus Copernicus, On The Revolutions of the Heavenly Spheres

| | |
|---|---|
| **ERA:** | Renaissance |
| **BRANCH OF KNOWLEDGE:** | Physical Science |
| **DEVELOPMENT:** | Optics (requires Mechanical Clock) + 2,880 |
| | Production Units = GALILEO'S TELESCOPE |
| **OBSOLESCENCE:** | Robotics |
| **EFFECT:** | Increases effect of Scientists by 200% in |
| | Host City |

## Political/Economic Advantages

The Galileo's Telescope Wonder is invaluable for a civilization that is trying to advance rapidly. The 200 percent increase in scientific productivity allows for a faster pace of Advances. This, in turn, can really assist you in catching up to, or pulling ahead of, an opponent as you approach the early portion of the mid-game. Note, however, that the usefulness of this Wonder is localized. Since the increase is predicated on the number of Scientist units in the city where the Wonder is built, you should only build this Wonder in a city where you have sufficient population to be able to exploit it. The more Scientist units that can logistically be assigned to the city, the faster those Advances will accumulate.

Remember that the increase is predicated on the number of Scientist units in the one city,

Galileo Galilei finished his life as a blind man. It is unclear whether or not this came about as a result of his peering directly into the sun with his telescope, but it is very clear that he opened the eyes of mankind. As late as 1597, Galileo was still supporting the idea that the Earth was stationary. When Johannes Kepler published his *Mysterium Cosmographicum*, defending the Copernican idea of the Earth revolving around the sun, Galileo was attracted to his reasoning but remained unconvinced.

By 1610, however, Galileo refined the refracting telescope, used it for astronomical purposes, and observed something amazing: the four satellites of Jupiter. Recognizing that if Jupiter could have four satellites rotating around it and still orbit the sun, the Earth could orbit the sun with its one satellite. The telescope so influenced Galileo's cosmology that he hoped to convince some of the church fathers of the Copernican theory in 1611. Though some of these

but the effects of the Wonder (increased scientific output) impacts your entire civilization. If you are an empire-building player who is more interested in winning by economic and cultural advancement than by conquest, such Wonders as Galileo's Telescope can make the difference between lagging behind the computer civilizations and pulling ahead. Once you get the Wonder, crank up the number of Scientist units in the host city by a magnitude and milk the Advances until the Robotics Advance negates your productivity during the early part of the Genetic Era.

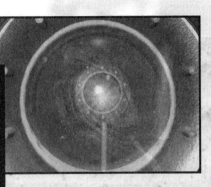

luminaries were impressed by the phenomena, they would not accede to the correctness of his theory. Fortunately, many people did recognize the truth by using this new invention. As a result of the evidence provided by the telescope, alongside Galileo's reasoning, the orthodox Christian doctrine that the Earth was the crown of God's creation and the center of the universe was threatened. Therefore, in an attempt to silence the threat, Galileo was tried before the Inquisition during the first half of 1633. During a period of house arrest following the trial, Galileo wrote a work entitled *Dialogue of the Two New Sciences* in which he advanced gravitational theory and the understanding of pendulum mechanics, greatly advancing the later work of Isaac Newton in gravity and Christiaan Huygens with the pendulum clock.

It is extremely appropriate that *Civilization: Call to Power* requires the Optics and Mechanical Clock Advances prior to being able to build the Galileo's

## Military Advantages

Galileo's Telescope is going to be rather peripheral for your overall strategy. Since it increases the scientific productivity in the host city, it can be useful for pushing forward on the branches of knowledge which can improve your military capacity. But the main reason to build Galileo's Telescope at the early mid-point of the game is to keep one of your closest competitors from getting it, and thereby leapfrogging past you in economic-cultural growth. At this point in the game, the Emancipation Act is potentially more useful to you. The Emancipation Act will throw your slave-holding enemy into disorder, which can be exploited by incursions of your troops.

Telescope Wonder. This reflects both Galileo's refining of the refracting telescope and his research into gravity and pendulum movement. It is also appropriate that the Galileo's Telescope Wonder usually appears late in the Renaissance Era of the game and appears in the flow chart at approximately the same point as the Age of Reason Advance. This is because both the philosophy surrounding the Age of Reason and the revolutionary scientific knowledge unveiled by Galileo's work caused great shock waves in the religious world of the time. Since the historical result of Galileo's work was the stimulation of further research into gravity and mechanics, it is appropriate that the Galileo's Telescope Wonder increases the Science level of production for every Scientist unit in the city where the Wonder is located. Also, since the later works of Galileo had to be smuggled out to Leyden and published under an assumed name (because of the papal verdict), it is appropriate that the effects of Galileo's Telescope Wonder is limited to the immediate vicinity of the Wonder itself.

Should your enemy build Galileo's Telescope, however, you will want to advance along the Mechanical Discoveries branch of knowledge as rapidly as possible. Not only will advancing on Mechanical Discoveries give you such advantages as Submarine and Destroyer units, but reaching the Robotics Advance will obsolete your opponent's Galileo's Telescope and give you both War Walker and Spy Plane units, two units more readily useful for your overall strategy.

# Genome Project

*"Begun in 1990, the U.S. Human Genome Project is a 15-year effort coordinated by the U.S. Department of Energy and the National Institutes of Health to: identify all the estimated 80,000 genes in human DNA; determine the sequences of the three billion chemical bases that make up human DNA; store this information in databases, and develop tools for data analysis."*

—The Human Genome Program, the U.S. Department of Energy

| | |
|---|---|
| **ERA:** | Modern |
| **BRANCH OF KNOWLEDGE:** | Medicine |
| **DEVELOPMENT:** | Genetics + 7,200 Production Units = GENOME PROJECT |
| **OBSOLESCENCE:** | Alien Archaeology |
| **EFFECT:** | Increases Production by 10%, +10% Health for all Units |

## Political/Economic Advantages

Any time you can increase Production, you'd be crazy not to consider it. The best thing for the economic-minded player is that the Genome Project comes at a mostly convenient time. The only real obstacle is that you might have to choose between this Wonder and Hollywood, or worse, between Genome and the Internet, with the latter being one of the great Wonders in the game.

If you have a choice, you should make the Genome Project a medium-high priority, even if it's only to keep this Wonder out of the hands of a military-minded enemy. Our only other complaint is why should this Wonder ever expire? Alien Archaeology is

*"We have the technology. We can rebuild him. Make him better than he was: stronger, faster."*

—*The Six Million Dollar Man*

Few pieces of fiction read as well as the exciting real-life discoveries of Francis Crick and James Watson. These two scientists combined forces to discover the double helix in 1953, unlocking the secrets of DNA, often called the "stuff of life itself." After gaining the Nobel Prize for Science, both men went on to unravel even more of the mysteries of the human design, including the functions of RNA and amino acids. Their activity, and that of thousands of other scientists and doctors, led eventually to the founding of an entirely new industry.

Genetic engineering has brought us everything from AIDS treatments and better vaccines for our kids to

the key to the game, certainly; but wouldn't you want an enhanced human (as opposed to an obsolete one) fighting for the alien spoils?

## Genome Project

skin replacements for serious burn victims. It has also brought new controversy in the form of cloned sheep, with the most obvious question being "Can a cloned human be far behind?"

For answers, we might turn to science fiction, which has speculated on the potential of a *Homo Superior* since H. G. Wells put pen to paper more than a century ago. Theoretically, humans could be faster, stronger, more intelligent, and the best news for the average Joe, we could live a long, long time. It is this idea that is explored in *Call to Power*, where the completion of the Genome Project enhances not just the way of life, but the individuals themselves. More food and manufactured goods are produced, but the

## Military Advantages

This Wonder is doubly effective for the Alexander-style leader, because you not only gain Production for your war machine, but all of your units, new and old, benefit from the ten-percent bump in strength. And this bump is crucial to your plans of world conquest. Think about it: You'd much rather have the ten-percent improvement on your side than that of your enemy, because it's a potential *20-percent edge* in combat quality—the difference between plus-ten-percent and minus-ten-percent.

If you have a chance to build the Genome Project, take it over Hollywood any time, even if the world is filled with

fighting soldier is more potent as well. All of which bodes well for the gamer: Regardless of which style of play you choose, you'll benefit from this Wonder.

TV sets. Unless, that is, you're planning on putting down your weapons for fights over Neilsen ratings instead...

# Global E-Bank

*"Trade curses everything it handles; and though you trade in messages from Heaven, the whole curse of trade attaches to the business."*

—*Henry David Thoreau*, Walden

| | |
|---|---|
| **ERA:** | Diamond |
| **BRANCH OF KNOWLEDGE:** | Economics |
| **DEVELOPMENT:** | Digital Encryption + 15,200 Production Units = GLOBAL E-BANK |
| **OBSOLESCENCE:** | Never |
| **EFFECT:** | Gives 10 gold for every Trade Route between two foreign civilizations |

## Political/Economic Advantages

You would think that the Global E-Bank Wonder would be the ideal Wonder for an empire-builder at this point in the game. After all, the operative words for empire-builders are trade and income. Since the Global E-Bank Wonder celebrates new efficiencies in Trade, it should be perfect for you, right? The problem is that the income from the Global E-Bank is not predicated upon your style, but on the style of your rival civilizations. If they don't have any Trade Routes, you don't get any income. So, if you're trying to build up and stay out of the way of a prospective Alexander-style conqueror, and you know that your rivals are mostly interested in the military aspects of the game, you shouldn't bother with the Global E-Bank option.

The only exception to the above counsel would be if you have plenty of bandwidth and there are no other Wonders eligible within the Modern Age. Then, you might build the Global

Although the documentation in *Civilization: Call to Power* rightly sees the idea of a Global E-Bank or digital bank for electronic currency as a 21st century offshoot of the Internet and the World Wide Web, the roots of a global economic currency are much older. Electronic currency on an international basis would, to some degree, accomplish for the world of the future what the gold standard accomplished for the world of the past. In the 19th century, the world economy functioned much like the domestic economy. Goods were free to move across borders with moderate or no tariffs, while gold provided both a stable universal exchange rate and transparent convertibility (i.e., your capital was always potentially liquid). In the 20th century, a combination of protectionist barriers, combined with the unwillingness of poorer, developing nations to tie their local currency to a standard which would cause said currency to deflate, had the impact of significantly complicating the international trade process.

**[ 245 ]**

E-Bank Wonder as a defensive mechanism so that your rivals cannot collect the ten gold per turn off of *your* Trade Routes. As you can tell, however, the likelihood of such a scenario is fairly unlikely.

At this point in the game, you're probably trying to decide whether to start the Eden Project, the Immunity Chip, or the Global E-Bank Wonder. Obviously, if your rivals don't have many Trade Routes, you'll need to consider one of the other two. In this case, we lean toward the Immunity Chip Wonder. A boost in Happiness is always welcome, and the ability to render innocuous the Infect City special attack could save your cities from a depopulating blow. We also think The Eden Project Wonder has plenty to commend it at this stage in the game. That way, you can eliminate one of the heavy polluters in the game at the same time as you gain the Eco-Ranger attack (the ability to turn enemy cities and tile improvements within two squares into parklands) at the same time.

As a result, from just prior to World War I to the restoration of currency convertibility in Western Europe (AD 1958), capital was not free to travel across international borders. Some investment instruments, such as ADRs (American Depository Receipts) allowed U.S. investors to purchase foreign stocks without actually converting currency (AD 1927), and the rise of the Euromarkets in the 1960s brought about an increase in foreign investment. Yet, the main beneficiaries to date have been arbitrageurs, those traders who make their money in the time-lapse between currency conversion and interest rate deviations.

The Global E-Bank hypothesizes a one-world global currency. In *Call to Power*, this currency is purely digital and relies upon an advancement in Digital Encryption to be effective. Obviously, a one-world currency would greatly simplify international trade,

## Military Advantages

If your rival civilizations are engaging in a significant amount of Trade, here is your chance to gain a lot with very little investment. Building the Global E-Bank Wonder means that you get to collect gold from foreign Trade Routes. You didn't build them. You don't have to maintain them, but you'll probably average as much profit as your empire-building competitors. Selecting this Wonder seems like a very Alexander-style approach to this section of the game.

As always in *Civilization: Call to Power*, there is a trade-off. Do you establish the Global E-Bank at the expense of not building either the Immunity Chip Wonder or the Eden Project Wonder? Again, the decision rests on your current game situation. If Happiness is low or you suspect that

as it would clear up the lapses and aberrations in currency conversions and interest rate changes. In such a world, the "banker" would undoubtedly profit. Hence, the builder of the Global E-Bank Wonder would get to profit from the Trade Routes owned by rival civilizations, making this a potentially lucrative resource to create.

your enemy may use the Infect City special attack derived from the Infector unit built after the Genetics Advance), the Immunity Chip is your best bet. If one of your competitor's civilizations is a stand-out polluter, you gain a lot of extra firepower by immediately wiping out three of your rival's cities

with the Eden Project (as well as gain the ability to build Eco-Ranger units that can turn rival cities into beautiful, new parklands).

Just remember that the more Trade Routes that belong to your opponents, the more valuable the Global E-Bank is. Without plenty of foreign routes, forget the E-Bank and go for something more pragmatic.

# GlobeSat

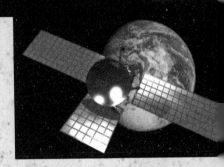

*"Clearly there was a sense of urgency after the launch of Sputnik 1, and especially after Sputnik 2 on November 3rd, so that the December 6th launch of Vanguard (1957) had a lot riding on it. Now, it was an untried rocket—that was a real problem— and there must have been a lot of pressure put on the engineers. Much of the pressure was self-directed. The rocket exploded spectacularly on national television."*

—*NASA Chief Historian Dr. Roger D. Launius,* New York Times *interview*

| | |
|---|---|
| **ERA:** | Modern |
| **BRANCH OF KNOWLEDGE:** | Economics |
| **DEVELOPMENT:** | Globenet + 7,200 Production Units = GLOBESAT |
| **OBSOLESCENCE:** | Cloaking |
| **EFFECT:** | Gives you radar coverage of the entire world |

## Political/Economic Advantages

The big problem with choosing whether to build the GlobeSat Wonder is that there are so many Wonders potentially available to you at the end of the Modern Era. If for some reason neither you nor anyone else has yet built the Contraception Wonder, it should take precedence. Happiness is a key when trying to win via the peaceful, research-oriented path.

And for a peaceful society, it's always tempting to fill the treasure chest with gold, which would have you leaning toward the Hollywood Wonder. But this is dependent on how many TV sets your rivals are building. If they aren't modernized enough to do that, how big of a threat can they be? Do you really need to see the

*"But knowledge of when, where and how the enemy will strike is no guarantee of victory. Forewarning cannot produce ships, or multiply trained pilots and their aircraft, like the miracle of the loaves and fishes."*

—*Gordon W. Prange,* Miracle at Midway

George Orwell tried to tell us 50 years ago that Big Brother was watching, but it's doubtful he could have imagined how much of our lives would be digitized, filmed, and recorded even before the 21st century. Consider the following simple examples: After we go to our automatic teller and get our cash, we walk into a convenience store and spend it, or maybe we just use our electronic debit card to buy gasoline. Either way, we're captured on a security camera, our smiling face recorded for posterity. We carry photo identification, we buy goods and services sometimes without walking into a store, and we use our social security number, which was originally supposed to be

whole map to protect yourself from potential threats?

In the end, it comes down to how Orwellian you feel. Those who are more paranoid will build the GlobeSat, regardless of the costs. Those comfortable with living in the postmodern world will save

their gold and production for another Wonder.

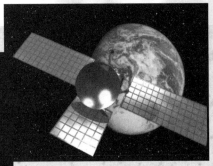

reserved for government use, to identify ourselves for everything from bank loans and tax returns to the simple opening of a new credit card account.

As what used to be science fiction now becomes mundane, we have to wonder where it all started. Our vote would be for the launch of the Sputnik. This Soviet satellite didn't simply achieve orbit around the Earth, it also became a defining moment of the Cold War and launched our culture into the Space Age. While we don't remember the launch itself (thankfully, we're not quite that old), we do recall that when Nixon visited China in the early 1970s, *Life* magazine ran a satellite photo of a man on a bicycle, riding down the streets of Beijing. Though a bit blurry, you could clearly read the make of the bicycle.

## Military Advantages

From Sun Tzu to General Schwartzkopf, military leaders have always stressed the importance of knowing more about the enemy than he knows about you. In that vein, the Globesat Wonder represents the quintessence of military intelligence. Much

like the Apollo Program in *Civilization II*, GlobeSat lets you see the entire map at once. Better yet, this Wonder (unlike Apollo in the older game), doesn't give someone else the chance to win the game because you're not much more than halfway

through a game of *Call to Power* at this point. It's the best Wonder to build if you are trying to find the last few cities to conquer and either knock out a crippled rival, or to win the game entirely.

With this Wonder, you can avoid most any conventional sneak attacks because you see

With such capability 25 years ago, it staggers the imagination to conceive of the future of surveillance 50 or 100 years from now. Thus, the GlobeSat Wonder in *Call to Power* may be science fiction, but it's more likely than most sci-fi predictions to come true. And what leader could resist the chance to spy on his enemies from a discreet distance?

them as they develop. This is also helpful against rival civilizations that have Nuke capability, because it gives you the opportunity, even if you can't stop the Nuke, to see exactly where it came from and plan your reprisal accordingly. Often, you can threaten other civilizations into concessions because you can call their bluff a lot easier than they can call yours. All in all, the GlobeSat gives you nearly unlimited intelligence for almost the remainder of the game, even against Stealth Aircraft, as Cloaking is one of the very last Advances to be discovered. GlobeSat is a bargain that no self-styled conqueror can afford to be without.

# Gutenberg's Bible

*"The advent of the cannon killed the feudal system; ink will kill the modern social organization."*

—Napoleon Bonaparte, quoted in Bertaut, Napoleon in His Own Words

| | |
|---|---|
| **ERA:** | Renaissance |
| **BRANCH OF KNOWLEDGE:** | Cultural Advancement |
| **DEVELOPMENT:** | Printing Press + 2,880 Production Units = GUTENBERG'S BIBLE |
| **OBSOLESCENCE:** | Mass Production |
| **EFFECTS:** | Gives 10% Science Bonus |
| | Gives Immunity Against Convert City Attacks |

## Political/Economic Advantages

Once you have Stonehenge and Confucius Academy, which are the optimal Wonders to start with in an economic-cultural approach, or in the next best configuration, one of the former and the Labyrinth Wonder, you'll need to choose between the Philosopher's Stone or the Gutenberg Bible Wonder. The former will put you in a stronger defensive position, but the latter has some significant advantages.

*Civilization: Call to Power* recognizes the efficacy of movable type in accelerating the transmission of information. Therefore, the most immediate effect from creating the Gutenberg Bible Wonder is to get a ten percent bonus for Science.

More important for the empire-builder might be the resistance to the Convert City command, particularly if your enemy is a Theocracy with the Hagia Sophia Wonder. In such a case, you'll need to raise the priority on the Gutenberg

Although the western world usually thinks of Gutenberg's Bible as the initial implementation of movable type, this invention really dates back to China. In China, block printing was common during the eighth or ninth century and movable type was used as early as the eleventh century. When Gutenberg actually printed his bible in AD 1456, the Chinese had been using movable type for centuries.

The most logical reason for the delay between the introduction of printing technology in China and its dissemination into Europe was the relative scarcity of inexpensive paper. As long as parchment was primarily made of animal skins, it wasn't significantly cheaper to use movable type over human copyists. In this case, labor was the inexpensive part of the equation. Even when Johannes Gutenberg introduced his printing press, it is estimated that it took the skins of 300 sheep to provide parchment enough to print his first bible.

Bible Wonder. The Hagia Sophia Wonder is a nightmare for the empire-builder because it increases the effectiveness of Cleric units when they use the Convert City command. It's bad enough when you start losing 20 percent of your city's income as a tithe, but losing 10 percent of a city's gold each turn is not merely regressive, it's anti-growth whether you believe in Keynsian or supply-side economics. If you are an empire-builder and don't have Gutenberg's Bible by the time you start receiving messages that a rival civilization has nearly finished the Hagia Sophia, you'll need to get the Gutenberg Bible Wonder as a defensive move—right away. Fortunately, both the Hagia Sophia and the Gutenberg Bible Wonders expire at the same time, with the Mass Production Advance.

If, however, there are no Theocracies on the board when it's time to consider this Wonder, but there are hostile civilizations, you might want to consider the Forbidden City option instead of Gutenberg's Bible.

Because the power of the printing press is both an impressive agent of social change through the dissemination of knowledge and a touchstone for providing constancy and continuity through its capacity for preserving knowledge, *Civilization: Call to Power* empowers the Gutenberg Bible Wonder with both effects. Representing the former, it provides a ten percent boost in scientific advancement throughout the civilization. Representing the latter, it allows civilizations to resist the Conversion command. In an age coexistent with the Hagia Sophia Wonder and the Cleric units associated with a Theocracy, this is an important function. No one wants to lose a percentage of their revenue as a "tithe" to the representatives of a foreign or rival Theocracy.

## Military Advantages

There are really only two good reasons for the Alexander-style player to create the Gutenberg Bible Wonder. First, if you already have the Forbidden City Wonder as a defensive tool, you should create the Gutenberg Bible Wonder in order to accelerate Science production. In this way, the ten percent bonus will permit you to build toward faster deployment of more advanced weaponry, letting you walk over your opponents as if they were escargot.

Second, even if you already have the Forbidden City Wonder to keep people from declaring war on you directly, you should build this Wonder immediately to stave off the effects of a Theocracy. If there are Theocracies in your world, create this Wonder. Cleric units can bleed you to death with the Convert City

Gutenberg's Bible is a major defensive move for any civilization facing an enemy Theocracy, but has too short of a lifespan to be worthwhile merely for its Science bonus. Think before you become a "publisher." It may be more expensive than you think.

command, and that inimical potentiality reduces the funds available for your war machine. If there is a Theocracy anywhere on the map, be sure to create the Gutenberg Bible Wonder. Obviously, this advice is doubly true if the Hagia Sophia Wonder has been completed or is near completion.

Finally, if you are steamrolling all of the civilizations that are near your borders, you may be able to leapfrog the Forbidden City Wonder and jump right to the Gutenberg Bible Wonder (if there are Theocracies in operation), or build the Hagia Sophia yourself (if you want to make some quick gold pieces and

play havoc with some rival civilizations in an indirect way). Just remember, it's better to be printing bibles than to be paying a 40 percent (or even a 20 percent, for that matter) "tithe" to your enemies.

# Hagia Sophia

*"Glory be to God who has thought me worthy to accomplish so great a work! O Solomon! I have vanquished you!"*

—*Emperor Justinian, December 26, AD 567*

| | |
|---|---|
| **ERA:** | Ancient |
| **BRANCH OF KNOWLEDGE:** | Theocracy |
| **DEVELOPMENT:** | Theocracy + 3,240 Production Units = HAGIA SOPHIA |
| **OBSOLESCENCE:** | Mass Production |
| **EFFECT:** | Doubles the Happiness associated with temples and cathedrals; Doubles the tithe exacted from any city successfully converted. |

## Political/Economic Advantages

Just as Justinian believed that he was building God's empire, empire-builders need to look seriously at the Hagia Sophia Wonder. If you weren't able to complete the Confucius Academy before a rival civilization did so, the Hagia Sophia Wonder is a marvelous stop-gap measure. Doubling the effectiveness of temples and cathedrals until the Mass Production Advance appears is extremely valuable. Of course, this does have the disadvantage of costing gold and production units in order to construct temples and cathedrals in each city in order to take advantage of this Wonder's feature. So, the Confucius Academy is more valuable to you at this point in the game if all you want to do is shore up your Happiness quotient.

If, however, you would like to conquer economically by using the Theocracy advance to convert other civilizations to the orthodoxy of your civilization's thinking, the Hagia Sophia becomes more valuable than the Confucius

After a rebellion in Constantinople, where the Senate building, public baths, imperial palace, and Church of Saint Sophia were destroyed (AD 532), Justinian immediately began to rebuild all of the public works in a grander style than ever before. The Senate house was replaced with a white marble edifice. The Baths of Zeuxippus were rebuilt in a multi-colored marble. A palace with marble buildings and brilliant mosaics on the ceilings replaced the wing destroyed in the revolt. A new summer palace was built across the Bosperus. And most importantly, the Church of Saint Sophia was no longer dedicated to one particular saint, but to the *Hagia Sophia*, the holy wisdom of God himself. The new cathedral, with its central dome was to become an architectural work synonymous with Byzantine architecture, as well as have influence on mosques and cathedrals throughout the world.

Academy. Once you've built the Hagia Sophia, your Cleric units become twice as effective at extracting income from cities who have been converted using the Convert City attack. Since the 20 percent of a converted city's gold "tithe" is doubled to 40 percent, this is the equivalent of the latter portion of the game, where a Televangelist unit extracts 40 percent of a converted city's gold when the foreign city has TV. This is an extremely powerful economic advantage, but requires you to stay in Theocracy mode in order to harvest its potential.

If you don't want to spend most of the early to mid-game mired in Theocracy, don't bother with the Hagia Sophia Wonder. There are better ways to glean Happiness points, and the economic advantage simply isn't there for any other form of government.

It took five years, 10,000 workers, and 320,000 pounds of gold to complete the Hagia Sophia. Justinian used Anthemius and Isidore, the most famous architects of the era, and spent a great deal of his own time at the construction site. The basic construction of the edifice was in the plan of a Greek cross, 250 feet by 225 feet with a small dome at each end of the cross and a central dome over the intersection of the crosspieces. The central dome was made of bricks in 30 different panels (half of which collapsed during the earthquake of AD 558 and had to be rebuilt by Isidore's son).

Many historians cite the eyewitness account of unnamed contemporaries with regard to the dome of the Hagia Sophia. It was called, "a work at once marvelous and terrifying, it seems rather to hang by a golden chain from heaven than to be supported by solid masonry." That the masonry was all too solid was indicated in the damage done in AD 558.

## Military Advantages

Naturally, you'll want to consider yourself to be the "Scourge of the Lord" if you activate this Wonder. As noted in the strategic considerations for the empire-building player, the Hagia Sophia Wonder simply isn't worthwhile unless you plan to form a Theocracy and stay in that form of government for quite a while—essentially from early game through mid-game. There are better ways to harvest Happiness units, and the Convert City attacks will work only if you plan to use an army of Cleric units as part of your offensive strategy.

If you already have a Theocracy, you should think about building the Hagia Sophia and performing the stealth fund-raising strategy. Remembering that the Convert City attack has only a 25 percent chance of detection should your Cleric unit fail (50% chance of success), you can send a wave of Cleric units into an allied civilization's

In *Civilization: Call to Power*, the Hagia Sophia Wonder reflects the influence that the architecture of the great cathedral had upon both Christian (primarily Eastern Orthodox traditions) and Islamic architecture. As such, constructing the Hagia Sophia Wonder immediately doubles the effectiveness of any temple or cathedral within your civilization. With the Happiness factor being a variable that is expensive to maintain, this is valuable in itself. However, the Wonder also has an offensive value. Should you change your civilization into a Theocracy, you can build Cleric units and start using the Convert City command to extort, er, fund raise, er, accept an offering from the target cities. The Hagia Sophia Wonder doubles the effectiveness of these efforts.

territory. Unless a Spy, Diplomat, or Cleric unit spots the Cleric units, they will be able to operate in stealth mode for a while. This can yield a significant amount of income for your war machine without having to actually go to war with a neighboring civilization. And it means that you can be operating on two fronts without having some of the inherent disadvantages of operating on those two fronts (i.e., you don't have to maintain two separate defensive perimeters). Of course, should you opt to take this approach and one of youe Cleric units get caught, you'll need to be prepared for a two-front war.

So, the Hagia Sophia Wonder isn't a high priority for the Alexander-style gamer, but it does offer some interesting possibilities for an Alexander who is willing to play Constantine for a while. It can be fun to extract funds and conquer in the name of the divine.

# Hollywood

*"I'd rather do an honest commercial than act in a dishonest film."*

—Orson Welles,
as quoted in Frank Brady's Citizen Welles

| | |
|---|---|
| **ERA:** | Modern |
| **BRANCH OF KNOWLEDGE:** | Economics |
| **DEVELOPMENT:** | Mass Media + 7,200 Production Units = HOLLYWOOD |
| **OBSOLESCENCE:** | Alien Archaeology |
| **EFFECT:** | Earns two gold per each foreign city that has TV |

## Political/Economic Advantages

You can never have too much gold in your coffers. Fortunately, the Hollywood Wonder provides a marvelous opportunity to continually exploit your enemies and enrich those coffers with no downside. If the graphs of rival civilizations seem to be keeping relative pace with your civilization, and you have a chance to build the Hollywood Wonder, take the opportunity by all means. Although the Wonder is relatively expensive by early mid-game standards, you don't have to do anything else to collect the income, and its obsolescence is quite a way down the line. If your rivals have Television studios in their cities, this Wonder can be amortized over a long period of time.

Hollywood has become representative of the *Weltanschaaung,* or philosophical/cultural value system of all popular culture. In the 20th century, the movie making industry turned into not only a big business that followed and reflected popular culture, but also an agent of change in facilitating cultural shifts within said culture. During numerous wars, but particularly during World War II, the propaganda value of film came to be realized. Later, the anti-Communist films of the 1950s and the pro-Civil Rights films of the 1960s, proved that film could be a solid instrument for social change.

Hollywood wasn't always the "film capital of the world." For a time, that distinction belonged to the eastern United States, where access to the stars of the legitimate theater made New York a desirable center for filming. This was fine as long as filming was largely a matter of capturing stage performances on

As is the current case in the film industry, where it takes effort to lose money due to international rights, television broadcast rights, and videocassette sales, the world very literally beats a path to your door when you control this industry. Further, it doesn't matter whether the world map for your game is small, medium, or large, the benefit from this Wonder accrues immediately upon completion, assuming that your rivals have the Television studios built in their cities. Naturally, if your rival civilizations are still building ancient units when you're ready to build the Hollywood Wonder, you may need to choose to build another Wonder first. After all, the income here is totally dependent upon the advent of Television among your rivals.

film, but as directors yearned to move the cameras outside, *a la* D. W. Griffith, the moderate climate and capacity to film all year round made Southern California seem more lucrative. As a result, most of the major studios moved to Hollywood by the 1920s, with First National Pictures being one of the last to move all of its production to Hollywood in 1927 (after leasing the old Biograph Studios in New York). That lot, after a buyout by Warner Brothers in 1928, became the existing Warner Brothers lot in Hollywood.

In *Civilization: Call to Power*, the Hollywood Wonder nets two gold pieces per foreign city with TV. This ability reflects the reality that U.S.-made films can be seen, both dubbed and with subtitles, on television in nearly every country of the world. Seeing old reruns of Vic Morrow in television's *Combat* dubbed into Japanese and shown on Tokyo television, or

## Military Advantages

Since funding for your war machine is always desirable, you need to consider the Hollywood Wonder when it becomes available to you. If you are already pulling well ahead of your rivals in Science advancements and number of cities and military units, you might want to hang onto your production units and build either the Genome Project Wonder or wait until you've nabbed the GlobeNet Advance and can build the GlobeSat Wonder. If your rivals aren't yet building Television studios in their cities, Hollywood isn't going to net you enough income in the short run to make up for the cost. However, the Genome Project Wonder enables you to boost productivity by ten percent (reflecting the superior abilities of your workers through eugenics) and, more importantly for an Alexander-style player,

viewing a dubbed version of *The Dirty Dozen*, where the protagonists talk about the Nazis while speaking German can be an amazing experience.

Residual payments (the two gold pieces per television-capable city) never seem to stop flowing in until this Wonder is made obsolete by the Alien Archaeology Advance. Apparently, the world will be more fascinated by artifacts from "real" alien civilizations than from viewing subtitled versions of *Star Trek*. Although initially expensive, the Hollywood Wonder is a marvelous gold mine with very little downside from any perspective.

dds an important hit point o every unit you command.

lso more valuable to the lexander-type than the Hollywood Wonder is the GlobeSat Wonder, which lets you see the entire map at nce. Hence, you can completely avoid any sneak ttacks. Hollywood becomes

a secondary priority to either of these Wonders.

If your rivals are making generous use of Television studios within their cities, the question becomes whether you want the immediate and lasting income of the Hollywood Wonder or will quickly be investing in the Genome

Project and the GlobeSat Wonders for more efficient military effectiveness. Although the choice seems clear to us, for every rule there is an exception.

# Immunity Chip

*"The programs in those computers that run your ships and your lives for you. Those bred what my body carries! This is what your sciences have done for me! You have infected me!"*

—Star Trek, *"The Way to Eden,"* Arthur Heinemann and Michael Richards

| | |
|---|---|
| **ERA:** | Diamond |
| **BRANCH OF KNOWLEDGE:** | Electricity |
| **DEVELOPMENT:** | Life Extension + 14,400 Production Units = IMMUNITY CHIP |
| **OBSOLESCENCE:** | None |
| **EFFECT:** | +5 happy citizens in owner's cities, also protects cities from biological attacks. |

## Political/Economic Advantages

Like the Cure to Cancer Wonder in *Civilization* and *Civilization II*, the Immunity Chip gives you additional happy people: in this case, five additional happy citizens per city. Therefore, if you are having trouble keeping your populace content, especially on the game's higher difficulty settings, then this is one medicinal cocktail you really should consider imbibing. Likewise, if your opponents, particularly in multiplayer games, are prone to play spoiler when you're in the lead, the Immunity Chip does offer peace of mind from unconventional bio-warfare attacks.

The Immunity Chip isn't particularly expensive to build, given where your economy should be by this late stage of the game (the Diamond Era). To put things in perspective, this Wonder is cheaper than the Global

Every time we have a chance in a game of *Call to Power* to build the Immunity Chip Wonder, we are reminded of some sage advice offered by Dr. Andrew Weil, the embodiment of the post-modern synthesis of traditional allopathic and "alternative" medicine: "If anyone offers you a miracle cure, and tells you that you'll never be sick again—find another doctor!"

Forgive us for being a bit cynical. But we live in an age when the United Nations must send inspectors to Iraq to make certain that Saddam Hussein's germ warfare stocks of botulism, anthrax, and influenza-of-the week are duly destroyed. Antibiotics, arguably the defining element of 20th-century medicine, have been over-prescribed to the point that some bacteria are now "wonder drug" bulletproof. Every year brings new retroviruses, and toxins increasingly infiltrate our environment. Bought any bottled drinking water lately?

-Bank, which you may actually be able to build earlier. till, as this stage also finds ou getting near the ndgame, you may be spending resources that could be etter used elsewhere. By ow, you should be trying ither to find the Wormhole o win via the "alien" method) or to conquer your nal opponents. If the folks at home are doing well enough, and there's no threat of a bio-war on the horizon, you should consider passing this Wonder by, unless you have a ton of resources to spend and/or you're trying to rack up the highest possible Civilization score. In any case, if you've reached the eighth Advance in Medicine (Mind Control), the AI Entity Wonder is a much better buy for assuring Happiness (see elsewhere this chapter).

## Immunity Chip

Amidst all this, the prospect that all disease might someday be eradicated seems a bit far-fetched, to say the least. On the other hand, while it's certainly possible for any would-be biologist to cook up something nasty in his home bathtub, the battle to conquer disease goes on as well, if for no other reason than that the potential rewards are so financially lucrative. Bought any stock in a genetic laboratory lately?

The most promising new technique is gene therapy, where the body's defensive systems, already so sophisticated that they are likened by many doctors to the complexity of the human brain and nervous system, are modified to recognize and respond to threats, even adaptable killers like AIDS and cancer. When and if those techniques are applied on a wider scale, they might cure even the common cold.

## Military Advantages

If you are trying to conquer the world, the Immunity Chip suddenly becomes much more attractive. In general, most players who commit to and carry out an aggressive military strategy tend to be less than understanding about environmental concerns. This makes them a target for Ecoterrorists and for Infector units, the latter of which the Immunity Chip can handle with no problem.

Also, if you are constantly sending out military units and carrying out wars under more advanced forms of government, such as Democracy or Multinational Republic, it's a constant struggle to kee the folks at home happy—th "CNN Effect," as we like to call it (see Chapter 4). The Immunity Chip, and the happiness the cure spreads, is a godsend when you are

Such is the implication in *Call to Power*, which assumes a future that even most science fiction literature shies away from—the total eradication of disease. In addition to making your citizens happier, the Immunity Chip (strangely enough, made possible through the final Advance in Electricity—don't ask) also protects you against some of the more wicked kinds of unconventional warfare in *Call to Power*: biotechnology that might make even old Saddam shudder.

rying to destroy your nemies, or simply wear hem down to the point hey can't stop you from winning by other means.

So, the Immunity Chip is by no means a substitute for the Sphinx (or the AI Entity Wonder), but it has its uses or those who think world peace is better served, even in the 28th century, with a sword (or a laser gun). It does make us think what a boring world the future must be, with no doctors, much less house calls. Then again, there won't be any HMOs.

# Internet

*1962–1969: "The Internet is first conceived in the early '60s. Under the leadership of the Department of Defense's Advanced Research Project Agency (ARPA), it grows from a paper architecture into a small network (ARPANET) intended to promote the sharing of super-computers amongst researchers in the United States."*

—www.pbs.org/internet/timeline

| ERA: | Modern |
|---|---|
| BRANCH OF KNOWLEDGE: | Electricity |
| DEVELOPMENT: | Computer + 7,200 Production Units = INTERNET |
| OBSOLESCENCE: | Alien Archaeology |
| EFFECT: | Gives a chance of receiving a free Advance every turn, but only from those known by foreign civilizations (an average of 10 Advances per age) |

## Political/Economic Advantages

The Internet is critical to the peaceful society. As the more militant empires in the game continue to stock their increasingly high-tech arsenals, you stand a very good chance of keeping up in the arms race through the Advances granted you by this Wonder. Keep in mind that because the Internet only gains you knowledge from foreign civilizations, it helps to make sure that you and your enemies (or your allies) aren't on a parallel research path.

The only reason we can think of that you wouldn't want to

*1998–99: "You've got mail."*

> —*Catch phrase that made America Online a household word,*
> *but couldn't be copyrighted*

If there is a true equivalent to the famed Great Library of Alexandria in the modern world, it has to be the Internet, that vast repository of easily downloadable data on nearly every subject imaginable. Originally, the World Wide Web, as it came to be known, was to be an area free of all restrictions on information, a way for common citizens to share experiences and ideas. But individuals and governments being what they are, the debate rages on what is "safe" or "appropriate" for everyone, especially kids, who often have access to the Internet in a way they never would have with "forbidden" books or magazines.

build this Wonder is if you are the paranoid type that simply has to have the GlobeSat instead, a Wonder generally of more use to a military leader.

So far, the Internet has managed to stay relatively free of regulation, controls, taxes, and the like. It's significant to note that when Gutenberg cranked up his printing press, the last comparable explosion of readily available information on such a cultural scale, he made the production of Bibles his first priority. It's hard to imagine the founders of the Web doing that. Thus, if the Internet can succeed on its own fiercely independent terms, it might be the most beneficial technological achievement for humanity, not just this century, but for centuries to come. It has already changed the way we think.

In *Call to Power*, the Internet offers an explosion of information. It gives you a chance of discovering an Advance for free every turn, which works out to 10 Advances per age in our experience. But there's a catch: You get only the Advances discovered by

## Military Advantages

Since the Alexander-style leader tends to focus on practical military applications, more mundane (or civilian, if you will) technology can often pass his civilization by. The Internet offers a rare opportunity to "fill in the holes" in your research tree without compromising your military machine. This Wonder is tremendously inexpensive, considering what you generally get out of it— 10 or more free Advances. Best of all, the more fervently your rivals try to increase their lead over you in scientific achievement, the more you tend to catch up, especially in games with seven or eight civilizations.

Unless you haven't built the GlobeSat Wonder yet, and you need the worldwide

foreign civilizations. We like this Wonder, not just because it gives you a lot of Advances for your money, but also because it makes you think globally. The founders of the Internet, both official and unofficial, would be justifiably proud of that achievement, especially since it takes place in a computer application.

nformation it provides to find and crush weaker foes, you should make the Internet a high priority. If you can build both without bankrupting your civilization, then by all means, go for it.

# Labyrinth

*"Furthermore he [Vulcan] wrought a green, like that which Daedalus once made in Cnossus for lovely Ariadne. Hereon there danced youths and maidens whom all would woo, with their hands on one another's wrists."*

—*Homer*, The Iliad (Book XVIII, 590)

| | |
|---|---|
| **ERA:** | Ancient |
| **BRANCH OF KNOWLEDGE:** | Sea Advances |
| **DEVELOPMENT:** | Ship Building + 2,160 Production Units = LABYRINTH |
| **OBSOLESCENCE:** | Age of Reason |
| **EFFECT:** | Allows host civilization to build free Caravan units |

## Political/Economic Advantages

Even for an empire-builder, the Labyrinth will often be the second Wonder to be built. Food is a primary consideration, so the Stonehenge Wonder with its 25 percent food production bonus is far more important. Plus, since the Labyrinth only allows you to build free Caravan units, it isn't going to do you a lot of good until you have other cities to engage in trade. So, the Labyrinth can be a nice second Wonder if you've decided to build plenty of cities on your own, or if

The Labyrinth Wonder is loosely based on the Labyrinth of Knossos (oft times Cnossos), a major portion of the famous palace of Minos, an early ruler of Crete. The first such palace was built circa 1900 BC. It was then destroyed and rebuilt around 1700 BC. Labyrinth comes from the root, *labrys*, which means sacred ax, indicating a ritual aspect to the site. Indeed, many of the classical Greek deities and rituals can be traced back to this culture.

Fittingly, the site of the Labyrinth of Knossos was discovered in 1878 by another Minos, Minos Kalokairinos. The great palace is located approximately five kilometers from the modern city of Iraklion. At the site are two palaces (the largest is 20,000 square meters), some dwellings for wealthy officials, a caravansary where travelers could bathe (complete with running water), and a royal tomb.

you've encountered a relatively friendly rival civilization with which to trade.

Of course, the more you plan to engage in trade, the better this Wonder is to procure.

Since each city with a Marketplace can maintain four incoming and four outgoing Trade Routes, and you are required to have one Caravan unit for every Trade Route, you potentially save a bundle of gold by building this Wonder, as well as eliminate the Caravan limit for the city where the Labyrinth resides.

The buildings feature elaborate frescoes and statues, indicating the luxurious and festive lifestyle that the ancient Greeks associated with Cretan civilization.

Within a smaller palace site, immediately west of Knossos' great palace, was discovered a magnificent statue of a bull's head. This statue is now in a museum in Heraklion and probably represents some connection with the "monster" that Minos' daughter assists Theseus in defeating. Bull's horns seem to be the significant sacred symbol of Knossos, and there are numerous reliefs of athletes vaulting over bull's horns and legends of women copulating with bulls to suggest that they are an important symbol of fertility for Cretan civilization. Thucydides was particularly impressed with the civilization of King Minos because of the extent to which these sea-faring peoples were able to trade and influence the rest of the Hellenic world.

## Military Advantages

Alexander-style players won't want to bother with the Labyrinth Wonder unless they already have Stonehenge and the Sphinx under their belts.

Stonehenge, of course, is vital to ensure valuable food production, and the Sphinx keeps your wartime expenses down. Since you'll want to conquer rival civilizations as quickly as possible, you don't want to keep building Trade Routes and losing them whenever you go to war with a rival civilization. Hence, the Labyrinth Wonder isn't a very high priority for you.

The stories of the Labyrinth and the so-called mino-taur fit nicely into this cradle of civilization. *Civilization: Call to Power* reflects the Wonder of the Greeks when they recognized the craftsmanship and luxuries provided by its trading orientation. To illustrate the fact that the citizens of King Minos' thalas-socracy were dependent upon the sea for their wealth, you must attain the Ship Building advance before you can build this Wonder. After you do, *Civ:CTP* rewards you for building the Labyrinth Wonder by allowing you to build free Caravan units and set up Trade Routes. This reflects the wealth brought about by this culture's sea-faring trade and expresses the high degree with which this civilization was generally held.

If, however, you are playing on a large world and you simply haven't found any victims by the time you complete the Ship Building Advance, it could be handy to construct the Labyrinth for two reasons. First, the extra gold from Caravan routes can certainly be useful for fueling the build up of your civilization's war machine. Second, building the Labyrinth early on denies the Wonder to any of your more peaceable empire-building rivals before you arrive in time to crush them. However, such a strategy is questionable for medium worlds and foolish for small worlds.

# London Stock Exchange

| | |
|---|---|
| **ERA:** | Renaissance |
| **BRANCH OF KNOWLEDGE:** | Economics |
| **DEVELOPMENT:** | Economics + 4,320 Production Units = LONDON STOCK EXCHANGE |
| **OBSOLESCENCE:** | Robotics |
| **EFFECT:** | Eliminates the Maintenance Costs for Improvements |

## Political/Economic Advantages

As observed in Chapter 2, any time you produce something, it takes the place of producing something else. This Guns versus Butter dilemma affects you whether you're building toward the Alien Synthesis Project endgame or trying to become the *Call to Power* version of Alexander the Great. Since each Improvement you produce has a fixed cost per round, the maintenance costs can ramp up regardless of the style of strategy you choose. The ability of the London Stock Exchange Wonder to privatize the Improvements within your civilization and eliminate the maintenance costs associated with those Improvements is a powerful consideration. It provides a net gain to your bottom line, a benefit any investor can understand.

The main problem with the London Stock Exchange is that it becomes obsolete a little too quickly for our taste. It is a late Renaissance Wonder that spoils us with those zero-cost services so that our civilization gets "sticker shock" when the first turn occurs after its obsolescence

During the period when the sun never set on the British Empire, private investors largely financed its industrial and economic expansion. Prior to the late 18th century, investors in London began to buy and sell shares in joint stock companies in various coffee-houses. As the number of joint stock companies expanded with the empire throughout the 18th century, the number of brokers and stockjobbers also increased. In 1773, the brokers opened their own subscription room in Threadneedle Street and voted to name the building the Stock Exchange.

The London Stock Exchange continued to expand as demand for new capital grew with Britain's industrial revolution in the 19th century. In 1801, a formal building was constructed in Chapel Court, Bartholomew Lane. Later that year, the rules of operation were agreed upon. Over 20 other stock

The good news is that completing this Wonder lets you build with impunity. The bad news is that you are likely to have to sell off some of the Improvements you build when the Wonder is cancelled. Of course, there is a way to avoid the sticker shock: Be certain that you are creating one Gold-producing Improvement or Wonder for every Production- or Happiness-enhancing Improvement or Wonder constructed. In this way, you will be using Keynesian economic theory to expand your income so that the potential "deficit" doesn't catch up with you at the time of obsolescence.

The London Stock Exchange is an outstanding purchase during this period in the game because it stimulates growth. Just make sure that you monitor that growth and don't get surprised when the party is over and, by decree of the *Call to Power* program, your economy faces potential recession or depression. The only rival purchase for an empire builder during this segment of the game is Galileo's Telescope. If this is still available and you're lagging behind your rivals in Science, Galileo's Telescope may be more critical to your needs than the London Stock Exchange. However, the London Stock Exchange gives you more flexibility.

exchanges were formed during that period of expansion. By 1965, the provincial exchanges had grouped together to form a Federation of Stock Exchanges. They amalgamated fully in 1973 and proceeded to merge with the Dublin Stock Exchange and London Stock Exchanges to form a unified body, which later became known as the International Stock Exchange of the United Kingdom and the Republic of Ireland. In 1996, when the European Union's Investment Services Directory ruled that each member state must have its own statutory regulation, the ISE-UK was split into a United Kingdom exchange and a Republic of Ireland exchange. In spite of this branching, the London Stock Exchange raised 2.7 billion pounds in Initial Public Offerings for international corporations in 1996.

## Military Advantages

As an Alexander-style player, the temptation is going to be to use the London Stock Exchange to accelerate Production and manufacture troops on an assembly line basis. Don't do it. If you do, you are likely to experience a severe contraction of your economy (and hence, your empire) when the Wonder becomes obsolete. Remember, more Gold makes it possible to build and, if needed, "Rush Buy" more troops. Therefore, it doesn't hurt to alternate a Gold-producing Improvement with a Production-enhancing unit (to spur military development), or a Happiness-inducing Improvement (to enable you to prosecute war without upsetting the home front).

The London Stock Exchange is the most versatile Wonder in this portion of the game because it frees your Gold

So, from the time of colonial expansion and industrial revolution forward, the London Stock Exchange has had a major impact on capital for the world's economy. Unlike securities markets in the United States (New York Stock Exchange, American Stock Exchange, and NASDAQ) which are influenced by governmental legislation, the London Stock Exchange is subject only to its own rules.

In *Civilization: Call to Power*, the capital formation provided by instituting the London Stock Exchange Wonder is abstracted into one simple, but valuable function. With the Wonder, you no longer have the maintenance costs for Improvements within your civilization. This function represents the privatization of these Improvements so that your citizenry will have the advantage of these institutions without the costs associated with them. This means, of course, a net gain in your civilization's treasury without having to worry about the discontent that would occur should you sell off one of them to balance your budget.

reserves to be able to build, produce, or accomplish nearly anything in the game. The period in which the capital formation associated with this Wonder is operative is a great time for shoring up gaps between your civilization and your rivals, as well as building some new units and moving your conquest timetable forward. In short, this is an ideal Wonder for any would-be Alexander.

Just remember to monitor your income potential as you use the London Stock Exchange so that you are ready to absorb the costs when you no longer have it. In this way, you don't end up losing most of your gains as soon as the Wonder becomes obsolete.

# Nanite Defuser

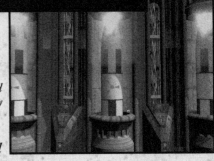

*"Nuclear weapons have become an international symbol of power and military prestige, what dreadnought battleships were before 1914."*

—A Quick and Dirty Guide to War, *James F. Dunnigan and Austin Bay*

*"Advances in microelectronic technology are just beginning to have an impact on medical care and should, in the long run, radically alter it."*

—Microelectronics: The Challenge of the Chip, *Simon Ramo and Max Weiss, from the 1969* Britannica Yearbook of Science and the Future

| | |
|---|---|
| **ERA:** | Genetic |
| **BRANCH OF KNOWLEDGE:** | Mechanical Discovery |
| **DEVELOPMENT:** | Nano-Assembly + 14,400 Production Units = NANITE DEFUSER |
| **OBSOLESCENCE:** | Never |
| **EFFECT:** | Eliminates all Nukes in the world |

## Political/Economic Advantages

If you are doing well in research, but you're worried about the threat of Nukes destroying your fair cities, the Nanite Defuser Wonder gives you peace of mind. This Wonder can often pay for itself within a reasonable amount of time, since you will no longer have to build Nukes to assure a Mutually Destructive deterrent.

However, by the time the Nanite Defuser is available, you are also getting close to the endgame. If you aren't

Microscopic hosts engineered to work within the confines of our bodies have existed in science fiction for decades. Sometimes, as in the movie *Fantastic Voyage*, they are human agents, scientifically shrunk to enter the bloodstream. The paradox concerning this potential technology is not so much whether the shrinking process could be done, but rather how to do it and still keep a human being functioning as a human being. In other words, does a human brain that's shrunk smaller than a microbe still have the intellectual capacity of a full-sized human brain? It's hard to say for sure, but it seems unlikely.

So, in more recent novels on the topic, authors have speculated exactly the opposite: How do we get agents already in the body to do what we want? In Greg Bear's *Blood Music*, a biologist genetically engineers improved white blood cells from his own

ahead in the research race, you should probably save your funds for the Primer and its scientific boost. We found during testing that in most cases where multiple civilizations survived to the endgame, one of the computer-controlled civilizations would build the Nanite Wonder, saving us the trouble. In a game with multiple human players (see Chapter 9), you can't count on that, and if your major rival in any game is Nuke-happy, you face a tough choice. If you make the wrong one, you either waste money, or you never survive to see the endgame.

## Nanite Defuser

blood, then injects himself with the improved product. As one would expect in a work of fiction, the white cells cooperate at first, but then develop a "mind" of their own. They refuse to stay within their host's body, moving by physical contact to the protagonist's girlfriend, by sneezing to his friends, and so forth.

So, maybe biological agents aren't the best idea. One alternative would be Nanites, microscopically small machines that would work inside the body. Generally they are assumed to be carbon-based so that the body being treated won't reject them while they're off killing cancer cells, clearing out clogged arteries, and whatnot. The idea is theoretically possible, according to some physicians and physicists.

## Military Advantages

For the military juggernaut, it's an easier choice to make. Building the Nanite Defuser makes a lot of sense:

1. For reasons we've already discussed elsewhere, the Gaia Wonder (available very soon after this) is not the best use of your production and gold.

2. It's probably too late to switch gears and go all-out for research at this late date, which means the Primer is out.

In the back story of *Call to Power*, Nanites are not limited to working inside the human body, however. They are able to be transmitted anywhere in the world, and their chief function is to enhance production (as an Improvement—see Chapter 6). But the most specialized function for Nanites, and the one we concern ourselves with here, is the ability to eliminate nuclear weapons through the creation of the Nanite Defuser Wonder. The great irony in *Call to Power* is that the Nanite Defuser doesn't actually defuse other Nanites.

3. You should have already built the Sensorium Wonder.

4. If you are doing well militarily, one of the few ways for your weaker opponents to strike a decisive blow at you is through the use of Nukes. By building this, you shift the emphasis back to conventional weapons, where you should have the edge.

All in all, the Nanite Defuser is relatively inexpensive, and it reduces your opponents' options. What more could a military commander ask for?

# National Shield

*"An electrical static-discharge forcefield? How primitive!"*
*"Yes, but still quite effective, don't you think?"*

—Doctor Who, *"The Stones of Blood"*
by David Fisher

| | |
|---|---|
| **ERA:** | Genetic |
| **BRANCH OF KNOWLEDGE:** | Electricity |
| **DEVELOPMENT:** | Unified Physics + 20,000 Production Units = NATIONAL SHIELD |
| **OBSOLESCENCE:** | None |
| **EFFECT:** | Creates a Forcefield in every City |

## Political/Economic Advantages

The first thing most gamers will do is look at the proliferation of Nukes around the map and seriously consider building this Wonder. Or worse, they'll have no good intelligence to rely upon, and will assume that Nukes are proliferating around the map, which leads down the road to panic. Regardless of your paranoia level, and to be fair, you may not be paranoid, you are almost always better off researching down the Mechanical Discoveries path and building the Nanite Defuser Wonder to destroy al the Nukes. After all, as a peaceful society, why would you ever want to build them

The use of energy fields to protect individuals and space vessels has been a staple of science fiction since before World War II, and the idea has been so popularized in movies and television shows, such as *Star Trek* and *Star Wars*, that it's become part of our culture. How many times have we been faced with a seemingly impossible task and joked, "Captain, the shields canna take any more! One more hit like that..."

ourself (except as a Mutually Assured Destruction defense)?

f it isn't Nukes you're worried about, but conventional warfare, the National Shield ffers a +500 percent defense or all of your cities. Then,

building it makes a bit more sense because the 24,000 spent toward the Wonder would otherwise build only four Forcefield improvements at 6,000 apiece. Just keep in mind that even a Forcefield in each city may not stop a

concerted conventional war effort or a series of Nukes. And if you build the National Shield, it's unlikely that you'll be able to afford the Sensorium with its gift of Happiness for your people.

Nowadays, such technology is not merely theoretically possible, it's actually used in practical devices, such as electronic fences around homes and aggressive anti-theft electrical devices on expensive cars. You can even replace that bottle of pepper spray with a handy and rechargeable electro-shock device to dismiss any muggers you might meet in a dark alley.

Even so, it's a big leap from individual, home, or car security to believe that we could protect an entire nation through the use of forcefields projected from satellites in orbit. But there are certainly surprises awaiting us in the next century, so we suggest you keep an open mind.

## Military Advantages

The National Shield Wonder can give you a strong defense, but this Wonder makes even less sense for the military-minded than for the peaceful society. If you build it, you are essentially saying that your strategy to conquer the world is not working out at all. It's a lot easier to justify the Nanite Defuser, or even the Sensorium. Pass this one by, unless your foes have ganged up on you and you are in danger of losing the game.

Our concerns center more around the utility of the National Shield as it works in a game of *Call to Power*. It's really expensive, particularly given when it's available in the game, fairly early in the Genetic Era. Before you decide on this Wonder, make sure it's beneficial to you in the game, and not just something you're building out of nostalgia to fulfill your Captain Kirk fantasies.

Having said that, there is one sneaky trick you might consider. If your research is going along fairly smoothly, start as if you were building the National Shield, then switch over to the Sensorium as soon as it's available (it's only one more Advance down the Electrical path). Not only will you likely snatch the Sensorium out from underneath another Civilization while you're "building" the National Shield, your rivals might also be so foolish as to think that you've gone on the strategic defensive. If so, it'll be a costly mistake on their part, perhaps their last.

# Philosopher's Stone

*"This Stone hath power to profite;*
*It maketh Multiplicacion*
*Of Gold and the fixacion,*
*It causeth and of this babite,*
*He doth the werke to be parfite:"*

—*John Gower*, "Concerning the Philosopher's Stone"

| | |
|---|---|
| **ERA:** | Ancient |
| **BRANCH OF KNOWLEDGE:** | Defensive War |
| **DEVELOPMENT:** | Alchemy + 2,880 Production Units = PHILOSOPHER'S STONE |
| **OBSOLESCENCE:** | Age of Reason |
| **EFFECT:** | Gives you an Embassy with every civilization |

## Political/Economic Advantages

Empire-builders should welcome this Wonder as soon as they can purchase it. The ability to have embassies in every rival civilization is invaluable. Want to avoid open warfare? Offer a quick peace treaty to an encroaching neighbor. Want to engage in a bit of gunboat diplomacy? Rattle your sabers by threatening any rival trespassers. Want to get a new Trade Route established? Make an offer to a distant civilization. You'll just need to watch out for Piracy if the Trade Route passes any hostile civilizations. In short, whether you're trying to create allies, stave off enemies, o find new consumers or goods the Philosopher's Stone Wonder is extremely useful.

The Philosopher's Stone is ideal for the early mid-game

The Philosopher's Stone was the name alchemists gave to the elusive, unknown metal which, when melted and combined with a common metal, would transform ordinary ore into gold. Obviously, modern man knows of no such element. So, it seems strange that *Civilization: Call to Power* would celebrate a "Wonder" which doesn't exactly exist. The logic is that the myth of a Philosopher's Stone is so powerful that it draws all of the civilizations in the game to its host civilization.

In general, gaining the Philosopher's Stone Wonder should be considered tantamount to having created a vast medieval chemistry laboratory. Although there is no empirical evidence of such a miraculous element, the practice of alchemy led humankind toward numerous chemical discoveries. Some would suggest that these discoveries were incidental, but the truth is that alchemy was probably the most scientific of all medieval disciplines in its methodology.

ortion of *Call to Power*. In ur testing, we found that the I civilizations are usually menable to peaceful over- ures. So, you can at least emporarily freeze your ene- nies from encroachment or ave off potential war while rying to build up your eco- omic power base or defen- sive capability. Since you will normally have the Wonder for only a short period of time in this portion of the game, be certain to create as many diplomatic and trade overtures as possible. Then, when the Age of Reason Advance sets in, you won't be hurt very much by losing the Wonder. Indeed, if you're planning to be strictly an empire-builder in the game, simply attempt to gain a peace treaty or alliance with every civilization in the game.

In *Call to Power*, the Philosopher's Stone Wonder represents some of the great medieval alchemists like Jabir ibn Hayyan (AD 702-765), to whom hundreds of later works were attributed. Many of ibn Hayyan's discoveries were influential on later European chemistry. The Philosopher's Stone also represents Franciscans prior to AD 1307, such as Brother Elias and Grosseteste. The latter alchemists argued for the transmutability of metal prior to the pronouncement by the church that alchemy should be considered to be a diabolical art. This did not stop European kings from employing alchemists in an attempt to enrich their treasuries, however.

## Military Advantages

Of course, the military side of the equation is a little more complex. Your goal as an Alexander-style leader is to confuse, disrupt, disable, and eliminate the enemy by any means possible. It is particularly advantageous to use your diplomatic communication to demand an end to trespassing with one civilization, while taking out another civilization simultaneously. If the rival civilization accepts your demand, that means it will take time for the civilization to find another direction to expand. This not only gives you time to destroy the other civilization, but time to mobilize forces on the unsuspecting civilization's border.

The best part of building the Philosopher's Stone Wonder at this point in time is that you get automatic embassies in every civilization. This opens up opportunities for spying on your potential enemies and knowing exactly what kind of strength they can bring to bear. Unless you rival civilization has the Forbidden City Wonder and can close off the military

*Call to Power*'s Philosopher's Stone sits on the border between the Ancient and Renaissance ages. Although it is soon made obsolete by the Age of Reason Advance, it is particularly valuable for the short time you are likely to have it. The Wonder automatically opens an Embassy for your civilization within every rival civilization. Whether you are playing on a small map and need to make contacts quickly, or playing on a medium or large map and want to have contact with civilizations prior to officially discovering them, the Philosopher's Stone is a terrific Wonder.

intelligence aspects of your embassy, this helps you pick out the right targets in a potentially target rich environment.

To further take advantage of the Philosopher's Stone, you'll want to open up some Trade Routes with those civilizations which are furthest away from your own. These foreign civilizations should be less likely to come after your civilization since the loss of income would be factored into the equation. Meanwhile, you'll be garnering gold to fuel the war machine, making it tougher than ever on the civilizations nearest at hand.

In short, the Philosopher's Stone is potentially the best Wonder to have in this period just before the early mid-game. It provides opportunities for garnering gold through trade, gaining ground through diplomacy, and grinding gains through application of military intelligence. If you don't have the opportunity to get this Wonder, you'd better invest in the Forbidden City Wonder right away.

# Nanopedia

*"In the end, our individual presence rests forever in the collective soul of the unfolding process itself."*

—Entropy, *Jeremy Rifkin with Ted Howard*

*"Tomorrow belongs to us."*

—*British Labour Party leader Harold Wilson, 1964 broadcast [Though echoed later by Margaret Thatcher, the slogan has rarely been uttered by youth groups, which it presumably represents.*

| | |
|---|---|
| **ERA:** | Genetic |
| **BRANCH OF KNOWLEDGE:** | Mechanical Discoveries |
| **DEVELOPMENT:** | Nano-Assembly + 14,400 Production Units = PRIMER |
| **OBSOLESCENCE:** | Never |
| **EFFECT:** | Doubles the effect of all Specialists in your civilization |

## Political/Economic Advantages

Choices, choices; what to do? You are faced with the possibility of building the Nanite Defuser, the Gaia Controller, and maybe even the Immunity Chip, all at around the same time. If you fear attacks from biological or nuclear means, you have to go with your gut feelings on the Nanite Defuser or the Immunity Chip (but be sure to check out our tips on those Wonders elsewhere in this chapter).

The term "interactive entertainment" gets thrown around a lot, as does "edutainment." Both of them refer to multimedia constructs that theoretically allow you to move at your own pace for entertainment or learning, though the structure and technology of today's programs tend to limit their range and utility, despite their lofty aspirations. In *Civilization: Call to Power*, the back story suggests that in the future, learning will happen all throughout our lives (which one could argue that it does anyway), and that this process will be enhanced through a variety of technology.

If your nerves are steely enough, we suggest that you go for the Nanopedia. Doubling the effect of your Specialists can bring you faster research, more food and growth, more money, more Happiness, or more production—whatever you might need on a given turn, all throughout your civilization. This boost can help you discover and build the Wormhole Sensor faster than your rivals, which is the most interesting way for a peaceful empire to win in *Call to Power*.

## Nanopedia

The culmination of all this technology is the Nanopedia Wonder, which so enriches everyone's lives that it doubles the effectiveness of all Specialists in the city in which it is built. If, like us, you're a little confused on exactly what the concept represents, don't question it. Just build the Wonder if you need a food, happiness, or research boost. The Nanopedia is a most versatile Wonder.

## Military Advantages

Given that you aren't likely to need the extra research, the only reason to build the Nanopedia would be if you needed extra cash to crack out units in a mad rush to win the game militarily before the Wormhole pops up.

Since you are also probably able to build the Nanite Defuser, the Eden Project, and possibly even the AI Entity by now, the Nanopedia simply doesn't make sense for your empire as you enter the endgame.

# Ramayana

*"There has to be a woman. There has to be a man. And there has to be a divine spark."*

—*Burton L. Visotzky, from Bill Moyers'* Genesis: A Living Conversation

| | |
|---|---|
| **ERA:** | Ancient |
| **BRANCH OF KNOWLEDGE:** | Physical Science |
| **DEVELOPMENT:** | Religion + 2,160 Production Units = RAMAYANA |
| **OBSOLESCENCE:** | Age of Reason |
| **EFFECT:** | Increases the Happiness of all your cities by 3 |

## Political/Economic Advantages

The "Hidden truth supports everything," according to the Ramayana, and we would be less than honest if we didn't recommend this Wonder wholeheartedly for a peaceful-minded society. If you aren't spending tons of money and production for defense, you can really boost your economy by building this Wonder. The Ramayana relieves you of placing extra garrison troops to keep up the Happiness level, and it also frees up workers and merchants (once you discover Trade) that would otherwise be needed as entertainers.

Best of all, this Wonder is available early on, as soon as you discover Religion, the first Advance in the Physical Science branch of technology. Thus, it's possible to build the Ramayana relatively early

The *Ramayana* is an epic poem from India, consisting of thousands of lines, that has often been compared to Homer's *The Iliad*. Both tales are mythic, with heroes that perform seemingly impossible feats, and the gods of each religion (Hindu and Ancient Greek, respectively) make appearances throughout each story. Both tales seem to have come to us originally from an oral tradition before they were written down and formalized. But while it is generally agreed that there is one "true" version of the *Iliad*, there are multiple versions of the *Ramayana*, each with significant differences that reflect changing social conditions at the time each version of the story was told.

The differences between the two epics go even deeper. Although the *Iliad* focuses on the vagaries of fate, the follies of men, their fallible nature, and even the infighting and jealousies exhibited by the Greek gods, there aren't any totally evil characters. After all, Paris abducted Helen of Troy because he was in love with

n the game. On lower levels of difficulty, should you be lucky enough to start the game with Religion (see Chapter 2), you could even reasonably start building the Ramayana as soon as you've founded your third city.

As a result, while the Ramayana tends to be effective for fewer turns than many of the other Ancient Wonders, it's still around plenty long to help your cities grow quite quickly before you reach the end of the Renaissance with the Age of Reason Advance. Combined with the effect of temples, which you should be able to afford since you don't have heavy military expenditures, the Ramayana can keep your empire happy and productive for a very long time, especially considering how very affordable it is compared to other Wonders.

her and because she was the most beautiful woman in the history of the world. Even if you don't agree with the guy's actions, it's easy to see where he was coming from.

In the *Ramayana*, however, our hero must take on Ravana, the ruler of the rakshasas (demons), who represents evil incarnate. Ravana has ten heads, 20 arms, and a bad attitude. He seems to exist solely to prevent the good people of Ayodhya from performing their religious rituals. The gods are angered by this, but they can't put Ravana in his place because he has been granted a boon that he can not be harmed. Since Ravana, like most grand evildoers, has the tragic flaw of arrogance, he has neglected to have the boon protect him from humans and monkeys.

Thus, the god Vishnu decides to reincarnate in human form, specifically as our hero, Rama, in order to defeat Ravana. Rama is born as the son of Dasaratha, the king of Ayodhya. As the epic

## Military Advantages

When you are planning to start a war, it never hurts to have the folks back home feeling good about it (and about everything else, for that matter). If you've been forced to garrison your cities with additional units to keep the populace content, the

*Ramayana* does relieve that burden by increasing the Happiness level by three everywhere in your empire. It also helps you to grow your cities a bit faster, though perhaps not as quickly as the Oracle did in *Civilization II*. All in all, a great Wonder. But

chances are, the Alexander-style leader isn't going to be able to build the *Ramayana* because there are so many other Wonders more critical to his success.

Even this early in the game, the military-minded leader should make the Sphinx a higher priority for the

unfolds, Rama is banished for 14 years to prove his worthiness (a common theme in mythic literature), and Ravana kidnaps Rama's beautiful wife. Assisted by the powerful Monkey King, an assortment of brave soldiers, and one of his brothers (who, like Rama, carries a divine spark), Rama defeats 14,000 demons and even convinces Ravana's brother to aid him in his holy cause. After the defeat of Ravana, Rama must, in most versions of the tale, banish his wife. Although we know she has not been unfaithful to him, she lived in another man's home for months, unacceptable under the law—the tale is not altogether a happy one.

The designers of *Call to Power* could have used any heroic epic, from the *Tale of Gilgamesh* to *Beowulf*, for a Wonder of the World. But they chose the *Ramayana*, with its emphasis on not just overcoming mighty odds, but also living a good and honorable life and the effects of performing one's duty, even when it causes personal pain and sacrifice.

advantage it gives him in Military Readiness costs. And by the time you finish building the Sphinx, it's likely, especially on higher levels of difficulty, that the *Ramayana* will have been built by a rival civilization. Should you have a chance to build the *Ramayana* after completing the Sphinx, the decision is still not an easy one.

For example, if it's productivity you're concerned about, you should consider building Chichen Itza instead to eliminate the gold and resources that you lose due to crime; always a huge problem when trying to mount an offensive against another civilization. With a Theocracy in the game, the Hagia Sophia is a great choice as well. And both Chichen Itza and the Hagia Sophia last until the discovery of Mass Production, a lot later in the game than the *Ramayana*, which expires with the Age of Reason.

# Sensorium

*"Nature has placed mankind under the government of two sovereign masters, pain and pleasure. It is for them alone to point out what we ought to do, as well as to determine what we shall do."*

—*Jeremy Benthan,* Constitutional Code

| | |
|---|---|
| **ERA:** | Genetic |
| **BRANCH OF KNOWLEDGE:** | Electricity |
| **DEVELOPMENT:** | Neural Interface + 20,000 Production Units = SENSORIUM |
| **OBSOLESCENCE:** | Never |
| **EFFECT:** | Eliminates the unhappiness penalties for pollution and overcrowding |

## Political/Economic Advantages

Controlling an expanding empire doesn't always give you the leisure of considering far-flung environmental impacts. So, it's likely that you're going to face Pollution and Overcrowding problems as your empire expands. This raises unhappiness, which, of course, impacts your Happiness quotient. Then, you find yourself spending gold on theaters and temples, as well as diverting entertainers from your productivity in order to increase your Happiness quotient. Any Wonder that gives you a chance to reduce that unhappiness is going to save your resources from being spent in less productive areas. Since it is unlikely that you are going to be confronted with a choice between Wonders at this point in the game, you

An outgrowth of the neural jack referenced in the AI Entity summary, the Sensorium is a far-future development that far outdistances the simple stimulation of the pleasure center. Currently, the idea of wireheads experiencing pleasure from a direct connection to a neural jack is found in many science fiction books. William Gibson (*Neuromancer*) and others saw opportunity within this vision to connect the "cybercowboy" user directly with the data matrix so that it was possible to virtually traverse the network and face the personified demons of the counter-intrusion AIs (ICE). Norman Spinrad (*Little Heroes*) perceived of the entertainment value of such devices if a modernized entertainment industry could chart a population's psychographics and design virtual entertainers to appease them. George Alec Effinger (*When Gravity Fails*) wrote of personality modification chips where individuals could change personalities to be the

can feel free to construct the Sensorium as soon as it is available.

One exception to this strategy could be used if you were afraid of a rival civilization using nuclear weapons against you. In such a case, you might want to save your gold for when the Nanite Defuser Wonder becomes available. If you can make a "Rush Buy" of the Nanite Defuser and disarm all of your rival's nuclear capacity, you'll ensure a longer life expectancy for your civilization.

celebrities of their dreams. He also wrote a short story where individuals paid to live in consensual realities, essentially the kind of virtual resorts described in *Civilization: Call to Power*.

In the fiction behind *Call to Power*'s Sensorium Wonder is a predictive nature to this stimulation of the pleasure center. According to this fiction, a researcher named Linus Traum figured out how to predict what the user wanted, generate appropriate sensations to reflect that desire, and mentally transport the user to such a location. As in the Effinger short story, these virtual locations could become shared experiences or consensual realities, where several people could share the vivid hallucinations together. As a result, Sensorium scenarios became a new portion of the overall entertainment industry.

## Military Advantages

Generally, you shouldn't have a real conflict here, because one of your rivals has likely already built the National Shield in an attempt to slow down your military juggernaut. If the National Shield is still available, we suggest that the unhappiness-reducing capabilities of the Sensorium outweigh the defensive capabilities of the shield. Also, building the National Shield essentially says out loud to your opponents that your strategy of conquering the world is going rather badly.

Moreover, building a war machine invariably pollutes. Engaging in warfare has Happiness costs, to boot. So, anything you can do to reduce unhappiness is a positive for your war effort. Having the Sensorium Wonder reduces the unhappiness associated with pollution and overcrowding, and it

The Sensorium is a valuable Wonder because the shared hallucinations or consensual realities that it creates make citizens forget their discontent due to Pollution and Overcrowding effects. Since the Sensorium never becomes obsolete, it is a great tool for canceling out the effects of all the negative aspects of your civilization's growth.

llows you to continue prosecuting your offensive front.
Since you are not usually
confronted with another
Wonder from which to
choose during this portion of
the game, the decision is
clear. Build the Sensorium in
order to move forward with
the war effort.

# The Sphinx

*"True history is no mere record of dates, treaties, battles, kings, and generals. Aristotle long ago recognized this vital fact when he placed poetic truth higher than historical truth."*

—*William Fleming*, Arts and Ideas

| | |
|---|---|
| **ERA:** | Ancient |
| **BRANCH OF KNOWLEDGE:** | Cultural Advancement |
| **DEVELOPMENT:** | Stone Working + 2,160 Production Units = SPHINX |
| **OBSOLESCENCE:** | Age of Reason |
| **EFFECT:** | Reduces military support costs by 75 percent |

## Political/Economic Advantages

We know what you're thinking: "Why build the Sphinx if I'm not going to try to conquer the world?" Keep in mind that there are only *seven* Wonders of the Ancient World in *Call to Power*. Any time that you pass on a chance to build one of them for short-term economic gain, you lose in the long run. Moreover, the Sphinx is a boon for your economy, because it reduces your Military Readiness costs by 75 percent. This allows you to build cheaper units, such as Phalanxes and Archers, *strictly for defensive purposes,* and still afford to keep them at full Military Readiness. Thus, your economic empire can thrive without having to compromise your safety against either those pesky Barbarians, or an opponent set on pirating your hard-earned Trade Routes and city improvements. Best of all, the

While there is considerable doubt that Egyptians were the first to domesticate wild cats, they certainly elevated the process into something approaching an art form. So obsessed were the Egyptians, in fact, that the furry creatures somehow touched virtually every bit of their culture. Not only were the great Pharaohs buried in the Pyramids with trusted servants and loved ones, they also evidently wouldn't have considered going on to the afterlife without the companionship of their favorite felines (and a few hundred jewels, of course).

The craft of mummifying cats seems to have been an honorable trade, and cats were often bred specifically for the purpose of selling as mummies to less regal families. Recent archaeological finds have even unearthed mummies with the head of a cat and various parts of humans—the pantheistic religion of ancient Egypt included such animalistic goddesses as Bast, who had the head of a cat.

Sphinx is a fairly long-lived Wonder, not expiring until the Age of Reason. So, the earlier you build it, the better.

An added benefit is that a few more military units of any type (which, again, you'll be able to afford with the Sphinx) can make a big difference in how your neighbors perceive you. The irony is, if you aren't perceived as a fat, easy target, you're less likely to have to go to war in *Call to Power*. And if you have the Sphinx, your neighbor, who might happen to be Genghis Khan or Napoleon, doesn't have it. All of which lets you make the world safer for capitalism, Zoroanthrianism, Utopianism, or whatever suits your fancy because you built a "military" Wonder. As Bugs Bunny would say, "Curious, ain't it, Doc?"

So it comes as little of a surprise that the ancient Egyptians built the Sphinx to pay homage to the lion, or big cat, if you will, but with the head of a *man*, presumably that of Pharaoh Khafre. Even viewed today in Giza (near Cairo), the Sphinx is in many ways the epitome of enigma; it's not hard to believe that the famous "Riddle of the Sphinx" found its way into even Western myth.

Cats have played their mysterious part in film and literature, and even a few computer games, ever since. Therefore, in *Call to Power*, one might reasonably expect the Sphinx to somehow increase the Fog of War, or to at least strike terror into one's enemies, which it does, however indirectly. The implication in the game is that only a strong government could have undertaken and completed such a tremendous project, and only a strong military could be worthy of its

## Military Advantages

If you want to rule the world at the point of a sword, the Sphinx has to be your foremost early priority. You are almost certain to discover the prerequisite Advance, Stone Working, early on (if you have doubts whether you need this knowledge so

quickly, check out our comments on Stone Working in Chapter 7). The ability to crank out military units and keep them at full Military Readiness is always difficult when fighting a prolonged campaign because of the high maintenance costs per unit,

which only get worse as the units get better. Samurai, for instance, always cost the full "at war" maintenance amount because they are elite troops, regardless of your true war or peacetime status. Thus, since the Sphinx reduces your Military Readiness costs by 75-percent, it becomes a boon in both war and those

achievement. The Sphinx essentially becomes the "watchful eye" of the empire, and reduces Military Readiness costs by 75 percent.

If all this seems a little abstract, it is. Every *Civilization* game has struggled with exactly how to depict, in game terms, the Great Wonder of the world from Egypt at the dawn of time, which is, in many games, the first Wonder that anyone builds. In the first *Civilization* game, the Pyramids were far too powerful, as they let you blithely change governments at will, hundreds of years before you could have discovered Democracy or Communism. In *Civilization II*, building the Pyramids gave you a Granary free in every city, meaning that you could grow far faster than your competitors in the early part of the game. It's obvious that the design team of *Call to Power* wanted to avoid either of these pitfalls, while still giving the great Egyptian civilization its place in history. On high difficulty settings, you'll probably build the Sphinx after the birth of Christ rather than centuries before, but it's still worth the trouble.

"pauses" between conflicts. As a result, you never have to tell your units to "stand ready" or "stand down" to reduce costs; with the Sphinx, you can afford to keep your troops always on the go, ready to react wherever danger arises! Sounds a lot like an ad for the U.S. Navy, doesn't it?

Once you build the Sphinx, you should focus on pressing your military advantage. Overwhelm weaker opponents, as you can afford to maintain a large army much more cheaply than they can. Keep in mind that even if you don't knock a nearby enemy completely out of the game, you can often force favorable terms, and afterwards, demand gold and/or Advances from weaker foes. Just be sure that you wait until you are provoked to start a war or demand tribute so that your reputation doesn't suffer unduly (see Chapter 4).

# Star Ladder

*"Again the space elevator was declared a necessity. 'They'll just pass us by if we don't have it, go straight out to the asteroids and not have any gravity well to worry about, eh?'"*

—Red Mars, *Kim Stanley Robinson*

| | |
|---|---|
| **ERA:** | Genetic |
| **BRANCH OF KNOWLEDGE:** | Flight |
| **DEVELOPMENT:** | Smart Materials + 12,000 Production Units = STAR LADDER |
| **OBSOLESCENCE:** | Never |
| **EFFECT:** | Free transportation into and out of Space; Free Space Colony at top of Star Ladder |

## Political/Economic Advantages

Since discovering the Wormhole and Alien Technology is the most likely route for you to win the game peacefully, this Wonder should be high on your "must have" list. We would certainly take this over the National Shield. But if you are in a race with another empire to build the Sensorium, you'll have to decide for yourself if the free Space route and Space Colony are worth more than additional happy citizens are. Even though the Star Ladder gives you an edge going into the endgame, remember that

*"When she gets there she knows/All that glitters is gold/And she's buy-ing a stairway to Heaven"*

—Stairway to Heaven, *from Led Zeppelin's Untitled album*

Ever since ancient man looked up at the heavens, he has longed for a way to get there. Some climbed the highest mountains, well past where they could easily breathe. The legend of Icarus is memorable because he got too close to the sun, his wings melted, and he plunged to his death. The story of Babel concerns the concerted effort of thousands of people building, so we are told, a tower to Heaven itself. God wasn't too fond of the idea, so He caused the various folks building the tower to be unable to communicate with each other. Thus, we now have quite a variety of

ou're still in the Genetic
ra, and there's more than
kely a lot of game left to
lay.

languages that we speak around the world—but no ladder to the stars.

Scientific interest in the subject of star ladders was rekindled not so much by the Moon landings, but by the increased search for ways to make space travel more cost-effective. Arthur C. Clarke, noted scientist as well as science fiction author, years ago proposed that a long cable could be run from the Moon or a planet, such as Mars, to a receiving station in Earth's orbit. This would allow raw materials to be shipped with a small bit of force along the line, and simple momentum would do the rest.

## Military Advantages

While we certainly don't think that you should spend too much effort on the National Shield, the Sensorium will soon be available, and that's a Wonder well worth having for a military regime, especially going into the endgame. The main reason that you would build the Star Ladder is for easy Space access, as well as a free Space Colony base that would allow you to launch spoiler attacks at any Alien-oriented activities conducted by more peaceful societies. It's even possible that this Wonder could put you

*Call to Power* takes the whole idea a bit farther. The Star Ladder Wonder allows you to have automatic entry into Space, and it also places a free Space Colony at the end of the cable. If it's tight going into the endgame, this could be the push you need to win the game.

irst in the race to get the
Vormhole, but making
uch a drastic change in
our strategy at this late
ate is risky.

# Stonehenge

*"We cannot properly estimate the achievements of prehistoric men, for we must guard against describing their life with imagination that transcends the evidence."*

—*Will Durant*, Our Oriental Heritage

| | |
|---|---|
| **ERA:** | Ancient |
| **BRANCH OF KNOWLEDGE:** | Physical Science |
| **DEVELOPMENT:** | Astronomy + 2,160 Production Units = STONEHENGE |
| **OBSOLESCENCE:** | Age Of Reason |
| **EFFECT:** | 25% increase in food production across host's entire civilization |

## Political/Economic Advantages

Whether you are an empire-builder or a conqueror, it's absolutely vital to grow your population and productivity as rapidly as possible. While the food bonus provided by the construction of the Stonehenge Wonder doesn't match the "free granary in every city" benefit of the Pyramid Wonder found in *Civilization II*, Stonehenge is still worthwhile for any style of player. Since the advance requires only the Religion and Astronomy Advances as prerequisites, Stonehenge can be built fairly early in the game and should accelerate population growth and production.

If you are playing on a medium to large-scale map and haven't encountered a rival civilization, Stonehenge certainly offers a more valuable productivity increase than th Sphinx's boost to your as yet

Throughout Europe, particularly in England and Ireland, may be found heaps of huge stones known as dolmens, menhirs, and cromlechs. Most have some sort of circular construction, while some (menhirs) are merely large, upright stones (reminding one of the monolith in *2001: A Space Odyssey*). There are numerous theories about the origin of these constructions. Some believe they suggest familiarity with the lunar calendar. Others offer ideas where circularity reflects rebirth and reincarnation. Some suggest that they were sites for civil and religious ceremonies, as well as burial sites. Still others have theorized that circular constructions, such as Stonehenge, are evidence that a second millennium incursion of steppe peoples or bronze-wielding warriors conquered the relatively peaceable Neolithic civilizations of Europe and the British Isles. The theory continues

on-existent war effort, or the Labyrinth's aid to your trade situation. If you are an empire-building player and have already encountered a rival civilization, by all means utilize diplomacy to placate the rival and build the Stonehenge Wonder first of all. If you build it faster than your opponent does, it will jumpstart your economy and help you to gain the edge.

## Stonehenge

that the conquerors then forced the conquered peoples to create these sites as powerful stone icons imitative of "tree-trunk circles." Although the initial phase, the so-called Aubrey holes date back to circa 3000 BC, there is some evidence that a later phase dates to around 1800 BC. According to William McNeill, carbon-14 dating of some charcoal found at Stonehenge suggests that the megalithic circle was definitely in use around 1785 BC (with an error factor of +/- 275 years).

Regardless of the theory behind the construction and shape of these stone structures, most archaeologists believe that they were sacred sites. Today, the Druids place particular significance on Stonehenge and have adopted it as one of their sacred sites, even though its use probably predated the apex of their religion. Local guides will be glad to demonstrate the magnetic sources of power, or "ley lines," which allegedly pass

## Military Advantages

Even if you're an Alexander-type player, you are likely to want to build Stonehenge as your first Wonder. The across-the-board food bonus is simply too important to pass up unless you are playing on a small map and expect to conquer your opponents rapidly, or you are playing on a larger map and have already encountered a rival civilization. In the case of these two exceptions, the Alexander will probably choose to build the Sphinx first in order to reduce the cost of military readiness. If possible, however, it will be wise to pick up Stonehenge via conquest or to build it rapidly using the "Rush Buy" option after you've built the Sphinx.

If you're lucky, you might take out the civilization that is building Stonehenge. If you're phenomenally lucky, you'll finish off the rival civilization just as it finishes Stonehenge. That way, you'll get the Wonder without

through the site, and such demonstrations add to the site's reputation as a powerful supernatural locale.

In *Civilization: Call to Power*, the flow chart suggests that Stonehenge was definitely built to aid in astrology, since it follows so directly upon the Astronomy Advance. Its primary purpose within the game structure is to aid in the production of food, since it provides for the ability to use the lunar calendar in order to gauge seasons, aid planting, and placate the agrarian gods and goddesses. Assuming such a cultic use of the site, *Call to Power* gives you a 25 percent increase in food production across your entire civilization once you have finished building Stonehenge. Recognizing the age-old belief that the powers of the gods and goddesses begin to wane once the population fails to believe in them, Stonehenge is made obsolete by the coming of the Age of Reason Advance (along with other Wonders of the Ancient Era, such as the Sphinx, Labyrinth, Forbidden City, *Ramayana*, and Philosopher's Stone).

aving to build it. If you merely take out the rival civilization *while* it's building tonehenge, you should gain reasonable chance of completing it before another rival ivilization does. If this second rival is as far along as the ne you took out, however, ou'll just need to use the Rush Buy" option. Your onquest should have given ou a net gain of a couple of cities, boosting your overall income. If you're fortunate, you should be able to start building Stonehenge as soon as the Sphinx is complete. In this case, use your extra gold to make a "Rush Buy" as soon as you receive the inevitable message that you're running out of time to construct Stonehenge because a rival civilization is nearing the completion of the same Wonder. It is particularly satisfying for those with an Alexander complex to steal a Wonder right out from under the nose of a rival civilization.

# Wormhole Sensor

*"These singularities are points at which the very structure of space-time breaks down and the laws of physics no longer apply."*

—*E. David Peat*. Superstrings and the Search for the Theory of Everything

| | |
|---|---|
| **ERA:** | Diamond |
| **BRANCH OF KNOWLEDGE:** | Physical Science |
| **DEVELOPMENT:** | Wormholes + 20,000 Production Units = WORMHOLE SENSOR |
| **OBSOLESCENCE:** | Never |
| **EFFECT:** | Makes Wormhole visible to all civilizations |

## Political/Economic Advantages

This is it. This is the Wonder that demonstrates the superiority of your civilization and its ethos of empire-building. If you can build the Wormhole Sensor first, you'll have five full rounds to launch your probe and capture the alien DNA before your rivals get a chance to do so. After that, it will depend on how efficient you can be with regard to building the Xenoform Laboratory Improvement, along with the extra Improvements to enhance your chance of success within the Alien Synthesis Project. Since you've come this far without taking a tremendous number of risks, be sure to build two Gene Splicer Improvements so that there is only a ten-percent chance of failure. If you happen to hit the unlucky 20-percent chance (or 10-percent using two Gene Splicers) and destroy the lab,

Black holes, singularities, and wormholes are mysteries within the present world because they defy our previous understanding of physics. Much science fiction revolves around the idea that the physics of relativity no longer apply near a singularity. Therefore, these wormholes could be used to travel through space in a manner that the *Star Wars* hyperdrive and the *Star Trek* warp drive suggest. The thesis in *Civilization: Call to Power* is that the alien civilization uncovered through the Alien Archaeology Advance came through the wormhole. Therefore, the only way to locate the alien civilization is to find the wormhole, send a probe through it, and capture alien DNA. Some additional Advances must then be used to duplicate the alien, artificially creating a new alien child to influence the future of civilization. This alien, the *Call to Power* equivalent of Arthur C. Clarke's "star child" in *2001: A Space Odyssey*, presumably moves

ou have to relaunch a probe, ecapture the alien DNA, and tart the Alien Synthesis Project all over again.

The Wormhole Sensor Wonder is the gateway to the most interesting ending of the game. Be certain that you're ready to exploit the Wonder as soon as it's complete. It would be a shame to build this Wonder and have some warmongering civilization steal this satisfying victory from you after you located the wormhole itself.

## Wormhole Sensor

humankind to the next phase of evolution. Obviously, this Wonder is part of the endgame for those who are not satisfied with merely conquering the world or lasting until AD 3000 with the highest score.

In the fiction behind *Call to Power*'s Wormhole Sensor Wonder, your civilization has determined that the secret to the alien civilization depends on locating the wormhole through which the aliens previously visited your world. In order to locate the wormhole, you build a vast, ambitious project to measure the gravimetric flux within space in order to pinpoint the wormhole. This Wonder is absolutely essential for gamers who want the most advanced victory within the game. Upon discovering the wormhole, you can't sit idly by. The wormhole is constantly moving through space. You'll have to monitor it continually in order to successfully launch the probe and have a chance of success. Also, remember that after five

## Military Advantages

The only reason for an Alexander-style player to build this Wonder is that the world was too large for him to be able to conquer all of his rival civilizations in the time allotted. Then, building the Wormhole Sensor allows you to beat your strongest rival at his own game. For most conquerors, however, it will be more satisfying to let your rival build the Wormhole Sensor and start the Alien Synthesis Project. The rival will be attempting to keep the location of the Xenoform Laboratory secret, but if you can find it and capture the city, the X-Lab will be destroyed and your rival will have to start the endgame all over again.

Most Alexanders will simply continue their path of conquest during this period. The Wormhole Sensor doesn't add to this effort, assuming that

turns, your opponents will be able to see the wormhole, too. They will also have a chance to successfully launch the probe and build the Alien Synthesis Project, the bonus Advance that leads to the most fascinating endgame.

The Alien Synthesis Project is really intricate. Once you start the project, you'll build a Xenoform Laboratory and follow that up with an Embryo Tank, Containment Field, Gene Splicers, and Extraterrestrial Communication Device. And, you still aren't guaranteed success. There is a 20-percent chance of cataclysmic failure unless you build two Gene Splicers. Then, you reduce the chance of disaster to 10-percent and you're ready for the optimal endgame.

you believe you can conquer your rivals before they can finish the Alien Synthesis Project. So, the Wormhole Sensor Wonder shouldn't be atop your priority list during the endgame, unless you feel like your overall strategy has failed.

# Chapter Eight:

# Concerning the Method of Devious Play

## Advanced Cheats, and Tips for *Call to Power*

*"It is customary for those who wish to gain the favor of a prince to endeavor to do so by offering him gifts of those things which they hold most precious, or in which they know him to take especial delight."*

—The Prince, *Niccolo Machiavelli*

Cheats allow you to find the hidden +8 Sword of Impending Doom and make it to the last level of an adventure game. Hacks allow you to put your favorite classic Super Bowl team into the most recent football simulation. But with strategy games, gamers who would think nothing of using a cheat in one of the games listed above sometimes feel uneasy, as if they are compromising their honor as a cyber-warrior.

Let's get one thing straight: We like cheats. Regardless of what a well-intentioned game designer tells you, all computer games cheat in some way. Having a few good cheats on your side is a nice way, in our minds, of restoring the balance, so long as you don't use them as such a crutch that you never even try to play the game as it was designed.

This chapter will give you some ideas on how to indulge your inner strategist, if you will, that more devious, mischievous side of you who wants to build a starship in the year 1750, or conquer the world before the Age of Reason.

# Starting Over

*MIGHTY EMPIRE OF THE CELTS: In* Call to Power, *there are no differences between the various civilizations, so have some fun with it and conquer the world with your favorite clan.*

In all previous versions of *Civilization*, who you were was as important to beginning game balance as where you started. The Egyptians and Babylonians, for instance, always got the cushy starting positions, more Advances, and more often than not, extra Settlers to boot. Winning with the Japanese or the Aztecs really gave you bragging rights because they always started at a disadvantage.

Well, none of this is true any more. In addition to giving us more civilizations to lead in *Call to Power*, the designers have made them all the same, with Advances determined by difficulty level rather than nationality (see the following table). Thus, you're just as likely to be surrounded by green fields with the Celts as the Portuguese are to have a plentiful seafood harvest, or the Egyptians are to begin with Stone Working. So, don't think too much about which civilization you want to play—at least not for some perceived edge, because there isn't one.

## Number of Starting Advances

Human and Computer players get a number of chances for Advances based on difficulty level:

| Difficulty | Human | Computer |
|---|---|---|
| Chieftain | 6 | 2 |
| Warlord | 6 | 2 |
| Prince | 4 | 3 |
| King | 3 | 4 |
| Emperor | 3 | 6 |
| Deity | 3 | 8 |

As you can see, the more difficult the level, the more the Tech deck is stacked in favor of the Computer player. What can you do to overcome this initial Computer advantage?

1. Don't panic. It's a computer, and it tends to think literally. Use this tendency against it (check out the tips in Chapter 3 for some ideas).

2. Most computer games think better tactically than strategically. Luckily, *Call to Power* isn't a chess program, where the entire universe consists of 64 squares, and the tactical proficiency of brute force number crunching could destroy you. Keep the strategic situation complicated for the computer, and don't give it clear-cut tactical decisions to make. If you are having trouble on higher levels of difficulty, play on a large map, which in our playtesting seemed to give the AI the most trouble over the long haul.

3. Make a point of trading to gain critical Advances. As we've said throughout this book, an AI ally gained early on is beneficial throughout the early- and mid-game for a lot of reasons.

4. Don't bother with Public Works in the early stages of the game, except to build roads for Mobile Defense (see Chapter 3). Instead, put as many resources as possible toward research.

5. When you get a chance to change Governments, maximize your research. You'll be surprised at how quickly you can catch up in the Tech race. If you are having problems with discontented citizens, you're still better off under Martial Law than spending Tech dollars on Happiness.

## Specific Advances Granted at Start

For each Advance chance from the previous table, the program "rolls" for you on the chart below. It starts this process at the top of the list and goes down until you fill out your Advances. It is possible on very low levels (like Chieftain) that you might go through the list without "rolling up" all your Advances, but that's very unlikely from a mathematical standpoint.

| Advance | Human | Computer |
|---|---|---|
| Tool Making | 100% | 100% |
| Agriculture | 90% | 99% |
| Mining | 90% | 99% |
| Domestication | 90% | 99% |
| Bronze Working | 50% | 99% |
| Stone Working | 50% | 99% |
| Jurisprudence | 5% | 5% |
| Ship Building | 50% | 50% |
| Writing | 5% | 5% |
| Geometry | 5% | 50% |
| Iron Working | 5% | 50% |
| Religion | 80% | 50% |

So, it's a given that you'll start with Tool Making. It's also likely at Prince level
and above that you'll start with Agriculture and Mining, or maybe
Domestication. Most everything else seems out of reach on higher levels of
difficulty.

But this doesn't have to be the case, not if you treat the start of a game of *Call to
Power* as if you were rolling up a character in a role-playing game. It's a little
more difficult process, to be sure, because you have to restart the game every
time you get a less-than-desirable set of Advances. Nevertheless, it works. One
time Terry rolled up an empire on Prince level that had Tool Making, Bronze
Working, and Religion, along with the automatic Agriculture. He had
Ramayana, Stonehenge, and the Sphinx built before the Computer opposition
was barely past stone knives and bearskins, along with Phalanx garrisons in all
his Cities.

Regardless of what Advances the Computer players might get, you deserve a
chance to determine your own playing style and strategy from the start of the
game. Therefore, we strongly believe that this "roll your own" approach is
critical on difficulty levels from King to Deity, where you get only three
Advances. So, use it, live it, and don't be embarrassed by it!

# Predicting AI Behavior

How the Computer players react varies from game to game, with a myriad of factors too confusing to get into in the space we have available here. It also seems that the controlling files for AI behavior are shielded in the final version, so that it's basically impossible to modify them without locking up or otherwise compromising the game. However, there are certain tendencies that you can use to your advantage in dealing with Computer players.

First, the program assigns a personality to each Computer player at the beginning of the game.

Some of these personalities are predictable. We never played a game, for instance, where Genghis Khan was anything other than warlike and heavily expansion-oriented. But what does "warlike" specifically mean in a game sense, or "peaceful," for that matter? Here's how the process works.

*A. There are four basic Computer personalities:*

1. **Huge Empire with Science Emphasis**—This Computer player places Cities farther apart as its empire expands, typically two to three spaces outside of normal City boundaries. It tends to spend 10- to 20-percent on Public Works and tries aggressively to get new Advances, usually in five to six turns. As the game goes along, this empire tends to expand over its continent, and is more likely to settle areas overseas from its starting position.

2. **Compact Empire with Science Emphasis**—This Computer player places Cities right on top of each other as its empire expands, and some City boundaries may overlap. It spends little or nothing on Public Works in the beginning of the game, and it is also very aggressive in terms of research. It is less likely to build Cities on islands early in the game, and even its Undersea Colonies tend to be relatively close to its original capitol.

3. **Huge Empire with Military Emphasis**—This empire expands much like #1 above. While it spends a similar amount on Public Works, this goes for other constructs like roads and mines, implying an aggressive military stance in another's territory, where it presumably won't need City Walls. Science is less of a concern, as this empire only receives new Advances every eight or nine turns. This empire is a deadly, if predictable early game threat.

4. **Compact Empire with Military Emphasis**—This empire expands like #2 above, choosing to spend its production and gold on cranking out military units. Science emphasis is to target new Advances every eight or nine turns. Generally speaking, this military empire is a threat over the long term because it tends to build up a sizable, potent force before launching an assault.

*B. After selecting the personality of each Computer player, the program sets the production for each of the starting AI cities.*

1. The program sets the number of Workers, Entertainers, and Scientists.

2. It then places the Workers on specific spaces to work them.

3. As the City grows in population, the program assigns them to food or production spaces, according to the Computer player's personality.

Therefore, if a City had a population of 3, chances are that a compact empire with military emphasis (our #4 personality) would assign the odd worker to production rather than food so that it could build military units faster. If a City had a population of 5, our #2 personality would have a better than average chance of turning the odd citizen into a scientist for additional research.

Keep in mind that there are several randomizing factors during this process, one of which is a subroutine that keeps similar empires, such as two #2 Computer personalities, from carrying out the same exact strategy in any given game.

If you want an example of how the AI prioritizes the placement of citizens, just check out your own Cities. Every time that your population grows, the program places a worker, usually where it will gain a balance of food and production.

*C. After setting the production for each of the AI cities, the program selects a strategic plan for each Computer player.*

While the specific tactics used to carry out these plans vary considerably from one AI empire to another and one game to the next, the overall strategies available fall into the following main categories:

1. **Science Domination**—The Computer personality will attempt to reach a pivotal discovery, such as University, before the other empires in the game. It will also beef up its defenses rather than building attack-oriented units.

2. **Military Domination**—The Computer personality will attempt to discover a pivotal type of attack-oriented unit, such as the Knight, before the other empires in the game. After discovering this unit, it will build it at a two-to-one or better rate over more defensive fare.

Keep in mind that this strategy "cycles" throughout the game. An empire bent on military domination will try to build the Knight, then the Tank, and then the War Walker, while the scientific-oriented will try to monopolize Electricity to the Wormhole.

*D. The program reconciles any contradictions between the personality and the strategic path chosen.*

It is possible, for example, that you can have a compact, scientific Computer society in the game that strives for Military domination. What the AI might do in this case is to pump up its scientific research, so that it could fulfill both its civilian and military ambitions. Still, it would move toward the Knight rather than the University at every opportunity, and it would still put a low profile on Public Works.

Such a society would be a good one to trade with, because you could help to satisfy its research hunger. You'd be well advised to gain the confidence of this empire and ally with it if possible. For should such an empire achieve its goal, gaining its Knight unit before anyone else, you could be in a lot of trouble.

An outright military dictatorship, on the other hand, might have the same goal. But you'll get a lot of warning signals from diplomacy screens to tip you off that this Computer player is dangerous. It's the more "balanced" Computer player that's the greater threat to you in *Call to Power*, rather than the unsubtle military one. Plan accordingly.

## Assorted Tips & Tricks

* Keep in mind that when investigating a village in the hope of a bonus advance, there's about a fifty-fifty chance that the free Advance you discover will be the one you are already researching. So, you might take a chance and bump down your science output this turn, until you see what gifts you get.

* Corny it might be, but when you are about to enter a battle, especially one that involves ten or more units, save the game for goodness' sake. Doing this three or four times a game is probably sufficient to keep you from pulling out your hair over a bunch of bad dice rolls, while also keeping you from feeling like you're coasting.

* If you want to have some control over the amount of Barbarians, don't choose the top setting, where their occurrence seems to be totally at random. On the next highest setting, you can cut down on Barbarian incursions.

* If a Barbarian is making progress against another empire, send a Spy or Cyber Ninja to shadow the Barbarian. If the Barbarian gets lucky and captures an enemy City, you can Incite Revolution and grab the city without starting a war with the former owner of that City.

* Normally, we prefer using the Nuke N' Go method (see Chapter 3) as a prelude to a general invasion. However, if you are in danger of being lapped in research by a science-oriented opponent, you may not be in a position to launch a full-scale invasion of his country. In such a situation, consider using a Nuke followed by a Paratrooper for a hit-and-run raid on one of his key Cities. First off, you'll stop any Wonders he is currently producing in that City. Then, you can sell the most expensive building that remains after the nuclear explosion. This should pay for the Paratroop you will almost certainly lose, and even after your opponent recaptures his city, he will have lost a tremendous amount of resources and time.

* Alternatively, you could rush in and Bombard an enemy City with conventional weapons, then follow up with a succession of Paratroops until you crack through its defenses. This does avoid a thermonuclear war, but it also carries a higher degree of risk. The approach works best on enemy coastal cities, where you can bring your Battleships to bear, as well as your Bombers.

* Keep track of your opponent's Aircraft: Some of them are almost certainly operating at the farthest range of which they are capable. In such a case, all you have to do is to place a row of Air units between them and their refueling base. When the enemy Air units can't get home, they crash—quick, simple, and deadly. Remember that there are no aerial ZOCs, so your aerial blockade must consist of a solid line of aircraft, with no holes. When executing this tactic, Terry especially likes using obsolete Aircraft.

## Menu of Cheat Codes

The game has cheats that can be accessed directly from the *Call to Power* Options menu.

## Rules to Live by When You Cheat

1. Copy all of your saved games to a safe directory (C:\JOHNNY\PEACEOFMIND, or whatever).

2. Don't try these cheats in combination with other cheats, not even the ones we list elsewhere in this book.

3. Type the cheat listed within the quote, not the quotation marks themselves.

4. Don't whine to Activision when these cheats don't work on your system; Activision does not support the cheats.

5. Likewise, we've tried to authenticate all of these cheats. But we can pretty much guarantee that you won't be able to get all of them to work. So, we suggest that you try them one at a time. Find one or two you like, such as the Unit Cheat, and stick with them.

6. Know before going in that a lot of these cheats work only if the Fog of War option is turned off. We think that not seeing the whole map at the beginning of the game is one of the most fun aspects of the *Civilization* series, but you'll have to make up your own mind.

7. If you completely corrupt your install of *Call to Power*, uninstall the game (don't just delete it), and reinstall from scratch. Remember: If you're following our advice, you can copy your old saved games over to the new install, and all will again be happy in your gaming kingdom.

## Cheats Accessible from the Interface

On the Options menu, there is a button called "Cheat Mode." Cheats are more easily used when Fog of War is toggled OFF [tfog] by hitting the Show Map button. They can also be used with fog on. The Main Map and Game are disabled while Cheat mode is ON. To resume playing, close the Cheat Tools.

## Button Cheats

Five buttons appear when you choose Cheat Mode from the Options menu: Gold, Public Works, Show Map, Advances, and Units.

## Gold

If you hit the Gold button, you can type in the amount of gold you want to give your civilization.

## Public Works

If you hit the Public Works button, you can type in the amount of Public Works you want to give your civilization.

## Show Map

Show Map is a toggle button used to toggle Fog of War off and on.

## Advances

The Advances button brings up two columns. The right column indicates your current advances. The left column lists every other advance in the game. To add any advance to your column, highlight the advance and hit the arrow pointing to your column. (You can also remove any advance from your column if you wish.)

## Units

1. Click on the Unit button.

2. If you would like to create any unit (i.e., for which you may or may not have the enabling Advance), click the Legal button; it will change to All Tech.

3. You can only create units and cities on tiles for which they have the movement ability. You will *not* be able to create Triremes on land, or Tanks in the ocean.

4. To create Army Units, from the Army tab, click on the icon for the army unit you would like to create, then click the tile on which you would like to place the unit.

5. To create Naval Units, from the Navy tab, click on the icon for the naval unit you would like to create, then click the tile on which you would like to place the unit.

6. To create Air Force Units, from the Air Force tab, click on the icon for the air force unit you would like to create, then click the tile on which you would like to place the unit.

7. To create Space Units, from the Space tab, click on the icon for the space unit you would like to create, then click the tile on which you would like to place the unit.

8. To create Special Units, from the Special tab, click on the icon for the special unit you would like to create, then click the tile on which you would like to place the unit.

# Chapter Nine:

# Concerning the Domination of Other Human Civilizations

## Multiplayer Tips & Tricks in *Call to Power*

*"For to win one hundred victories in one hundred battles is not the acme of skill. To subdue the enemy without fighting is the acme of skill. Thus, what is of supreme importance in war is to attack the enemy's strategy."*

—Sun Tzu, The Art of War *(around 500 BC),*
*translated by Samuel B. Griffith, 1963*

*"It's more fun to blow up the world with a friend."*

—Terry Coleman,
*Computer Gaming World, 1996*

Much of the advice we've passed on in earlier chapters is still very applicable to a multiplayer game. But Human leaders tend to be craftier than computer opponents. They notice things an AI would miss. You have to pull out all the stops. Here, then, are our favorite tricks to play on our own friends and "enemies for an hour" when we play *Call to Power* over the office network.

*SNEAKING A PEEK: When you reload the saved multiplayer game, you can check to see who's winning and who's losing. In the old versions of Civilization, you had to retire to do this.*

*PING ME: Call to Power has an excellent counter to accurately judge "ping" rates for your Internet connection. Although you are free to hang out wherever you like, it's best to choose ping rates listed in green.*

## Practical Joke Department

Every civilization is password-protected, which keeps you from restarting a saved multiplayer game and selling off all of your buddy's City Improvements and military units. Moreover, most cheat commands render a multiplayer game unplayable, and they generally corrupt multiplayer saved game files. However, here is one trick you can try:

## 18 Steps to Better Understanding (and a Few Laughs)

1. Make sure that you are the one hosting the game.
2. Copy the saved multiplayer game to a safe directory (C:\TERRYISSILLY, or whatever).
3. Take the original saved multiplayer game, and invoke the Cheat Mode from the Command Bar (see Chapter 8 for a refresher if you need it).
4. Turn off Fog of War.
5. You should now be able to see the entire map

6. Click on the Strategic Map (in the corner of the main screen display) where your first rival is.
7. Hit the "Print Screen" key on your keyboard.
8. On your main Windows 95/98 toolbar, click on "Start."
9. Go two selections up the toolbar and select "Run."
10. Type "pbrush" (without the quotation marks)
11. This puts you into the Windows Microsoft Paint program.
12. Now, select "Edit" from the pulldown menu at the top of the screen.
13. Next, select "Paste," and "As new document."

14. Paint will ask you if you want the screen enlarged; select yes.
15. You are now the proud owner of a map of your opponent's empire, which you can view at any time from Paint, or any other viewing program, like Photoshop.

16. Repeat steps 6 through 11 for any other rival civilizations' maps you desire.
17. If the program locks up, you can delete the corrupt save and copy the save that you placed in the safe directory in step 2.
18. When you are done, delete the saved game you were using for screen capturing, and copy the multiplayer save from the safe directory. It now becomes the "real" saved game for your next multiplay session—none of your opponents will be the wiser.

## Never Trust a Telepath

The ESP Wonder is a great Wonder to have at the end of the game, because it prevents other nations from starting wars with you. Since (at least as of press time) this Wonder worked as well against Humans as Computer players, we tried the following strategy with considerable success:

After completing the ESP Wonder, begin building up your military. As you grow stronger, make increasingly tougher demands on nations around you. Concentrate on those civilizations without allies. Ply medium-range nations that are in a position to help you with Trade or Tech gifts. Try to sign an alliance with them.

The ESP Wonder prevents your *enemies* from starting a war, but *not you*. So, when you are ready, go to war. After conquering one of your enemies, continue to make deals where applicable.

Repeat the process (if you can) in the endgame, where it will give you a huge edge.

## Nuke, Then Nanite

During the turn before you are about to complete the Nanite Defuser Wonder, fire off all of your Nukes at an enemy. At the beginning of the next turn, the Nanite Defuser will eliminate your opponents' Nukes before they can reply to your attack. If timed correctly, this can take one of your closest competitors effectively out of the game. By the way, don't try this in an email game, or you'll be cursing mushroom clouds over your own cities.

## Join the Moral Majority

Televangelists are always effective in *Call to Power*, but they are a real nuisance in a multiplayer game. Their basic economic attack, like those of priests, is the Convert City command. Unlike Cleric units, which have only a 50-percent chance of success in using this command and a 25-percent chance of being caught should they fail, Televangelists enjoy a 75-percent chance of success and have only a 20-percent chance of being caught upon failure. This might reflect multicultural tolerance in the modern age, who knows? Whatever the reason, that extra 5-percent of safety should encourage you to use them aggressively.

Each Convert City attempt costs 100 gold, but this is extremely cost-effective since each success means that the converted city will pay 20-percent of its gold as a "tithe." Better than this, a city with a TV is affected twice as much, meaning that 40-percent of its gold supports the Televangelist's "worthy cause."

> TIP: Break Out the Spotlights—While we have made a point of downplaying the Hollywood Wonder throughout this book, we've noticed a tendency for Human players to build a lot of TV sets. This makes Hollywood, when combined with the Televangelist Convert City ability, a quick way to fill your coffers for a long time in a multiplayer game—television executives should have it so good.

Should you want to use the Televangelist unit to aid an ally, you can use the Sell Indulgences command. This command costs nothing and immediately provides a Happiness boost within the target city. The forgiven sinners immediately reward the Televangelist with an "offering" in gold. There is no "cheap grace" in *Call to Power*. Best of all, you don't need your buddy's permission to do this.

Should you choose to completely disrupt the enemy, you can spend 500 gold to use the Soothsay command. This attack always works and immediately drops the Happiness quotient in the target city by five points. It seems it's always good to convince people that God isn't on their side prior to invading them. Alternatively, you can often provoke a Human player into an ill-advised war by using your Televangelist activities easier than you could a Computer opponent.

## So Sue Me

Corporate Branch units are expensive—about seven times as expensive as a Cleric. By the time Corporate Branch units are readily available, there are plenty of ways for your enemy to kill or evict them from his territory. And Human leaders tend to find your units, where an AI might miss them.

So, if you are going to use legal tactics, it's best to buy three or four of these units and flood an opponent's defenses with them. At least one, and probably two of your Corporate troops are almost sure to get through to the target. Then you just watch the money roll in. Your opponent is then faced with the choice of either taking several turns to mount a legal defense, or starting a war for which he is likely unprepared. The Corporate Branch tactic is particularly effective against Democracies and Republics, and against any player adopting the "research first" strategy.

## Multiplicity of Wonders

Here are our favorite Wonders for multiplayer games, in addition to those discussed above:

| Wonder | Why to Build It |
|---|---|
| East India Company | Often better than in a solo game, as there's usually more Trade between Humans |
| Eden Project | Trust us: One of your aggressive buddies will be a polluter *nonpareil* |
| Edison's Lab | Not as good as the Internet, but still helps you a lot |
| Forbidden City | Shuts off information to your enemies; drives 'em nuts |
| Hagia Sophia | The multiplayer game without a thriving Theocracy is rare indeed |
| Internet | Almost guaranteed to keep you in a multiplayer game |
| London Stock Exchange | Being more cost-efficient than fellow Humans is a key to winning |
| Philosopher's Stone | It's more important to know what a Human is thinking than an AI |
| Sphinx | As combat-happy as most gamers are, this gives you peace of mind |
| Stonehenge | Grow fast and grow strong before your neighbor does |

## No Chance for Chunnel

Undersea tunnels exist in New York, San Francisco, and even under the English Channel. And let's face it, being able to build them in a game is very cool. However, you can use this fact to take advantage of your Human opponents:

1. Capture an Undersea City by underhanded means with your Spy or Cyber Ninja.
2. Place a cheap unit, preferably one that's obsolete, into the undersea tunnel about two spaces from the opponent's next city.
3. Place another cheap unit one or two spaces back in the undersea tunnel, toward the City you just captured.
4. Have a Park Ranger ready to go in the Undersea City you just captured, preferably by transporting it in the same ship that brought the Spy.
5. The opposing empire will counterattack. Unlike a computer opponent, he will probably attack with mobile units, like a Tank. Your defense in depth, the second cheap unit behind the first, should stop him. However, by this time, your Human opponent has probably succumbed to a bit of emotion and a desire for revenge. Therefore, it's highly likely that he will push forward with a larger force into the tunnel.
6. At this time, you release the Park Ranger—basically, a mobile Nanite Bomb—into the undersea tunnel and blow it up. This destroys all the enemy units in the tunnel. It also effectively isolates the Undersea City you just captured, allowing you to build up its defenses and thereby prevent its recapture. Best of all, it only cost you one Park Ranger and a couple of cheap, maybe even obsolete, units.

## Using the Map Editor

✤ On the devious side, you can design a multiplayer scenario with certain terrain features that only you know about. A good way to surprise your office buddies, for example, is to build a land bridge between two continents along the South Pole—they'll never expect it (unless they've played with you before, maybe).

*NELSON NEVER HAD IT SO GOOD: If you are setting up a multiplayer game, there's nothing illegal about playing to your strengths. In this case, I know more about Naval warfare than my opponents, so I adjust the map to have lots of oceans and islands.*

✤ On the positive side, you can use the editor to balance things to make the game fun for everyone, even those just learning how to play *Call to Power*. The easiest way to do this is simply to give less experienced players three or four additional Advances to start the game.

*A CIV FIT FOR A KING (OR A CHIEFTAIN): One of the nice things about setting up a multiplayer scenario is that you can handicap the sides to even things up between players with different experience levels.*

✤ Keep in mind that while *Call to Power* is a turn-based game, during a multiplayer game, the program is sending several packets of information back and forth. The better ping rate you have, the better the conditions will be for conducting the game. This is something you can easily check before starting an Internet game; it's built into the *Call to Power* code.

[ 335 ]

As far as using outside scenarios: We suspect that there will be dozens of multiplayer scenarios available on the Internet within weeks of the game shipping. After all, *Civilization II* has somewhere in the neighborhood of 350 scenarios and counting…

Still, don't simply trust that everything you download will work. Always check scenarios out with a good anti-virus program (we recommend Norton AV 5.0), and be sure to set the options to "check all files," not just executables.

After you determine that you have a healthy file, play through a few turns of the scenario solo before springing it on your buddies. If you have an ethical problem with seeing the map before your opponents, tell yourself that you're engaged in worthwhile research. Failing that, you can always play a different civilization when you finally get a multiplayer game going.

## To Everything There Is an End

Well, that's about all the time we have here, folks. We hope you have as much fun using these various schemes as we've had in devising them. We also hope we've made you think a bit along the way, as well, because that's one of the things we find so fascinating about *Call to Power* and the rest of the *Civilization* series, that's kept us so addicted for nearly a decade.

May you always build an empire "to stand the test of time," or at least have a lot of fun making the attempt.

*Terry Coleman*
*Johnny Wilson*
*February, 1999*

# Appendix

## Data and Statistics Tables

### Governments

| Name | Growth | Production | Science | Gold | Military |
|------|--------|-----------|---------|------|----------|
| Anarchy | Awful | Awful | Awful | Awful | Awful |
| Communism | Average | Excellent | Awful | Bad | Good |
| Corporate Republic | Average | Good | Good | Excellent | Average |
| Democracy | Average | Average | Good | Average | Bad |
| Ecotopia | Good | Bad | Good | Good | Good |
| Fascism | Average | Good | Average | Bad | Excellent |
| Monarchy | Bad | Average | Bad | Bad | Good |
| Republic | Bad | Good | Average | Average | Bad |
| Technocracy | Good | Excellent | Good | Average | Average |
| Theocracy | Bad | Good | Bad | Good | Average |
| Tyranny | Awful | Average | Awful | Bad | Average |
| Virtual Democracy | Excellent | Bad | Excellent | Good | Bad |

### Terrain

| Terrain Type | Food | Production Bonus | Gold | Movement | Defense | Possible Construction |
|--------------|------|------------------|------|----------|---------|-----------------------|
| Beach | 10 | 5 | 5 | 1 | | Fishing, Undersea Tunnels |
| Continental Shelf | 10 | 10 | 5 | 1 | | Fishing, Undersea Tunnels |
| Dead Tile | 0 | 0 | 0 | 1 | | |
| Deep Water | 5 | 15 | 5 | 1 | | Fishing, Undersea Tunnels, Undersea Mines |
| Desert | 0 | 5 | 0 | 2 | | Roads, Farms, Mines |
| Desert Hill | 0 | 10 | 5 | 2 | 50% | Roads, Mines |
| Forest | 5 | 20 | 0 | 2 | 50% | Roads |
| Glacier | 0 | 0 | 0 | 3 | | |
| Grassland | 10 | 5 | 0 | 1 | | Roads, Farms, Mines |
| Hill | 5 | 10 | 5 | 2 | 50% | Roads, Mines |
| Jungle | 5 | 20 | 0 | 3 | 50% | Roads |
| Mountain | 0 | 20 | 5 | 4 | 100% | Roads, Mines |
| Plains | 5 | 10 | 0 | 1 | | Roads, Farms, Mines |
| Polar Hill | 0 | 10 | 5 | 2 | 50% | Roads, Mines |
| Rift | 5 | 25 | 5 | 1 | | Fishing, Undersea Tunnels, Undersea Mines |
| River | +5 | +5 | +5 | 1/2 | | As Underlying Tile |
| Shallow Water | 10 | 10 | 5 | 1 | | Fishing, Undersea Tunnels |
| Space | 0 | 0 | 0 | 1/20 | | Food Pods, Assembly Bays |
| Swamp | 0 | 5 | 0 | 3 | 50% | Roads |
| Trench | 10 | 10 | 5 | 1 | | Fishing |
| Tundra | 5 | 0 | 0 | 2 | | Roads |
| Volcano | 5 | 45 | 10 | 1 | | Fishing, Undersea Tunnels, Undersea Mines |

# Units

| Name | Cost | Assault Strength | Range Strength | Defense Strength | Movement Points | Vision Range | Special Functions | Obsolescence |
|---|---|---|---|---|---|---|---|---|
| Abolitionist | 225 | 0 | 0 | 1 | 3 | 1 | Free Slaves, Aid Uprising | Emancipation Act |
| Aircraft Carrier | 3,000 | 8 | 8 | 8 | 4 | 2 | Transport 5 Small Aircraft | |
| Archer | 270 | 1 | 2 | 1 | 1 | 1 | | Explosives |
| Artillery | 1,200 | 4 | 20 | 4 | 1 | 1 | Bombard | Robotics |
| Battleship | 2,000 | 20 | 20 | 15 | 5 | 2 | Bombard | Ultra-Pressure Machinery |
| Bomber | 2,250 | 10 | 20 | 4 | 10 | 1 | Bombard, Transport 1 Nuke, 5 Turns of Fuel | Advanced Composites |
| Cannon | 540 | 2 | 6 | 2 | 1 | 1 | Bombard | Explosives |
| Caravan | 750 | 0 | 0 | 1 | N/A | N/A | Create Trade Route | |
| Cargo Pod | N/A | 0 | 0 | 2 | 10 | 2 | Transport 1 Unit | |
| Cavalry | 720 | 5 | 0 | 3 | 4 | 1 | | Robotics |
| Cleric | 270 | 0 | 0 | 1 | 2 | 1 | Convert City, Soothsay, Sell Indulgences | Mass Media |
| Corporate Branch | 2,000 | 0 | 0 | 1 | 5 | 2 | Franchise | Subneural Ad |
| Crawler | 3,750 | 0 | 0 | 8 | 3 | 1 | Transport 5 Units | |
| Cyber Ninja | 2,000 | 0 | 0 | 3 | 4 | 3 | Spy, Plant Nuke, Incite Revolution. 25% Spy Defense, Steal Advance | |
| Destroyer | 1,000 | 10 | 10 | 10 | 6 | 3 | Bombard, Spot Submarines | Ultrapressure Machinery |
| Diplomat | 135 | 0 | 0 | 1 | 2 | 2 | Establish Embassy, Spy | |
| Eco Ranger | 3,750 | 0 | 0 | 1 | 5 | 1 | Create Park | |
| Ecoterrorist | 5,000 | 5 | 0 | 5 | 3 | 2 | Plant Nano-Virus, Conduct Hit, | |
| Fascist | 1,000 | 16 | 0 | 8 | 2 | 1 | 25% Spy Defense | |
| Fighter | 1,125 | 10 | 10 | 10 | 10 | 2 | Land On Aircraft Carriers,3 Turns of Fuel | Space Flight |
| Fire Trireme | 720 | 2 | 1 | 1 | 2 | 1 | Transport 1 Unit, Shallow Water Movement | Machine Tools |
| Fusion Tank | 3,250 | 20 | 20 | 15 | 8 | 2 | Shallow Water Movement | |
| Infector | 3,750 | 0 | 0 | 1 | 3 | 1 | Infect City | |
| Interceptor | 1,500 | 15 | 12 | 12 | 15 | 3 | Active Air Defense, 2 Turns of Fuel, Land On Aircraft Carriers | Smart Materials |
| Knight | 540 | 3 | 0 | 2 | 4 | 1 | | Cavalry Tactics |
| Lawyer | 450 | 0 | 0 | 1 | 3 | 1 | File Injunction, Sue | Robotics |
| Legion | 200 | 2 | 0 | 1 | 1 | 1 | | Gunpowder |
| Leviathan | 9,000 | 40 | 40 | 40 | 1 | 3 | Active Air and Space Defense, Bombard, Only Moves 1 Tile per Turn | |
| Longship | 720 | 2 | 0 | 2 | 3 | 1 | Transport 2 Units | Mass Production |
| Machine Gunner | 800 | 8 | 0 | 8 | 2 | 1 | | Robotics |
| Marine | 1,000 | 12 | 0 | 8 | 3 | 2 | Amphibious Assault | Space Colonies |
| Mobile SAM | 2,000 | 4 | 12 | 4 | 6 | 3 | Active Air Defense | Robotics |
| Mounted Archer | 270 | 1 | 1 | 1 | 3 | 1 | | Gunpowder |
| Musketeer | 560 | 4 | 4 | 4 | 1 | 1 | | Mass Production |

| Unit | Cost | Attack | Range | Defense | Movement | Vision | Special Functions | Obsolescence |
|---|---|---|---|---|---|---|---|---|
| Nuke | 4,000 | Special | 0 | 1 | 20 | 1 | Destroys 75% of City Population and All Units Within 1 Tile, 1 Turn of Fuel | Nanite Defuser |
| Paratrooper | 2,500 | 10 | 0 | 10 | 3 | 2 | Paradrop | |
| Phalanx | 135 | 1 | 0 | 2 | 1 | 1 | | Agricultural Revolution |
| Phantom | 6,750 | 40 | 0 | 10 | 3 | 1 | Cloak | |
| Pikeman | 270 | 3 | 0 | 3 | 1 | 1 | | Explosives |
| Plasma | 4,500 | 30 | 15 | 15 | 8 | 2 | Active Air Defense, Bombard | |
| Destroyer | | | | | | | Spot Submarines | |
| Plasmatica | 4,500 | 15 | 0 | 15 | 6 | 2 | | |
| Samurai | 335 | 3 | 0 | 1 | 2 | 1 | | Explosives |
| Sea Engineer | 4,500 | 0 | 0 | 1 | 5 | 1 | Settle Sea Colony | |
| Settler | 540 | 0 | 0 | 1 | 1 | 1 | Settle City | |
| Ship of the Line | 855 | 4 | 4 | 4 | 4 | 1 | Bombard, Transport 3 Units | Space Flight |
| Slaver | 270 | 0 | 0 | 1 | 2 | 1 | Capture Slaves | Age of Reason or Emancipation |
| Space Bomber | 7,500 | 6 | 50 | 6 | 2 | 2 | Bombard Land from Space | |
| Space Engineer | 7,500 | 0 | 0 | 3 | 5 | 1 | Settle Space Colony | |
| Space Fighter | 2,250 | 16 | 16 | 16 | 15 | 3 | Active Air Defense, 2 Turns of Fuel, Space Launch/Descend | |
| Space Plane | 2,250 | 0 | 0 | 3 | 15 | 1 | Transport 5 Units, 2 Turns of Fuel, Space Launch/Descend | |
| Spy | 1,500 | 0 | 0 | 1 | 4 | 3 | Spy, Plant Nuke, Incite Revolution, 25% Spy Defense, Steal Advance | Neural Interface |
| Spy Plane | 2,815 | 0 | 0 | 2 | 10 | 5 | 10 Turns of Fuel | |
| Star Cruiser | 7,500 | 30 | 30 | 20 | 5 | 2 | Bombard | |
| Stealth Bomber | 3,375 | 16 | 22 | 8 | 10 | 2 | Bombard, Transport 2 Nukes, 5 Turns of Fuel | |
| Stealth Sub | 6,000 | 30 | 30 | 10 | 5 | 2 | Bombard Sea Units, Transport 4 Nukes | |
| Storm Marine | 4,500 | 24 | 0 | 20 | 3 | 2 | Amphibious Assault | |
| Submarine | 1,500 | 20 | 20 | 8 | 5 | 2 | Bombard Sea Units, Transport 2 Nukes | Sea Colonies |
| Subneural Ad | 2,250 | 0 | 0 | 1 | 5 | 2 | Advertise, Franchise | |
| Swarm | 5,250 | 20 | 0 | 20 | 5 | 1 | Space Descend, Amphibious Assault | |
| Tank | 2,000 | 16 | 16 | 10 | 6 | 2 | | Fusion |
| Televangelist | 1,000 | 0 | 0 | 1 | 5 | 2 | Convert City, Soothsay, Sell Indulgences | |
| Trireme | 540 | 1 | 0 | 1 | 2 | 1 | Transport 2 Units, Shallow Water Movement | Machine Tools |
| Troop Ship | 1,200 | 0 | 0 | 2 | 5 | 2 | Transport 2 Units | |
| War Walker | 3,000 | 12 | 24 | 12 | 5 | 3 | Transport 5 Units | |
| Warrior | 135 | 1 | 0 | 1 | 1 | 2 | Active Air Defense, Bombard | Explosives |
| Wormhole Probe | 9,375 | 0 | 0 | 3 | 5 | 1 | Enter Wormhole | |

# Tile Improvements

| Type | Cost | Bonus |
|---|---|---|
| Farms | 200 | +5 Food |
| Advanced Farms | 500 | +15 Food |
| Hydroponic Farms | 1,400 | +25 Food |
| Nets | 200 — 400 | +5/10 Food |
| Fisheries | 500 — 900 | +15/30 Food |
| Automated Fisheries | 1,400 — 2,000 | +25/50 Food |
| Food Pods | 600 | +20 Food |
| Food Modules | 1,400 | +40 Food |
| Food Tanks | 2,200 | +60 Food |
| Mines | 300 — 400 | +5/10/15 Production, +5 Gold |
| Advanced Mines | 800 — 1,000 | +10/20/30 Production, +5/10 Gold |
| Mega Mines | 1,600 — 2,200 | +15/30/45 Production, +10/15 Gold |
| Undersea Mines | 400 — 600 | +30/40/50 Production, +5 Gold |
| Advanced Undersea Mines | 1,000 — 1,400 | +60/80/100 Production, +10 Gold |
| Mega Undersea Mines | 2,200 — 2,800 | +90/120/150 Production, +15 Gold |
| Assembly Bays | 600 | +30 Production, +5 Gold |
| Advanced Assembly Bays | 1,400 | +60 Production, +10 Gold |
| Mega Assembly Bays | 2,200 | +90 Production, +15 Gold |
| Roads | 60 — 400 | Movement Cost 1/3 |
| Railroads | 120 — 800 | Movement Cost 1/5 |
| Maglevs | 240 — 1,600 | Movement Cost 1/10 |
| Undersea Tunnels | 1,200 — 2,400 | Movement Cost 1/10, Allows Land Units to Move in Water Tiles |
| Listening Post | 1,000 | Vision 8 |
| Radar Station | 1,000 | Vision 1, Radar 25 |
| Sonar Buoy | 150 | Vision 1, Spots Submarines |
| Air Base | 1,000 | Vision 2, Radar 3, Refuels Air Units, Paradrop |
| Fortification | 1,000 | Vision 2, +150% Defense |

# City Improvements

| Name | Cost | Effect | Maint. Cost | Exclusions |
|---|---|---|---|---|
| Academy | 540 | +50% Science, +1/2 Science per Citizen | 4 | Land Only |
| Airport | 2,500 | +50% Gold, +100% Pollution | 20 | Land Only |
| Aqua-Filter | 8,000 | -5 Overcrowding | 5 | |
| Aqueduct | 405 | +20% Food, -2 Overcrowding | 3 | Land Only |
| Arcologies | 5,000 | -4 Overcrowding | 15 | |
| Bank | 1,125 | +50% Gold, Allows Merchants | 10 | |
| Beef Vat | 3,000 | Prevents Starvation | 3 | |
| Bio Memory Chip | 2,800 | +50% Science, +1 Science per Citizen | 5 | |
| Body Exchange | 10,000 | +3 Happiness | 50 | |
| Capitol | 405 | Capitol | 0 | |
| Cathedral | 2,475 | +3 Happiness (+1 Under Communism, +5 Under Theocracy) | 10 | |
| City Clock | 1,620 | +1 Gold per Citizen | 5 | Land Only |
| City Wall | 405 | +4 Defense, Prevents Slavery, Prevents Conversions 50% of the Time | 3 | Land Only |
| Coliseum | 1,035 | +2 Happiness | 8 | Land Only |
| Computer Center | 2,400 | +50% Science, +1/2 Science per Citizen | 24 | |
| Courthouse | 270 | -50% Crime | 2 | Land Only |
| Drug Store | 3,000 | +3 Happiness, +25% Production | 10 | |

| Name | Cost | Effect | Maint. Cost | Exclusions |
|---|---|---|---|---|
| Eco-Transit | 3,500 | -200% Pollution | 15 | |
| Factory | 2,025 | +50% Production, Allows Laborers, +100% Pollution | 20 | |
| Forcefield | 6,000 | +12 Defense | 30 | |
| Fusion Plant | 10,000 | +50% Production, -100% Pollution | 30 | |
| Granary | 540 | 50% Less Food Required to Grow | 1 | Land Only |
| Hospital | 2,250 | -3 Overcrowding | 10 | |
| House of Freezing | 5,000 | +50% Gold, +5 Happiness Under Theocracy | 25 | |
| Incubation Center | 2,500 | +25% Production | 25 | |
| Marketplace | 675 | +50% Gold, Allows Merchants | 5 | Land Only |
| Micro Defense | 3,500 | Prevents Infect City and Nano Attacks | 15 | |
| Mill | 1,125 | +50% Production | 10 | Land Only |
| Mind Controller | 10,000 | No Unhappiness, Prevents Slavery, Prevents Conversion 50% of the Time | 50 | |
| Movie Palace | 1,500 | Lowers War Discontent 50% | 10 | |
| Nanite Factory | 4,000 | Gold = Production for Rush Buy | 30 | Space Only |
| Nuclear Plant | 5,500 | +50% Production, -50% Pollution | 45 | |
| Oil Refinery | 3,500 | +50% Production, +200% Pollution | 20 | Land and Sea Only |
| Publishing House | 540 | +25% Science, +1/2 Science per Citizen | 6 | Land Only |
| Rail Launcher | 6,000 | Launches Units into Space | 15 | Land and Sea Only |
| Recycling Plant | 3,000 | -200% City Pollution, Lowers Worldwide Pollution | 5 | |
| Robotic Plant | 4,500 | +50% Production, +100% Pollution | 45 | |
| SDI | 5,000 | Prevents Nuke Attack on City | 10 | Land and Sea Only |
| Security Monitor | 4,000 | +25% Production, -50% Crime -100% Pollution | 10 | |
| Television | 3,000 | +5 Gold Per Citizen | 50 | |
| Temple | 270 | +2 Happiness | 2 | Land Only |
| Theater | 495 | Doubles Effect of Entertainers, +1 Happiness | 1 | Land Only |
| University | 1,350 | +50% Science | 12 | |

# Wonders of the World

| Name | Age | Cost | Effect | Obsolescence |
|---|---|---|---|---|
| The Agency | Modern | 7,200 | Gives the Protection of a Spy in Every City | Alien Archaeology |
| AI Entity | Diamond | 12,000 | Makes All Citizens Content | |
| Chichen Itza | Ancient | 2,160 | Eliminates Crime in Civilization | Mass Production |
| Confucius Academy | Ancient | 2,160 | Eliminates Unhappiness Due to Distance from Capitol | Mass Production |
| Contraception | Modern | 7,200 | Increases Happiness by 5 Throughout Civilization | Alien Archaeology |
| Dinosaur Park | Genetic | 7,200 | Quadruples Gold from Goods in Host City | Cloaking |
| East India Company | Renaissance | 4,320 | Gives Player 5 Gold for Each Foreign Trade Route Crossing Water, Increases Boat Movement by 1 | Mass Production |
| The Eden Project | Diamond | 8,000 | Destroys Top 3 Polluting Cities; Ecotopias Can Make Eco Rangers | |
| Edison's Lab | Modern | 7,200 | Grants 10 Free Advances per Age On Average | Alien Archaeology |
| Egalitarian Act | Diamond | 20,000 | Causes All Revolting Foreign Cities to Join Owner's Civilization | |
| Emancipation Act | Renaissance | 5,760 | Converts All Slaves in All Civilizations into Citizens; All Foreign Slave Cities Suffer -3 Happiness for 5 Turns | |
| ESP Center | Diamond | 14,400 | Earns Higher Regard from All Other Civilizations, Opens Embassies (Even Those at War), Prevents Civilizations from Attacking Owner First | Age of Reason |
| Forbidden City | Ancient | 2,160 | Closes All Foreign Embassies, Prohibits Foreign Civilizations from Starting War With Owner, Earns Higher Regard From All Other Civilizations. | |
| Gaia Controller | Diamond | 20,000 | Ends Threat of Global Disaster, +25% Food in Civilization | |
| Galileo's Telescope | Renaissance | 2,880 | Increases Effect of Scientists by 200% in Host City | Robotics |
| Genome Project | Modern | 7,200 | Increases Production by 10%, +10% Health for All Units | Alien Archeology |
| Global E-Bank | Diamond | 15,200 | Earns 10 Gold per Trade Route Between Foreign Civilizations | |
| GlobeSat | Modern | 7,200 | Radar Coverage of the World | Cloaking |
| Gutenberg's Bible | Renaissance | 2,880 | Increases Science by 10% in All Cities, Eliminates Conversions in Civilization | Mass Production |
| Hagia Sophia | Ancient | 3,240 | Adds 100% to Fees Paid by Converted Cities, Doubles Effectiveness of Temples and Cathedrals | Mass Production |
| Hollywood | Modern | 7,200 | Receive 2 Gold per Citizen in Foreign Cities with Television | Alien Archaeology |
| Immunity Chip | Diamond | 14,400 | Adds 5 Happiness and Protects All Cities from Infect City Attacks | |
| Internet | Modern | 7,200 | Allows 10 Free Advances per Age Known by Another Civilization | Alien Archaeology |

| Labyrinth | Ancient | 2,160 | Gives Free Caravans | Age of Reason |
|---|---|---|---|---|
| London Exchange | Renaissance | 4,320 | Eliminates Building Maintenance in Civilization | Robotics |
| Nanite Defuser | Genetic | 14,400 | Eliminates All Nukes | |
| Nanopedia | Genetic | 14,400 | Increases Effect of Specialists by 100% in Civilization | |
| National Shield | Genetic | 20,000 | Creates a Forcefield in Every City | |
| Philosopher's Stone | Ancient | 2,880 | Opens an Embassy in Every Civilization | Age of Reason |
| Ramayana | Ancient | 2,160 | Increases Happiness by 3 throughout Civilization | Age of Reason |
| Sensorium | Genetic | 20,000 | Eliminates Overcrowding Unhappiness, Eliminates Pollution Unhappiness | |
| Sphinx | Ancient | 2,160 | Reduces Military Readiness Costs by 75% | Age of Reason |
| Star Ladder | Genetic | 12,000 | Gives Free Transportation In and Out of Space in City (Top of Ladder is a Space Colony) | |
| Stonehenge | Ancient | 2,160 | Increases Food by 25% in Civilization | Age of Reason |
| Wormhole Sensor | Diamond | 20,000 | Makes Wormhole Visible to All Civilizations | |

# Index

[ A-C ]

## B

## C

Index

[ A-C ]

[ C–I ]

## D

## E

## F

## J–K

## L

## M

**[ I–P ]**

## N

## O–P

## Q-R

## S

[ P–U ]

[ P–U ]

[ V–Z ]